THE SiNS OF
JACK SAUL

THE TRUE STORY OF
DUBLIN JACK AND THE
CLEVELAND STREET SCANDAL

BY

GLENN CHANDLER

Grosvenor House
Publishing Limited

The right of Glenn Chandler to be identified as the author of this
work has been asserted in accordance with Section 78
of the Copyright, Designs and Patents Act 1988

The book cover picture is copyright to Jon Bradfield

This book is published by
Grosvenor House Publishing Ltd
28-30 High Street, Guildford, Surrey, GU1 3EL.
www.grosvenorhousepublishing.co.uk

A CIP record for this book
is available from the British Library

ISBN 978-1-78148-991-8

Glenn Chandler is best known as the creator and writer of *Taggart*, which became the longest running television detective series in the world. He has also written true crime television dramas, notably those on William Palmer the poisoner, George Joseph Smith the 'Brides in the Bath' killer, and John George Haigh, the acid bath murderer. His books include *Burning Poison*, a true account of a Georgian Liverpool murder mystery, and two fictional novels about Brighton detective Steve Madden, *Savage Tide* and *Dead Sight*. He is also an award-winning theatre writer, producer and director.

The reader interested in keeping up with research about Jack Saul and the Cleveland Street scandal, the subjects of this book, can log on to www.jacksaul.co.uk

For Peter Bull, Robert Love and Diana Tyler.

CONTENTS

FOREWORD

I first encountered Jack Saul when I was writing a stage show called *Cleveland Street – The Musical*. It was a satirical romp based on the notorious homosexual scandal which centred on a male brothel in Victorian London, one that rocked the British establishment in 1889. I produced it at the Above The Stag Theatre, London's only LGBT space, then in Victoria but now carrying on its sterling work at new premises in Vauxhall, south of the river. (1)

All theatre production is a risk, financially and artistically, but thankfully the show was a sell-out. Audiences were keen to see how we would present a story of sodomy and sex-for-sale in Victorian back streets with songs and, yes, an upbeat and happy ending. In fact, the musical format complimented the true story very well indeed, allowing us to escape from the grim reality of the subject – which had we gone down that route would have necessitated a very serious and worthy drama – and concentrate instead on what was essentially a story of conspiracy and hypocrisy, truly appalling Victorian values, and larger-than-life, colourful characters.

The clients of the brothel at 19 Cleveland Street included Members of Parliament and the House of Lords, wealthy bankers, high-ranking figures in the military, and very possibly the grandson of Queen Victoria and Heir Presumptive to the throne, Prince Albert Victor Edward, Duke of Clarence. Prince Eddy's role was never proven, but the merest hint of the involvement of the son of the Prince of Wales and heir to the throne elevated the affair into the major sex scandal of Victoria's reign.

The other factor, which made the brothel infamous, was that telegraph messenger boys from the General Post Office were recruited to sell their bodies to supplement their wages. One of the lads was only fifteen. The house was managed by Charles Hammond, who had been a male whore or 'professional sodomite' himself, and his French wife Caroline. They appear to have enjoyed a good few years running it with impunity. John Saul, otherwise known as Jack Saul or Dublin Jack, lived and worked there for a time and was intimately associated with the Hammonds. He was a rent boy (or renter as they were known then), a little past his sell-by-date but nevertheless still actively pursuing clients around Piccadilly and the Haymarket, even as the police gathered evidence to be used in prosecutions.

Jack Saul – we shall call him that from now on – was the most notorious male prostitute in Victorian London. He is, for that and many other reasons, the most intriguing character of the whole affair. He has long been an enigma. Students of gay history, and particularly that of the late nineteenth century, have speculated on his identity.

Why should he be so fascinating? Because if we are to believe everything that is written, and that which he wrote himself, he was involved in not just one, but three major 'gay' scandals in the space of two decades without anyone knowing where he came from, what happened to him afterwards, or if indeed John or Jack Saul was his real name.

Jack intrigues for another reason. He is the central character in a controversial and 'autobiographical' work of Victorian pornography called *The Sins of the Cities of the Plain*. This was clandestinely and anonymously published in 1881, years before his involvement with the Cleveland Street brothel, giving weight to the theory that the name was originally a pseudonym. For who on earth would put their real name to a book which provides, in highly explicit detail, a long and relentless list of their sexual acts which, if proven, could earn the author a long period of imprisonment?

Not only did Jack Saul contribute his name, but also the street where he lived, so that anyone might look for him.

Jack was the first person in literature, if one dares call it that, to give a personal account of meeting Ernest Boulton and Frederick William Park, the two transvestites otherwise known as Fanny and Stella, who shocked Victorian society eleven years earlier by going around the West End of London dressed as women, picking up men for sex and having a high old time with a succession of male lovers.

That case was the first in a twenty-five year period of Victoria's reign, which culminated in the trial of Oscar Wilde and his imprisonment in Reading Gaol. Between them, in the course of that quarter century, lay the so-called Dublin felonies, during which a number of men had their lives laid bare and ruined, and the grandfather of them all, the Cleveland Street affair. Had Jack Saul been connected only with the writing of *Sins*, and his recollections of Boulton and Park, his name would be forgotten today, consigned to an ancient book locked away in the 'forbidden books' section of the British Library.

But he wasn't. Like a tarnished penny, he rolls out from between its pages and through the next two decades, turning up in Dublin to give evidence against a soldier with whom he had enjoyed a sexual relationship, and finally at the Old Bailey, to stand up in court, at great risk to himself, on behalf of a man he had never met, in one of the three trials that followed on from the discovery of Charles Hammond's boy brothel.

The two previous books on Cleveland Street were both written in 1976 when the files on the case were finally opened to researchers after a period of eighty-five years. There is a sense that the authors were competing with each other to get them on the bookshelves. *The Cleveland Street Scandal* by H. Montgomery Hyde largely concentrates on the legal manoeuvring in high places to bring an appalling business concerning brothels, buggery and boys to a swift conclusion. It was diligently researched and Montgomery Hyde was well placed, being gay himself and a Belfast-born barrister.

The Cleveland Street Affair by Colin Simpson, Lewis Chester and David Leitch is the more rollicking of the two and more fun, devoting a whole chapter to Jack Saul's colourful world of dormitory shenanigans in boarding schools and goings-on in the boudoirs of the aristocracy. Both books take as their starting point the moment when the brothel at 19 Cleveland Street is discovered, at which point the more low-life participants are soon dispatched so the authors can concentrate on the machinations of government to keep Prince Eddy out of the scandal.

In a way, Prince Eddy has hijacked the Cleveland Street story. The very suggestion that the Queen's grandson might have visited the house, incognito, at night, while Royal aides waited nervously outside in a hansom cab with a driver paid handsomely to keep his eyes out front and his mouth shut, is alluring to the conspiracy theorist in us. His spectre hangs over the house. It was the reason for the whole business being hushed up so quickly.

Neither of the books mentioned above uncovers the real Jack Saul. They get his age wrong (hardly surprising as Jack himself laid the groundwork for the confusion as we shall see) and coldly dispense with him at the end.

More recently, Jack the Ripper Internet forums have buzzed with speculation about him, for two reasons. Inspector Abberline, the policeman in charge of the Ripper hunt, was the following year put in charge of the Cleveland Street case. And there are still those convinced that Prince Eddy was behind the Ripper murders, joining the two cases at the historical hip. No one has yet suggested that Jack Saul was Jack the Ripper but in the inexhaustible search for suspects and the ever-expanding canon of (many totally ridiculous) Jack the Ripper books, it is bound to happen one day.

The best and most serious attempt so far to pin down Jack Saul has come from Justin O'Hearn, a Victorianist doctoral student who took a PHD in English at the University of British Columbia. Justin in his first year decided to specialise in Victorian literature, and as a sub-speciality, clandestine publications like *The Sins of the Cities of the Plain*. To put it in Justin's own words, he likes to study naughty books.

In his brilliant and incisive essay on Jack, Justin explored three personas. In Saul the author, he analyses *The Sins of the Cities of the Plain*; in Saul the professional sodomite, he admits that little is known about Jack Saul except that he was supposedly a male prostitute in London originally from Ireland. In the third, Justin maintains that we can point to another Jack – Saul the individual – as an early gay rights activist. It is a fascinating proposition. (2)

Finally, however, Justin admits the complications of pinning him down. As has everyone up to this moment.

I would point to yet another Jack. Saul the survivor. He worked the streets putting himself at risk every day; he finally got off the streets and eventually tried to do something with his life. He had a family, a mother he loved and who loved him. He had brothers and sisters, aunts and uncles. He was once a boy who stood on the brink of manhood and decided, for better or for worse, which way he should go.

Jack's story is also the story of Charles Hammond, with whose life his became inextricably intertwined, the wily, unscrupulous, money-grabbing pimp and brothel owner about whom it is impossible to say anything very kind. Except perhaps that he too, like Jack, had a family he loved and was a survivor. Many monstrous men love their families. Had he lived today Hammond would have been branded a paedophile. His crimes however were of their time and while it is no excuse to say that in Victorian London child prostitution was rife, he was certainly not the most guilty of the guilty. Which is more than can be said for the titled upper classes and landed gentry who used his services.

Nothing much, it seems, changes. At the time of writing, the British media is obsessed with the subject of VIP sexual abuse of minors. Whether or not it is proven to be as widespread as they suggest, the story of Jack Saul and the Cleveland Street scandal seems suddenly very prescient.

It is possible to trace most of the protagonists of the Cleveland Street affair. The boy telegraph messengers with one or two exceptions married and raised families. The aristocratic clients of the house are all in *Who's Who*. But Jack Saul has never been found,

Yet Jack did leave a few footprints in the sand, which enable one to discover where he came from and, just as importantly, what happened to him. (3)

My discovery of one of those footprints was a combination of luck and research, as are so many genealogical 'eureka' moments. It was fortunate that householders in the 1901 Irish census were required to sign their form, unlike in England where it wasn't required until 1911. I was perusing one such Irish census entry on line, courtesy of the National Archives of Ireland, when a signature struck me as faintly familiar. My mind raced back five years to when I was writing *Cleveland Street – The Musical*. Then, for research purposes, I had photocopied a police statement signed by Jack from our own National Archives, and subsequently filed it away. I still had it. I dug it out and looked at Jack's signature. The signatures on the police statement and the much later householder's census form were unmistakably those of the same person. It would no exaggeration to say that it took my breath away. From that moment on, everything else fell into place, and a trail that took me back and forth to Ireland began.

Jack Saul was no pseudonym. He was as real as Dublin potatoes. And Dublin is the city where we have to go to find him.

* * * * * *

Chapter Notes

1. The word homosexual was not used in Jack's time, and gay had a very different meaning. However, for ease of narrative, I use both terms and some others at times throughout the book.

2. Justin O'Hearn's paper on the historical and literary Jack Saul can be read online at http://graduable.com/2013/04/15/victorian-pornography-part-vi-jack-saul/

3. Regrettably, I have not been successful in discovering a photograph of Jack Saul. That is not to say of course that one does not exist somewhere. The reader hopefully will conjure up his or her own image, and can keep up with any new and further developments on my website at www.jacksaul.co.uk

CHAPTER ONE

THE ROAD TO HAROLD'S CROSS

It was a short journey but the last one the man would ever make in life. And it would pass almost every place south of the River Liffey that had meant something to him as he had grown up. The driver of the hackney cab, James Saul, thirty years old and newly married, would not care for some of the places known to his passenger, or wish to remember what had happened there. As for London, that was out of sight and out of his mind. His brother, lying in the back of the cab, knowing he was going to die, had lived the kind of life neither of his cab driving siblings wanted to know anything about. And he was taking the full story of it to his grave.

The journey began at South Frederick Street, a road of decaying Georgian tenements, where James had looked after his brother for as long as he was able. They turned right into Molesworth Street, close to the Masonic Temple, and down past the end of South Anne

Street where they had grown up together. Their old house, up a narrow passageway, just out of sight, held the memories of boyhood along with grinding poverty. It was where they once played, bare-footed and dirty-kneed with scores of other neighbourhood children. There were still children there now. There were always children. The streets of Dublin teemed with them, half-starved urchins selling wares to raise a few coins to take back to their families. At least James had a job, unlike the fathers of some of them, and he would raise his family as best he could. His brother had raised himself out of dire poverty too. It had brought money into the family. It had also brought shame, in not so equal measure.

They turned along the side of St Stephen's Green and down the more gentrified Harcourt Street, where his brother had worked for a while at a job that was respectable, but which he had left under a cloud of his own making. The corner house was still there, tall and solidly Georgian, still preserving an air of gentility though now looking rather shabby. As he always did here, James took care with the horse. The hooves tended to slide on the paving stones between the tramlines, which the Tramways Company once spread with sand in the days when they were horse-pulled. Since electrical traction had been introduced, the company had neglected the roads. The jarveys who drove the horse-drawn cabs were the casualties of that neglect. There had been numerous court cases involving injuries to horse and driver, but the Dublin roads remained in a dreadful condition.

They headed south towards the Grand Canal, which ultimately connected Dublin with the River Shannon to the west. His brother, sick and feverish in the back, looked right before they crossed the canal and saw for one last time the Portobello district with its barracks, soldiers and prostitutes that he had known so well, one of the many areas of Dublin which had seared itself into his consciousness as a boy growing up in the city. He had left all that behind a long time ago, and he was leaving it behind again.

Across the canal, James saw their destination ahead, the Hospice at Harold's Cross, a two-storey high building fronted with granite with limestone framing the windows and front porch. On the other side of the water was another institution, one that his passenger remembered well, also a granite building but one with an unwelcoming air. Within the Griffith Barracks was the Richmond Bridewell, a prison where his brother had spent a few uncomfortable nights as a young man contemplating his future. He would spend many more nights now contemplating his past, hopefully not so uncomfortable, though his health or lack of it would ultimately decide that. The district of Harold's Cross was a much healthier neighbourhood than the one they had just left. Here, at Our Lady's Hospice, he would be cared for until the end.

James left his brother to the love and mercy of the Religious Sisters of Charity and returned to the city, to his job. He would visit but he knew that there was little more that he could do.

It was 1904. An era had ended three years earlier with the death of Queen Victoria. Lord Salisbury, four times Prime Minister, across whose desk had once passed the name of the man now in the care of the Sisters, but who had as quickly forgotten it as new crises absorbed him, had only recently died. The dream of Irish Home Rule seemed as far away as ever, while the British Empire spanned a fifth of the globe and Edwardian Britain basked in the hope and sunshine of a fresh millennium.

At Harold's Cross, Jack Saul had plenty of time now to look back on a life that had been described in court as one of 'infamy'. He knew that in the great reckoning – he had been a Catholic all his life if not a good one – he hadn't been completely bad, even if his family considered him to be so. He had at least done one good thing, had stood up to the establishment and to the foreign occupier of his country of Ireland no less, in order to prevent an injustice. Was one good thing enough to balance the books?

As he lay in his bed in the ward, lightweight cotton dimity curtains hanging by the side of him and moving gently in the soft breeze from an open window, Jack Saul reflected that it wasn't bad for a boy from the Dublin slums who had been born without any hope in sight.

* * * * * *

CHAPTER TWO

THE LIBERTIES

Dublin in the middle of the nineteenth century was a city blighted with slums, decaying Georgian tenements most of which were unfit for human habitation. Whole families lived in wretched vermin-infested single rooms where the only bedding was a filthy straw mattress. Poverty was crippling. It was by no means unusual for a hundred people to share one tap and primitive outside toilet. Human excreta and horse dung lay about backyards. Infant mortality was shockingly high and frail wraiths of children, filthy and malnourished, played in streets that were no better than open sewers.

The photographs of the time tell only part of the story. Grim monochrome buildings frame groups of ill-clad youngsters in bare feet with sunken eyes, skinny limbs and haunted expressions. The odd child whose parents can afford to buy him boots stands out with a look of smugness on his grimy face. Young girls stare at the camera, as old and as worn out as their mothers, and wearing the same clothes. Boys in cloth caps and threadbare shirts look like their fathers. It appears to be a different world entirely; Dickensian, awful, beyond salvation. The sun never seems to shine. Yet the tenements, putrid alleys and courts have a strange romance about them, their neat rectangular Georgian frontages redolent of a more prosperous age, now home to the people of the abyss.

Transpose the children to any British city at the time and they would look the same. But Dublin wasn't like any other British city. It didn't have the burgeoning major industrial base of Manchester or Glasgow or Birmingham. It didn't have the wealth or growth of London. Those cities had slums too but they had populations drawn there because of the opportunities to work. Dublin was different. It seemed fated to sit across the water from mainland Britain, neglected and forgotten, a city that wasn't going anywhere in a hurry.

It had not always been so. The previous century, the once fine mansions had housed a large civil and administrative population. Ireland had its own governing body, albeit one in thrall to London. But the ruling Irish Protestants had demonstrated a woeful incapacity to keep law and order and rebellion at bay. The consequent Act of Union in 1801 and the abolition of the Irish parliament by its English neighbour had an unintended consequence. No longer needed to run the affairs of the country, most of the middle class population in the already hopelessly over-crowded city centre sold their stately residences and moved to the more pleasant suburbs, leaving their homes to stand empty and rot. Those were bought up by rapacious and profiteering landlords who divided and sub-divided them and crammed their tenants into increasingly smaller spaces.

Some of the most dilapidated slums were to be found south of the River Liffey in The Liberties, so called because historically the area lay outside the original city walls, which stood around the hill of Christ Church. At its heart today is the famous Guinness Brewery. A number of streets, including Kevin Street, The Coombe, Francis Street, Cork Street and Chamber Street, all in the vicinity of St Patrick's Cathedral, had long been regarded as the worst in the district.

It was here, just off Kevin Street in a block of houses called Ferns Court, that Jack Saul was born, in the parish of St Nicholas on 29 October 1857, and baptised shortly afterwards at home, which was the common practice, as was the recording of both his and his father's name in Latin by the parish priest. He was christened Johannes (John) Saul, son of Guilelmus (William) Saul and Eliza Revington. He was to be the eldest son of eight children, preceded only by a sister Maria born in 1853. Both she and Jack were born out of wedlock, their parents not marrying until six months after Jack's birth.

If Ferns Court possessed any claim to fame prior to Jack Saul's birth, it was quarter of a century earlier when Aaron Botts, a Chelsea Pensioner said to be a hundred and six years old, died there. Eight years before his death, it was reported, he was summoned for paternity of a child. His longevity and virility probably had little to do with the health of the place in which he lived.

The name is deceptive. In Dublin any address at that time with the word *court* in it generally indicated a group of broken-down houses, two or three storeys high, built on land round the back of other houses and accessed by a narrow passageway. The only things that grew large in the vicinity of Ferns Court (it was sometimes referred to as Fearons court) were not ferns, but the rats that were reputed to come out at night and feed on the milk of lactating mothers as they slept.

At the time Jack was born, Ferns Court and the neighbouring tenements of Kevin Street teemed with large families as did the whole of Dublin. It was the Great Famine of the 1840s that had brought thousands including his father William Saul, his grandfather also called William and his grandmother Maria, along with at least four of their grown up children and aunts and uncles from the clean air of the countryside to the horror of the Dublin slums, in search of food and work.

Saul is not a common name in Ireland. It is of Norman origin and their ancestors settled originally in the south around Tipperary and Waterford. By the time Jack's father was born, they were centred mainly about Rathdrum in County Wicklow and Drumcondra in County Meath.

His father, uncles and grandparents in actual fact came from the area around Killiskey in County Wicklow, just to the north of Rathdrum, a large parish which extended from near the coast up onto the slopes of the Wicklow Mountains. Lewis' Topographical Dictionary of Ireland described it as,

'in the highest state of cultivation, and the system of agriculture is generally improved; there is neither bog nor waste land, except some tracts of mountain, which may be easily reclaimed. The surrounding country is remarkable for the boldness and impressive magnificence of its features; and within the limits of the parish are several gentlemens' seats.'

This was written eight years before the famine and might give the impression that the potato blight did not touch that part of County Wicklow. But it did, though not quite so severely as the west and the south of Ireland. It's proximity to Dublin and the fact that there was more arable and cultivated land meant that it escaped the worst, but at the height of the hunger the workhouses were still full, much of the population was starving, and government relief works were inundated with men desperate to earn enough to feed their families. The Sauls, landless labourers or peasant farmers of probably only a few acres at most, lived through the failures of the potato crop year after year, but in 1847 when the disease devastated the crop for a third year running, like thousands of other families they sought a way out. And so the slow march north began, from a countryside in crisis to a city unable to cope.

Many – such as Jack's father and siblings – were born and baptised into the established Church of Ireland at the ironically named Nun's Cross Church on the edge of Ashford, but had left their Protestant roots behind and married as Catholics, rearing Catholic children. This was not uncommon in the age after Catholic emancipation.

Jack's baptism was attended by two sponsors, or Catholic Godparents. One was John Saul, a farmer's son, probably his father's cousin, the other his fifteen-year-old aunt Elizabeth Reilly, daughter of his great-aunt Susan. If he ever needed more aunts and uncles, there were at least eight other Reillys around Ferns Court and Kevin Street. Through their marriages, his world as he grew up would also be populated with Hickeys and Connors, Briens and Greys, and Brennans and Hutchinsons through his paternal grandmother's side. Hardly a year went by without another baptism, sponsors and families and friends crowding into rooms made to look pretty for the occasion.

It was hard to feel a special little boy when surrounded by so many cousins, but he was the first boy in his own family and that gave him a special relationship to his mother Eliza. She was a Revington, which is not a common name in Ireland either, though her origins are obscure. The name comes from England, as her ancestors would have done, settling in the south of Ireland where there was a Revington clan.

She was much younger than his father, by about fifteen years, and was likely a minor when she had their first child, hence the delayed marriage. Her own mother, Elizabeth Revington, born around the time of the French revolution, would move in with the family. Eliza was illiterate, which was nothing unusual at the time. On the deaths of two of her future children she simply signed the register with a cross, the 'mark' of Eliza Saul.

Hers would be the fate of thousands of Irish wives and mothers, poverty and a life of domestic toil, tempered and alleviated only by the dream of watching her children grow up to make better and more prosperous lives. As her firstborn son, Jack was her pride, and would in time learn to read and write. He would learn to do a lot of other things besides, which would bring anything but pride to a poor labouring class Irish Catholic family. For the moment however, there were few indications he was going to turn out differently from the scores of other children who congregated about the courts and alleyways.

William Saul set himself up with a second-hand cab of the London type, specially built and light enough to be pulled by one horse, to hold four people and carry luggage on the roof, and became a 'jarvey', one of a tough, hard-drinking breed of men of which there were two and a half thousand in Dublin. The hackney trade was huge, but the economics were harsh. William could not survive as a hackney cab driver with just one horse. Two were needed for if one went lame or died suddenly it could spell disaster for the family, plus the fact they were required to be fed and stabled, vets bills needed to be paid, and the carriage maintained. William stabled his horses close to where the family lived, probably in accommodation little better.

Jack grew up with horses, climbing up onto the seat with his father, for one day as the eldest son he would be expected to take the reins. Eliza stayed at home and did her best to make ends meet with the sixpence a fare her husband brought home, or didn't. The culture was hard to escape from. Countless cab drivers spent their money in the pubs while their womenfolk suffered and starved.

There was a strong sense of community in The Liberties. It didn't matter that you went hungry and without boots on your feet, or your clothes were crumpled and tattered cast-offs plucked from rough nails in damp candlelit cellars up the Coombe, or that your diet of bread and cabbage and potatoes left you malnourished and prone to disease, or that you itched and scratched from the plagues of tiny creatures that crawled out of the walls and shared your bed.

When you fell on hard times, the community helped. When the merciless Dublin 'Corpo' booted you out because you couldn't pay the rent, or the landlord took the door off your room to drive you out, or the wet got through in winter and chilled you to the bone, or you fell sick and just couldn't move for days, an army of mammies and grannies would step in to help. They were the unsung heroes of the Dublin slums, applying remedies passed down to them on to the next generation.

Jack's parents could not afford a doctor. Such gentlemen were expensive and indeed beyond the pockets of most slum dwellers. The stigma of poverty was attached to those who were forced to attend the infirmary, and many used it as a last resort. Everyone became their own chemist, mothers and aunts and grans in particular dispensing homemade ointments and herbal medicines. When Jack fell ill, his mother would be the first port of call, and if she couldn't help then her own mother would step in, or one of his aunts or older cousins would come to the rescue. There were professional chemists in The Liberties who stood in for doctors and were there in times of dire need. They knew their customers as well as any doctor, if not better, and some of them became legends in The Liberties.

It was a Trojan undertaking for a family to lift itself out of the Dublin slums, and it took much more than the money earned by a cabdriver to do it. The most anyone could hope for was a change of address, which frequently meant flitting from one hovel to another, often with the purpose of escaping a grasping landlord and escaping a demand for rent.

The Sauls did not stay long at Ferns Court. Jack was born within yards of the police barracks in Kevin Street, close enough to hear the marching of boots as they paraded during training, but by the time he was four his parents had moved. It may well have been necessitated by the overcrowded and appalling condition of their accommodation.

Not that they were moving to anywhere more salubrious or healthy. They went to Duke Lane, a short narrow road that connected South Anne Street with Duke Street, near St Stephen's Green and a stone's throw east of the fashionable shopping thoroughfare of Grafton Street.

A stone's throw could be a long distance in Dublin. While ladies strolled along Grafton Street under parasols in their fine crinoline, gazing into windows at the latest fashions, South Anne Street and Duke Lane at the 'back end' were being described in a scathing report by city inspectors as unsanitary. Grafton Street itself was like a lady in a beautiful skirt. Lift the hem and the vermin and filth were just inches from her dainty feet.

There was a system of National Schools in Ireland decades before they appeared in England. Jack's education was strictly denominational. The State had created them in the hope that they would unite Catholic and Protestant children, but by the time Jack went to school (possibly the one in Mill Street) they had become, after strong intervention by the respective churches, strictly segregated. No Irish was taught. Jack learned English, and anyway, it was the language that you needed if you ever decided to emigrate, as hundreds of thousands did.

Children mostly went out to work as soon as they were able, selling newspapers or wares on the streets, running errands, helping to clean out stables, anything a boy could do to bring a few coppers back into the house. One thing Jack learned to live with very quickly as a child growing up in a Victorian inner city, especially that of Dublin, was death.

At Duke Lane, he acquired a number of brothers and sisters, not all of whom lived through childhood. His second sister Anne's birth in 1861 was followed by two others, Teresa in 1863 and Susan in 1866, the latter dying of 'convulsions' at the age of three.

William Saul dug his hand deep into his pocket and bought a small plot for the burial in Glasnevin Cemetery to the north of Dublin next to the Botanic Gardens. It was cheap because there were already two bodies in the grave, those of two women called Mary Dunden and Anne Reilly who had no connection with their family. The grave was dug and the child laid on top.

He was just in time. The burial was quickly followed by that of Jack's seventy-seven-year-old grandmother, Elizabeth Revington, who had moved into 5 Duke Lane with the family, helping her daughter to raise her children. Eliza, her family growing, was left without a mother to help her and with a husband who was out all day and in all weathers.

Jack was eleven years old when his first brother came into the world and was given the name William Andrew Saul. He was followed two years later by a sister Margaret. It excited Jack to have a brother, instead of sisters, and as William started growing out of infancy it seemed to everyone that unlike Susan he was going to be a survivor. Then tragedy struck. At the age of five, William contracted tuberculosis and died.

TB, or consumption, or phthisis as the doctors often wrote on death certificates, was the curse of the Dublin slums. It stalked the houses of the poor, reaping a harvest of little mites and grown adults too. Once it struck a family, they were branded. The belief that it ran in families was widespread.

The Sauls were now a TB family. Jack's little brother William would be the third member and the second child to die at 5 Duke Lane in just over four years.

As a Catholic Jack was taught about Heaven and Purgatory. It did not matter how poor people were or how grim the living conditions, there was always a picture or a small statue of Our Lady lit by a votive candle in the corner of the room. Jack knelt down and prayed that someone so young as William might go straight to Heaven, for how could the soul of his little brother not be cleansed enough of sin so that he might go immediately to Heaven and sit with the angels? And while God and the Virgin were at it, could he please have another brother instead of more sisters?

His prayers were answered nine months later when James was born. Like Jack, James would survive into manhood. From an early age, Jack was raised with a second brother, Edward. There appears to be no baptism at Duke Lane for Edward Saul. He may have been adopted, though there was no official adoption in those days. When relatives or close neighbours died and young children were left orphaned, they would often be taken in by other members of the family. Edward was about four years younger than Jack, and when he married he would nevertheless name William Saul as his father.

Jack well knew the difference between a brother who just arrived, and a brother who was born. As with death, the facts of life were no mystery for a boy who grew up watching his mother go into labour in the same room where they slept and ate, the blood on the bed, the pails of water, the neighbours stepping in to help and telling him to keep out of the way, the cries as a new member of the family came into the world.

Like James and Jack, Edward would survive. Jack was still special though, and at fourteen years the eldest and only breadwinner of the family after his father. He was too young to be a jarvey but probably went out with his father and helped maintain the carriage, tend the horses and clean out the stable.

Dublin was not without its pleasures and excitements for three boys growing up in the back streets. Theatrical entertainments were chief among them, and there was no shortage of those. The Queen's Theatre, which advertised itself as the Alhambra of Dublin after the Alhambra of London (which one day would become very familiar to Jack) opened as a music hall in 1874. The Mechanics' Institute in Lower Abbey Street, where the Irish Dramatic Club performed, had a rougher reputation – and was where a young Irish boy who would become known as Sean O'Casey, the great Irish playwright, discovered his taste for the dramatic arts. Then there was always the new Gaiety Theatre, a few minutes from where the boys lived. But one place to which the brothers gravitated regularly was the Diorama at the Rotunda where there were nightly programmes of music accompanied by a raffle. *Freemans Journal*, the nationalist newspaper, reported the prizewinners in every issue and one night Edward won a set of japanned trays and took his prize home to their mother who was delighted.

In just a few more years, so the family hoped, Jack would be able to double the money being brought into the home by becoming a cab driver just like his father. But Jack would go a very different way.

The means by which he carved out a reputation and a career for himself would involve him stepping far beyond the borders of acceptable convention. Jack was aware that he was attracted to men just as much, if not more, than he was attracted to girls.

By the time he turned seventeen he became, to paraphrase his own words, 'ready for a lark' with a free gentleman at any time, and discovered that prostitution, if he played the game right, paid a young man of his abilities very well indeed.

* * * * * *

CHAPTER THREE

A CAREER OF INFAMY

To understand how a boy growing up in poverty in an inner city slum, where hope and prospects for the future are a rare commodity, became one of the most notorious male prostitutes in Victorian London, one has to go back and walk a few streets of that city.

London polished up Jack Saul, but Dublin moulded him. It was the cradle of the Dublin streets, where one could stroll from squalid alleys into fashionable shopping streets, where the poor might loiter in the shadows and watch gentlemen and their ladies pass by in fine carriages along handsome thoroughfares, that forged the young man who would learn to make a precarious living out of selling his body to the wealthy and influential.

Soldiers and prostitution were the abiding memories that many visitors to Dublin took away with them, and two of the elements that Jack could not avoid as he grew into young manhood, for where soldiers were garrisoned, prostitutes invariably followed in droves.

There was scarcely a neighbourhood he could walk around without seeing uniformed men on the march during the day and witness unsightly brawls between them and their paramours, for want of a better word, somewhere at night. At any one time, there were as many as six thousand military personnel garrisoned in and around the city.

A stroll up to and across the Liffey and a walk west would take Jack in no time at all to The Royal Barracks, simply known as The Barracks, on Dublin's North Quays. It was the largest in Dublin, and Barrack Street, which was named after it, was notorious as a meeting place between soldiers and prostitutes. As early as 1837, the *United Services Journal* warned – or one could say advertised – that 'riot, drunkenness and gross indecency' were common there, and that 'dens of filth and iniquity' abounded. Little more than a line of low public houses and brothels, it was renamed Benurb Street in a vain attempt to bury its reputation, but as long as The Barracks remained its image proved impervious to change.

Even closer for Jack, a young man who was becoming fascinated by prostitution, the sprawling Portobello Barracks, between the suburb of Rathmines and the Grand Canal, assured that the Portobello area too remained notorious. The Richmond Barracks in Inchicore had room for a thousand soldiers, and there were garrisons stationed in Phoenix Park itself as well as Dublin Castle.

Soldiers weren't just stationed in the city. Just outside Dublin, the Curragh Camp in County Kildare was home not only to the military, but to a species known as the Curragh Wrens. Of no interest to ornithologists, they were prostitutes who had actually set up tents complete with beds and crude furnishings in amongst the furze bushes on the open ground that surrounded the camp. The Prince of Wales, later King Edward VII, was based at Curragh a number of times and would not have been unacquainted with the Wrens. It was there that he met the actress Nellie Clifton.

But one district that Jack became intrigued by would become the most famous red-light district of all. Monto, north of the River Liffey, located between Lower Gardiner Street and Amiens Street and named after one of its most notorious thoroughfares Montgomery Street, put everywhere else in the shade.

It was renowned across Europe, and sailors after putting into port would head there in their droves. Like much of Dublin, it had once been fashionable, full of grand houses, but as Jack was growing up south of the river, it became more and more a place of brothels and raucous drinking dens where everything and any-one was for sale, and for a boy intrigued by the whole notion of selling sex it was an education second to none.

One can imagine his mother telling him to stay away from such evil places. All the more reason for him to explore the streets where all imaginable vice was avail-able for the right price. Jack may not have been able to afford every imaginable vice, but he could see where it was taking place and rub shoulders with those who practised it. As more and more houses deteriorated, and the respectable inhabitants and tradespeople moved out, more brothel-keepers moved in until a whole square mile began to resemble the most aban-doned sailortown in the world. Gentlemen in fashion-able garments mingled with soldiers, sailors, carousing medical students from Trinity College, noisy drunks, curious boys and the merely inquisitive in traipsing the streets of Monto to see what it had to offer.

And to Jack, growing up in poverty and seeing the grinding desperation of peoples' lives around him, the Monto had much to offer. If anything, it taught him that in a society where there were precious few jobs for women other than the demeaning ones of charring and washing other peoples' laundry, or going into service, there was one in which they could take charge of their own lives.

For not all the Monto prostitutes fitted the stereotype of fallen women. Some became madames in their own right, keeping 'flash houses' where a better class of woman was on offer. Some in their time had became famous, and their names still resonated, such as Margaret Leeson, known as 'Pimping Peg', and Mary Fagan who as far back as the end of the eighteenth century had opened a brothel in a fine house with the help of a wealthy admirer.

Yet Jack didn't even need to cross the river to see what Dublin had to offer in the way of sex for sale. Almost every day, the Monto came to him. The area around St Stephen's Green had its fair share of bawdy houses too, but a short step into Grafton Street introduced to him another phenomenon, horse-drawn carts brought down across the Liffey by enterprising madames to tout for business among Grafton Street's top-hatted shoppers. On the carts, displayed for all the world like a tradesman's wares, were young women in their finery, the better-dressed and more commercially acceptable of the brothel-keepers' girls.

Just as astonishing – to us, though it probably no longer astonished the inhabitants of Dublin – was the wide thoroughfare of Sackville Street, now O'Connell Street, where one side was practically reserved for 'respectable' pedestrians and the other for street walkers.

What Jack *didn't* see were the ravaged bodies of young abandoned country girls, thrown out of their families because of unwanted pregnancies, who would end up in the notorious Lock Hospital dying of venereal disease, some reputedly smothered to death out of kindness by nurses when they were past all hope.

What price a wealthy admirer then?

Of wealth in Dublin, Jack glimpsed a great deal. But it was all Protestant wealth. As a Catholic boy growing up he was made acutely aware of being a second-class citizen. His mother would be fond of pointing out the old decaying houses in the tenement-hedged streets around where they lived and telling him that Lords and Ladies used to live in them. Where were the Lords and Ladies now? When balls were held at Dublin Castle, Jack could not help but see them for they came back, as though by magic from the wealthier suburbs and corners of the Kingdom. The streets around the castle were thronged with coaches and broughams and cabs, a running stream of vehicles heaving with important personages, lords, ladies, earls and barons, honourables and most honourables, soldiers in uniforms with gold braid, their heads surmounted by spikes and plumes, accompanied by ladies in fine silk and rich lace.

Did any of them avert their eyes to see the boy who jealously regarded their world, who would in time invade it in his own surreptitious style?

Another way in which Jack became conscious of Protestant wealth and patronage was in the hunt for employment. Not only were Catholics treated like second-class citizens by the Protestant minority, but they were denied the better positions. While a Protestant youth could walk with ease into a good clerical vacancy, a Catholic slum boy like Jack was led only to expect the most menial job, being taken on as a floor sweeper or a messenger for a few shillings a week – if he was lucky. An Irishman's memory is long and many were still alive who remembered the pre-emancipation days when a Catholic couldn't sit in Parliament or hold public office. Times had changed, but many things had not.

To help get his family out of poverty, and perhaps into better accommodation, Jack needed to find a way of making money. But the wages from what was on offer were paltry and insufficient. Why work ten hours a day delivering newspapers or sweeping floors when there were richer pickings to be had practically on his own doorstep for doing something far more exciting and dangerous? He was seventeen. It was an ideal age to start.

As in London, though on a much smaller scale, Dublin possessed a flourishing trade in male prostitution.

Though Jack was attracted to both men and women and was possibly a bit confused by it, he was comfortable with the *demi-monde* of both. He had enjoyed plenty of opportunities to see how much could be earned if one played the game right. If women could win wealthy admirers, and pull themselves out of the gutter, then Jack was going to do it too. Some of those Lords and high-ranking military nobs in their posh carriages were going to be very grateful for a boy like Jack Saul, he decided.

The prospect of selling his own body came to him not only out of necessity but also as a way of discovering his own sexuality. Rent boys the world over would experience the first frisson of sexual pleasure with a paying companion. It added to the thrill as well as contributing to the pocket.

Jack was good-looking, stood five foot five and a half inches, with fair hair and a fresh complexion, and the developing look of a young adonis, if a somewhat effeminate one. (1) The Monto whores had commented on it, chatted to the pretty boy who hovered around their doorsteps, teased him by praising his good looks, and suggested what he might do with them if he had a mind to. What he could only achieve with them if he dressed flash like a young man on the town, cultivated an image, wore a nicely cut suit and carried a slim cane under his arm like a gentleman and looked less like a slum brat, posed endless possibilities.

To do that, to dress like a gent, Jack needed money.

It is a truth universally acknowledged, said Jane Austen in *Pride and Prejudice*, that a single man in possession of a good fortune must be in want of a wife.

It is also a truth universally acknowledged that a gay young man not in possession of a good fortune must be in want of a male lover who has one. Jack soon found what he was looking for. Or reckoned that he did.

Lieutenant Martin Oranmore Kirwan of the County of Dublin Regiment of Foot was no common soldier. In fact he was a bit of a snob who looked down on them. He was twenty-eight years old when he met Jack, probably in the vicinity of St Stephen's Green or Trinity

College, where he would typically pick up young men and students drawn to a man in full uniform, which he wore like a splendid cockerel attracting a mate. A photograph of Martin Kirwan, taken at a studio in Grafton Street when he was about Jack's age, presents him as a decidedly fey youth, his head turned somewhat nonchalantly to the side, leaning casually on a balustrade with an umbrella against his thigh. There is something very superior about the face, a disdainfulness that he carried into adulthood. Jack was instantly attracted by the haughty appearance, the red coat, the traditional scarlet of the infantry with its yellow facings, and the attentions of a man who obviously came from a very good family.

Quite how good, he soon learned. Lieutenant Kirwan's family lived at Upper Mount Street in the north of the city, far apart in the social spectrum. But Kirwan had friends in Dublin, friends who could lend him a room for an hour or two.

Jack would turn into a bit of a snob himself and a lot of that may well have rubbed off on him from Lieutenant Kirwan. For the handsome soldier was first and foremost a gentleman who was a cousin of the 2nd Lord Oranmore, or to give him his full eventual title, Geoffrey Dominic Augustus Frederick Brown Guthrie, 2nd Baron Oranmore and Brown of Carrabrowne Castle and Baron Browne of Castle MacGarrett, in County Mayo.

The Kirwans were one of the oldest tribes in Ireland. They left many splendid castles in their wake, and Kirwan's Lane, a mediaeval street in Galway City, is named after them. The family appear to have settled in Galway around the reign of Henry VI from which time they became one of the families which ruled Galway City for several centuries.

Martin's father, Richard Andrew Hyacinth Kirwan, was a Justice of the Peace who owned 4,308 acres in the county. Martin had been born at the family seat in Bawnmore, between Galway City and Tuam, but had resided with his family in Dublin since he was a boy. The Kirwans' true ancestral home was the seventeenth century Cregg Castle, bestowing on Martin the grand title of Martin Oranmore Kirwan of Bawnmore and Cregg, though he had never actually lived at Cregg, which is one of the oldest armorial stately houses in Galway. It was said that the Cregg Estate had been lost to their family in a card game. One castle to which Lieutenant Kirwan and his father were regularly invited was Dublin Castle, where they attended glittering balls of the kind Jack could only dream about.

Though their ancestors were Catholics, the Kirwans were staunch Protestants, though being from such an old Irish family not as despised as many. In fact the Kirwans were noted for being generous to their tenants. At a mass meeting of the Land League, Richard Kirwan had the privilege of being named as one of only two 'good landlords' in Galway County.

It is extremely doubtful that Mr Kirwan senior, sporting as he did the middle name of Hyacinth, realised that his son, while simultaneously helping to protect the city from riot and affray, was known affectionately among the secretive homosexual community of Dublin as 'Lizzie'.

Courting in Dublin between a Protestant soldier and a male Catholic youth ten years his junior was fraught with problems. The city was small and compact and all roads seemed to terminate in just two squares. One was constantly meeting the same people, and Kirwan knew many of the local gentry. Nevertheless it was necessary to take a few risks if one wanted the pleasure. There was always the Gaiety Theatre where it was possible to misbehave unobserved in a private box. Popular places outdoors were the Botanic Gardens at Glasnevin, next to the cemetery, with its hothouses where you could enjoy a secret assignation. Jack was not the first young man Kirwan would take to the gardens for an afternoon stroll and he certainly wouldn't be the last. Phoenix Park with its bandstand was another popular rendezvous. If one wanted to be really secretive it was necessary to travel out of Dublin, perhaps to the Wicklow Mountains or further afield to some small hotel where one was not known and would not be recognised.

Such potential dangers were tucked to the back of Jack's mind, and that of Lieutenant Kirwan. Kirwan was madly taken with the fair-haired working-class youth while Jack revelled in the fact that he was going out with an uncommon soldier who was also landed gentry and next in line to inherit his father's land.

This disparity between their backgrounds then was no minor concern in a society that was so riven by class-consciousness. Their affair was bound to attract attention.

As in all cities with barracks, there were plenty of men in uniform who, like their Monto counterparts, were prepared to prostitute themselves to supplement their meagre incomes. Lieutenant Kirwan, who on the surface seemed to have had little need to supplement his income, nevertheless kept company with much older men and may well have turned a trick or two himself. In spite of the family wealth, he very probably survived on an allowance, and army wages were notoriously bad. He soon introduced Jack to one of his older friends, Gustavus Cornwall, Secretary to the General Post Office in Sackville Street, the building that would later become famous as a flashpoint in the 1916 Easter uprising.

Cornwall had occupied the important position for twenty years. He had known Kirwan as a family friend since the younger man was about thirteen years old. Innocent though the origins of the friendship may have been, Cornwall, who was known endearingly in homosexual circles as 'The Duchess' and sometimes more grandly by his full title of 'The Duchess of Cornwall', had a penchant for soldiers and kept an album full of photographs of them. He was close friends with another militia soldier, the delightfully named Captain George Joy, a man of 'musical tastes', whom he had known almost as long as Kirwan.

Cornwall's reputation as a lover of young good-looking men as well as soldiers in uniform was an open secret. He also took a liking to the pretty young creature from Duke Lane. In his mid-fifties, bearded and imposing, he had married into the Scottish aristocracy. His wife, Elizabeth Grace Dalyell, was the daughter of Captain Sir William Cunningham Dalyell of the Binns, Linlithgow. Though they had been married fourteen years, there were no children to inhibit his private life, and as his wife was often away in Scotland visiting her family he was free to indulge himself in sexual activities with men and youths.

Cornwall was the kind of wealthy and well-positioned admirer Jack would search for, a man who could introduce him into society and to those others who, like Jack, wished to be introduced. He was a Mason who regularly attended the Freemasons Hall in Molesworth Street just a minute from Jack's home, and was a familiar figure strutting about the neighbourhood. He lived in Harcourt Street among the more elite residences of the medical profession on the other side of St Stephen's Green.

Another of Cornwall's young friends, though one who comes across as a more thoroughly unsavoury individual, was Alfred McKiernan, a clerk in the prestigious Munster Bank. They met at a 'musical party' – a popular euphemism – after which Cornwall began sending McKiernan gushing letters. He gave him a volume of Shakespeare's works for his nineteenth birthday, but they would fall out, with disastrous repercussions, over Cornwall's friendship with yet another army officer called Bulley.

Musical parties were perfect covers for meetings between homosexuals, useful places of introduction in a society long before there were bars or other public places for socialising, and Jack took full advantage of them. At some parties men dressed as women for informal balls, redolent of the scandalous entertainments enjoyed by Boulton and Park, the two London transvestites and stage performers who had been famously acquitted of conspiracy to commit sodomy a few years earlier.

Malcolm Johnstone, the fashionable and wealthy son of a Ballsbridge miller and baker, was one who frequently held such parties. We shall hear of him again.

Probably at one such party, Jack met another young man called Bill Clarke with whom he began to share an interest in amateur dramatics. The theatre was a good cover too for men of bohemian tastes to mix. Clarke worked as a cooper and lived by the Liffey on Ushers Quay with his family. Like Jack, Clarke worked as a rent boy, and the two quickly became friends. He was the shorter of the two, a rough-hewn little lad three years younger of barely over five foot three, and unable to read or write, though what he lacked in literacy he made up for in cunning.

Clarke entertained a 'customer' of particular standing and a member of the British Administration at Dublin Castle. James Ellis French was the head of the County CID and was horribly compromised in his job by his sexual liking for working class young men, and pretty careless about the way in which he went about his personal life. It was no secret in the police force that French kept company with male prostitutes and men much younger than himself. He would one day be accused of sexually assaulting a constable from the Kilcrea Barracks in County Cork.

Jack and his new friend began working as a pair, not always it has to be said in an honest capacity. The world of male prostitution was fraught with treachery. Boys robbed, punters cheated, relationships developed, relationships ended, love letters accumulated and gathered dust in drawers and trunks, and the threat of blackmail hung over all like a dark cloud waiting to descend. Alongside the thrill of illicit relationships there was always fear of discovery, of violence, fear of one's family finding out and always the fear of the law.

At that time, prior to the Criminal Law Amendment Act of 1885, things were a lot safer for men enjoying sex with other men. Anything that fell short of buggery was strictly speaking not against the law, but anal intercourse itself carried a penalty of life imprisonment, which in real terms meant a period of incarceration for not less than ten years. So foreplay was okay, oral intercourse had been deemed not to constitute buggery, but any movement *towards* anal intercourse could be interpreted as attempted buggery, which was also a crime.

The Bishop of Clogher had fallen foul of this in 1822 while indulging in sexual foreplay with a young guardsman in the back room of a public house in Westminster. A number of witnesses observed what was going on and did nothing to intervene until the bishop attempted actual penetration, at which point they burst in and held the pair down. The bishop was charged with attempted buggery but fled to Scotland. The young private was drummed out of the army.

In spite of this, long lasting relationships between men who might settle down together existed, but were extremely rare. Society was far from ready for such things and would not be for a very long time, especially in a Catholic country like Ireland, which had some similarity to the American Bible-Belt of today. Half a century after Jack fell in love with Lieutenant Kirwan, the two founders of the Dublin Gate Theatre, Hilton Edwards and Micheal MacLiammoir, known as 'the boys', were lovers whose propensities were much gossiped about, but they were prominent in the arts. The Gate and the famous Abbey Theatre were known respectively as Sodom and Begorrah.

There was no turning a blind eye for soldiers and coopers and male prostitutes, and men who dressed as women. When relationships developed, they were fraught with tension, especially when the ages and social positions of the partners were disparate, as with

Jack and his snobbish soldier. The taboo against such social classes mixing was almost as great as that against homosexual acts, if not actually greater. It couldn't last.

We do not know how it ended. It may have just fizzled out naturally when the difficulty of maintaining it became too great, or it may have climaxed in some argument, like the blistering row between Gustavus Cornwall and his young bank clerk. When romance and finance became muddled, conflicts were inevitable, and Kirwan might well have decided it was no longer worth taking the risk. One thing however is certain. Jack's relationship with Martin Kirwan lasted some considerable time and it became very well-known among their friends. To use modern parlance, they were a couple. What his parents would think of him even talking to a soldier, seen as a tool of the British occupation of their country, let alone becoming romantically involved with one, he didn't care to think about.

One factor that probably did put the brakes on the affair was Jack's friendship with Clarke. There was no shortage of places for the two youths to meet those who were searching for a quick sexual fix with young good-looking teenagers. St Stephen's Green and the environs of Trinity College would always produce a gentlemen or two searching for a willing boy. But if one wanted to meet in less-observed places, the underground urinals of the city were, in timeworn fashion, the places where encounters frequently took place, though one had to be constantly on the lookout for police officers in plain clothes.

The most notorious was at College Green, at the Meeting of the Waters, below the statue of Ireland's bard, Tom Moore. It was well-known to every homosexual man in Dublin, though Gustavus Cornwall, when accused of meeting a young man there, would strongly deny that he had ever been inside it or indeed had ever heard of such a place.

Jack could scarcely bring money back into the family home earned by prostitution without awkward questions being asked. He needed to find a job. And living in Harcourt Street, socially connected to a lot of its inhabitants, which included members of the medical profession, Gustavus Cornwall would have been in an ideal position to help Jack find employment.

The job that Jack found was not one popular with men, though it was with those of his sexual persuasion. He went into service. It could be said that the service sector was now to be the story of his life.

* * * * * *

Chapter Notes.

1. The description of Jack is taken from the Irish Prison Registers, the only reliable source.

CHAPTER FOUR

A GENTLEMAN'S GENTLEMAN

Jack Saul didn't become a servant for one of the most eminent doctors in Dublin without considerable patronage. He also needed at least one glowing reference.

A discreet word from a patient or a trusted neighbour, of which Gustavus Cornwall was one, about a young man who would benefit from a position of some trust might have persuaded Dr John Joseph Cranny of 82 Harcourt Street to give him a trial. Dr Cranny was young himself, just in his early thirties, newly married and eager to impress. Only the rich kept a male servant, for they were more expensive.

The Crannys were an incredibly wealthy family. They were also staunch old Catholics, many of them old enough to remember the days of Catholic emancipation. Dr Cranny's father, Patrick Cranny, had started life as a high-class bespoke bootmaker in South St George's Street, importing the finest leather from Florence and employing a number of Italian workers.

Many old-stagers in Dublin still walked about in boots hand-made by the famous Patrick Cranny. When mechanization came in, he gave up the boot trade and with a partner took up speculative building at which he made a fortune. He and his family, which included the young Dr Cranny then at medical school, moved to Muckross Park in Donnybrook where he bought up all the land and houses.

He was also fiercely involved in the Home Rule movement, and that passion spread throughout the family. One of his grandchildren would earn posthumous fame by being one of the sixteen shot by the British after the 1916 Easter Rising.

His wealth enabled his son John to enter the medical profession. Dr Cranny graduated from the University of Dublin and began his professional life by acting as assistant-physician at the Rotunda Lying-In Hospital, becoming a member of the Council of the Royal College of Surgeons. He had only been at Harcourt Street a few years when he took on Jack.

Jack was extremely lucky. Dr Cranny was the kind of medical practitioner his family would have been unable to afford. He also moved in a society that invited and displayed considerable snobbery. He made regular trips to the continent, which were assiduously announced in the society columns of *Freemans Journal*, as were his welcomed returns to the practice in Harcourt Street.

Jack's duties were numerous. Only on large estates would the jobs of butler, footman and groom be divided between different employees. In Dr Cranny's four-storey corner house, Jack was expected to wait at table, look after the silver in the house and clean the knives and shoes, look after his master's clothes, care for the wine cellar, wind the clocks, take letters from his master, answer the door to visitors who called, and be responsible for locking up the house at night.

It was a position that suited a young man who wished to escape his upbringing. Jack learned how to behave in polite society, mastered the graces needed to carry him through life. And he didn't need to travel far from home to do it, like many unfortunate girl servants who ended up sometimes miles from their families. On his time off, Jack could walk home across the green and visit his mother and brothers and sisters. His older brother Edward was now seventeen and about to follow his father into the hackney trade, his younger brother James only four years old and too young to contribute. His sisters, like all young girls from their social class, entertained no more ambition than going into service and marrying. His eldest sister Maria was already the wife of a labourer, Edward Donnelly, and both were living in the family home at 5 Duke Lane.

As the eldest boy, now turning twenty-one, and working for a respectable household, Jack must have delighted his mother. Some of his money he spent on clothes, some he gave to her. He would always do his best to care for her, even when he was not earning much money.

Jack learned much more at Dr Cranny's than just how to be a valet. In those days, physicians prepared and sold their own medicines, often with the help of an apothecary. Any education Jack learned at his mother's knee about the ointments and homemade cures shared among the poor in The Liberties was added to by what he learned at Harcourt Street. Long before antibiotics, doctors dispensed tonics and tinctures for headaches, coughs, stomachaches, itches and even hangovers. Jack was a young man eager to keep down a proper job and to learn as much as he possibly could, and his time at Dr Cranny's was spent furthering that education. Dr Cranny, who liked and trusted Jack, was clearly a willing teacher and Jack may well have helped him package and dispense drugs as part of his many other duties.

Jack was certainly intelligent enough to study to become anything he wanted to – if he had wanted to. He was literate, he was connected enough to find himself a job as a gentleman's valet in the first place, and clever enough to keep it, at least for a while. His journey out of the slums and escape from poverty was, at that moment, ready made for him. Good gentlemens' servants were in much demand and in time he might have found himself a senior position on a large estate. Not every Dublin kid got such an opportunity. Not every Dublin kid grew into the phenomenally good-looking boy that Jack had become. He must have been a source of pride to his mother Eliza.

And if Lieutenant Kirwan's snobbery had rubbed off a bit on Jack – the young Lieutenant had once chided Malcolm Johnstone, the rich miller's son, for keeping company with 'common soldiers' – Jack's position as a male servant to a gentleman in Harcourt Street puffed him up even more.

And then it all went wrong.

In his time off, Jack still worked as a prostitute. He wasn't the only servant or groom to do so. Along the road, Gustavus Cornwall was always happy to entertain. Jack was well-endowed. That salient fact would one day be immortalised for all time in a way that Jack couldn't yet begin to imagine.

There were male brothels too, though they were not sophisticated places, merely back parlours where curtains were drawn across to create small areas of privacy. It was an exciting, dangerous and addictive activity, one that Jack would find impossible to give up. A client who might take him to the theatre and entertain him with dinner and brandy was always welcome. Not all of them wanted to sodomise him, though some did, and though it doubtless hurt he grinned and bore it with thoughts of Ireland. And perhaps even Home Rule too. Some wanted you to 'gamahuche' them, in other words give them oral sex. Sometimes they wanted to return the favour. Jack enjoyed that, as did a lot of the boys who went on the game. And lest anyone think that S & M is a modern phenomenon, Jack was not beyond giving a customer a whipping, or being flagellated himself, with bondage thrown in for good measure.

Someone who lived as Jack did was well aware of the dangers posed by the host of venereal diseases that existed, particularly gonorrhea and the unmentionable syphilis, the latter carrying with it great social stigma and shame. In a city like Dublin, with its high proportion of soldiers and female prostitutes, it was reckoned that one in three soldiers was infected. There were no diagnostic tests in those days, and it is more than likely that at some point Jack contracted something. There were no cures. The old saying 'one night with Venus, a lifetime with mercury' summed it up. Mercury had been used for centuries to treat epidemic diseases, but its effectiveness was questioned. The side effects were horrible and it often killed you quicker than the disease.

Jack's most immediate problem was the criminal side of his life. He was no saint, no male tart with a heart.

It was easy to steal money or possessions from a client because they would be scared to go to the police, especially if it happened in a urinal, where robberies often did occur. In their homes it was just as lucrative. A boy invited into the home of an older man who made off with the family silver might well just get away with it as his victim would be reluctant to go to the police and subject himself to embarrassing questions. What was the boy doing there in the first place?

Whether Jack or Bill Clarke was the greater of the two tempted into villainy scarcely mattered. They both got into trouble one night in October 1878 and both ended up in prison.

Jack seems to have stayed out of trouble, or at least avoided prosecution, until that moment. And it wasn't buggery he was arrested for, it was burglary.

Between one and two o'clock in the morning, Constable 92B on patrol in the area of Harcourt Street heard the sound of breaking glass in Clonmel Place, the road which ran down the side of Dr Cranny's house. Clarke was leaning against the railings, and Jack Saul was leaning out of one of the lower windows. Jack had with him a coat, a walking stick, and upon investigation the pockets of the coat were found to contain a pair of gloves and a salt cellar.

The constable took both young men into custody then knocked on Dr Cranny's door and made a search of the house. A pane of glass had been broken in the window out of which Jack had been leaning. Dr Cranny confirmed that Jack was in his employment but he did not know Clarke. Jack had returned between nine and ten o'clock that night, and the coat found on him was, according to Dr Cranny, that of his brother.

Dr Cranny had two brothers. One, Gerald, was an architect. The other, Frank, had been sent abroad for embezzling his father and seducing a maid. If it was Gerald's coat, nothing was heard from him about it.

The youths were sent to the Richmond Bridewell at Griffith Barracks in the south of Dublin to await trial. The Richmond Bridewell had been built as a remand prison to relieve pressure on Dublin's Newgate Gaol, but was now a male penitentiary popularly known as 'The Richmond Pen'. Over the door was the motto 'Cease to do Evil, Learn to do Well'. Prominent Irish Nationalists were among its most famous historical prisoners. Jack and Bill Clarke were lucky to be only on remand, for the prison had recently become notorious for its 'plank-bed' system. Convicted prisoners were forced to sleep on hard deal boards, described by visiting Irish Justices as a form of torture. The fact that the torture had been decreed by English politicians was not lost on its critics.

They would spend only a few days in the Bridewell, a sobering experience nonetheless for both of them as it appears to have been the first occasion either of the two lads had spent time in captivity.

Their trial opened at the Green Street Court House (Dublin's equivalent of the Old Bailey) a few days later. Both boys would have been well aware of the history of the building. This was the same courthouse that had seen the trials of Wolfe Tone and Robert Emmet, the former for his part in the 1798 Irish Rebellion, the latter for his abortive and shambolic attempt to seize Dublin Castle with a handful of insurgents and very little weaponry. Both men had been hailed as heroes. There was nothing heroic about Jack Saul or Bill Clarke.

They were indicted for 'feloniously breaking and entering the dwelling house of Dr Cranny in Harcourt Street and also with burglarously breaking out of the house and stealing a coat, a stick, a pair of gloves and a salt cellar'. They were defended by Mr J. Byrne Wilson.

It was a strange charge, as Jack was legitimately employed at the house he was accused of breaking into and out of. And some odd new evidence emerged. Dr Cranny now stated that the coat and stick did not belong to him (there was no mention of his brother owning the coat) and Clarke, according to the brief report in *Freemans Journal* said that 'he was his (Saul's) brother and that he had come to tell Saul of his (Clarke's) mother's death', a statement that is hard to make sense of, though one has to allow for confusion and misreporting. (The *Irish Times* referred to Jack throughout as James Saul, which was the name of his four-year-old brother!).

The window out of which he was caught leaning had a broken catch anyway and could not be locked, so there was little reason to smash it.

If Jack said anything in his own defence, it wasn't reported, probably because the crime was not of great interest. The paucity and carelessness of reportage therefore leaves us with a mystery. The Lord Chief Justice said there was no case for burglary to go before the jury, however improper it might be for Jack to leave his master's premises in such a way, and he would leave it instead for the jury to say simply whether they thought the prisoners intended to commit a felony, bearing in mind that the property wasn't claimed by anyone.

The jury acquitted them both.

What is one to make of this? Why Jack should break out of a window in a house where he was employed as a servant is pretty strange. While it's impossible now to know what they were up to, we can hazard a guess, given the nature of their other activities as young rent boys. It's possible that Dr Cranny was originally mistaken about the ownership of the coat, and that Jack had stolen it and the other items or perhaps even taken them in kind from a punter that night who was understandably reticent to come forward and accuse him of theft. Clarke came to take the items off his hands and was leaning over the railings to grab them. Jack leant through the window, rather than going to the front door, and somehow accidentally the window got broken. Or the reverse might have been true. Clarke might have stolen the items, and Jack was receiving them.

Whatever the circumstances, they were unfortunate. A gentleman's male servant had to be above suspicion. Guilty or not guilty, it meant the end of Jack's employment. He would have no reference now. The chance he had been given he had blown out of sheer stupidity.

He still had a card left to play however. With his reputation tarnished, he made up his mind to go to London, a city in which he would make a name for himself that would define his life.

CHAPTER FIVE

JACK COMES TO LONDON

The winter of 1879 was a cruel one in Dublin. A smallpox epidemic, heavy snow and a stoppage of the sewers all combined to make life precarious and more unpleasant than usual. It was followed by a spring of relentless rain in which the potato crop blackened again in the waterlogged beds and Ireland seemed once more threatened by the spectre of famine.

The Sauls moved that year, out of the house at 5 Duke Lane, which the Sanitary Commission had recently condemned as unfit for human habitation, round the corner into Lemon Street. Lemon Street was a gloomy passageway that connected Duke Lane and Grafton Street. For all its unsanitariness, Duke Lane had been Jack's home for practically all his life. It was time to pull up his roots, and set off for adventure and independence.

It was Jack's first trip to London. Probably he intended to make it permanent but the journey was one he would get to know well. The speediest route was from Kingstown (now Dun Laoghaire) to Holyhead with the City of Dublin Steampacket Company. To catch the early morning mail boat he had to be up at half past four in the morning. Boarding the steamer he witnessed the chaos he had often heard about. Huge heaps of luggage belonging to passengers setting off on Continental tours were roughly manhandled, arguments ensuing among the clatter and uproar. The words 'With Care' were treated with so much contempt that the loading and the journey were often compared with travel on the sub-continent of India.

For a mother to see her eldest son pack up and leave home was always painful, and for Eliza Saul especially so. Jack was one of the only three bread-winners in the family. His departure would eat into the household budget on which she was struggling to bring up and feed three girls and a boy. With Jack gone, life wasn't going to be easy.

Maybe her good-looking darling would mend his ways; perhaps away from the influence of his less repu-table Dublin chums he would become a man she could be proud of. Perhaps, as good Irish sons did, once he stepped off the train at Euston Station, he would start to earn good money and send it home.

In one way, Eliza Saul's prayers would be answered.

In London, Jack tried to find employment as a butler or valet to a gentleman. There were lots of fine houses and no shortage of gentlemen, but without a reference or the patronage of such a man as Gustavus Cornwall he found it impossible. For the first time in his life he was among strangers.

London, too, he discovered had its share of dreadful slums, and he no doubt experienced the discomfort of living in a succession of wretched lodging houses, like the thousands of other young men from Ireland and the north of England who landed at Euston Station, stranded souls who knew no-one, looking for a job and a place to stay.

Another thing that went against him was his Irish accent. Many English distrusted the Irish. The newspapers were full of press warnings about Fenian risings and dangerous revolutionaries. Those in the Home Rule movement were becoming ever more vocal. A young Irish lad with no references in London at the end of the 1870s was treated with suspicion almost by default.

Fortunately Jack had a couple of assets, which needed neither references nor well-rounded vocals, and he already had the experience. He soon found his way into his old trade. And that meant Piccadilly Circus.

'The Dilly' as a pick-up place, if not yet known by that name, was well established. Created early in the century to link up the foot of Regent Street and Piccadilly, Piccadilly Circus was the stationary hub around which all life seemed to revolve – an ever-swirling mass of people, horses, carriages, omnibuses and cabs that created a cacophany night and day. The place never slept, and neither, it seemed, did the community of rent boys and their punters who established their ground along the pavement at the front of Swan and Edgar the haberdashers, under the adjacent arches – which would become popularly known as the meat rack – and in the concourse of Piccadilly underground station.

The boys did not welcome newcomers. It took nerve to stand there for the first time among runaways, post office boys, shoeblacks, newspaper sellers, office clerks, grooms, servants and a motley collection of others, all mingling in a dance of expectation, furtive glances thrown and met, sexual trade being constantly established in coded conversations.

In his tight suit and patent leather boots, with his fresh face and good looks, Jack was a new kid on the block, and new kids received their fair share of envious glances from other boys and offers of money from punters always on the lookout for an exciting new experience with a boy who had not been hardened by long exposure to the streets.

Oscar Wilde, a contemporary of Jack, who spoke of the 'exquisite poison' of such ambience in *The Picture of Dorian Gray*, is believed to have discovered the attraction of rough trade while waiting outside Swan and Edgar one day in 1888, and never looked back.

Neither would Jack, at least for some time.

It wasn't long before he got to know other boys on the game, and other places of entertainment and opportunity. London was vast compared to compact little Dublin, with a population of around four million. The Crown pub in Charing Cross Road and the Windsor Castle in the Strand catered for what in Dublin might have been called a 'musical' crowd but in London was for 'theatrical' types. Speakers Corner in Hyde Park was a popular meeting place. The Alhambra Music Hall on Leicester Square had a gallery at the rear where male prostitutes could promenade and pick up men, as did the Criterion Theatre. The Holborn Casino – far from being a gambling joint as the name suggested – was a debauched place where men regularly dressed as women and danced the night away with their admirers.

And was not Haxell's hotel on the Strand the place where famously, a few years before, Boulton and Park, two young theatrical gentlemen who rejoiced in the soubriquets Fanny and Stella, attended a ball with a dozen others all dressed as ladies, an event that had been used in evidence against them in court? They had been habituees of the Alhambra and the Holborn Casino.

Jack knew all about Fanny and Stella. Where were they now? What had become of them after their trial and largely welcomed acquittal?

Jack didn't need any education into the world of gentlemen who paid to sleep with soldiers. Though London did not have the concentration of barracks that Dublin possessed, there were plenty of soldiers, particularly guardsmen, who possessed a particular appeal, to be had for a price, and there were plenty of places to meet and go to bed with them. Dublin had nothing quite like the club off Portland Place to which Jack said he inevitably graduated. This was known as The Hundred Guineas Club, an establishment which catered for the sexual whims of the aristocracy whose paying members were obliged to fork out just over a hundred pounds for membership, and where it was *de rigeur* to adopt a female name. A hundred pounds in those days was about a quarter of what was needed to buy a decent London house, which made it a brothel well beyond the pocket of most of the population. (1)

It was here, according to Jack, that he met a youthful soldier in the Foot Guards called Fred Jones. Fred Jones (probably not his real name but the one given him by Jack in *The Sins of the Cities of the Plain*) was asked by the owner of the club Mr Inslip (definitely not his real name) to take the young Irishman under his wing.

Fred liked the look of his new friend and invited him to have a chop and cigars in his rooms, an offer that to modern ears has the flavour and aroma of true Victorian dining. According to Jack's riotous memoir, Fred Jones told Jack,

'We all do it. It's the commonest thing possible in the army. As soon as – or before – I had learned the goose step, I had learned to be goosed, and enjoyed it my dear. Don't you Jack?'

Considering Jack's relationship with Lieutenant Kirwan of the Dublin Militia, Jack needed little education in being goosed by – or goosing – a man in uniform.

Fred Jones then slapped Jack's thigh and said he meant to have Jack that night.

'Our old Major was the first to introduce me to it.' Jones told him. 'He made me drunk and next morning I found myself in his bed with him. Money was everything with me then. It always has been. Why, I used to be an office lad to a solicitor in Liverpool, where I forged his cheque for a hundred pounds and ran away to London, had a damned spree for a week, lost or spent it all, then enlisted. It was the safest thing to do. The military rig-out so changes the appearance of a fellow.'

The promised sex between Jack and his military companion may have been of the non-commercial variety, but Jack had little reason to complain. He was already making about eight or nine pounds a week on the game in his city of adoption, a considerable sum in those days when a labourer's weekly wage was about ten shillings, and on some days with luck he would make considerably more.

A gold sovereign – worth a pound – was the going rate for a paid sexual encounter of some quality with a gentleman who was well able to afford it. Ten shillings might do from others. From the money earned, Jack was able to send funds home to Dublin, ostensibly from the 'good job' he had found himself. If his brother ever came over to London, he might be in trouble, but until that day arrived he was quite safe.

Another acquaintance of Jack's was a young man called George Brown who had been sent away for four years to the reformatory at Red Hill in Surrey, a farm founded by the Philanthropic Society, run along the lines of an industrial school and to which boys could be sent for doing little more than begging on the streets.

George comes across as a particularly nasty piece of work.

'Jack,' George said to him one day, 'what a fool you are not to go in for the same lay as I do. You would get hundreds...'

George Brown's lay was to pick up a 'swell' and ride about with him in a cab. In the back of the cab he would get his 'prize' drunk, rob him of his wallet, and sometimes even steal the rings off his fingers.

Jack was no stranger to sex in the backs of cabs. In Dublin too, and in all major cities, they were popular places to have a bit of fun, particularly when it was too dangerous or impractical to take one's partner home. The cabbie was told simply to drive around. Jack had enjoyed sexual contact numerous times in the backs of cabs, in Dublin and in London. It was almost a sport.

Robbery was always a risk though. George Brown was proof of that. So was Jack himself, who had only got away with the theft of an overcoat and other items in Dublin because the owner did not dare to claim them.

This was the hard, brutal and off-kilter world in which Jack had set up his stall. A male prostitute couldn't afford to be soft. The soft didn't survive in that world. Selling your body put you in charge, not the purchaser. The relationship was two-way but it was heavily weighted.

For Jack, there were times, as in Dublin, when he could afford to just sit back and not do too much work. The gentleman who wanted simply to gamahuche him while he lay back with a brandy in his hand and a smile on his face, the customer who wanted nothing more than to talk to a stranger. There were always those. It sometimes surprised Jack that there was always someone who would pay a youth to sit on his lap while he droned on about his marriage or his job, as though no-one in his family would do instead. It had to be a stranger. A dangerous stranger.

To be a renter, you had to be a good listener. But danger was the thing that made the whole world of Piccadilly rent revolve on its axis. Oscar Wilde, in his letter *De Profundis*, when writing to his younger lover Lord Arthur Douglas from prison, termed it 'feasting with panthers'. The phrase is apt. In the jungle that was Piccadilly rent there were few pussycats.

As in Dublin, the police were an ever-constant danger, and Jack, like all the boys under the arches, learned to be always on the lookout for them. They had evolved to detect a policeman in plain clothes, a species still regarded as a continental invention, typically un-English and grossly unfair to those involved in the gentle practice of law breaking.

When Jack did encounter a policeman he was usually just asked to move on, or allowed to carry on his beat, depending on the bobby and amount of Irish blarney he could muster. Of course, there were always those bobbies who enjoyed a bit of fun themselves and were in the position to demand it. Though boys were arrested and charged, it was often the customers the police really wanted. The boys were bait; their customers were fish, often big fish.

Such would become clear in the two scandals in which Jack would later become involved, the Dublin felonies and the Cleveland Street scandal. In a way, he was already involved in the first, unable to do anything to check the series of interlinking events that would light the fuse and blow up into a disaster that would wreck so many lives.

The second was by no means inevitable. It was yet to depend on a chance meeting.

The first day of May 1879 was a holiday in London, as it was throughout the country. Jack had been in the capital barely a few months. Many Londoners took the opportunity of boarding the ferries that sailed down the Thames to the port of Gravesend, a popular destination in Victorian times. It was on that day that Jack was introduced by a mutual friend to Charles Hammond, whose family lived in the port, and who would have such an influence on his life.

Like Jack, Charles Richard Hammond was a 'sodomite' to use one of the few words available at the time. He was the son of a Thames waterman, one of the legion of river workers who ferried passengers across or up to London. The previous year Charles had married a French woman called Caroline Eugenie Cotte while both were living in Dean Street in the heart of London's Soho. Hammond must have possessed a considerable sense of humour for though he was only semi-literate he described himself on the marriage certificate as a professor of languages. Caroline recorded no occupation, but the one that would have described her best was whore.

She wasn't the first that Charles had lived with. Three or four years before, he had lived with a prostitute called Emily Parker who may not have been one until Hammond met her. She was literate and would write his correspondence for him.

Caroline was about ten years older than Charles, according to their marriage certificate, and he had met her on one of his youthful expeditions to the red light district in Paris. What the Hammonds thought of him bringing home a cigarette-smoking Frenchwoman old enough to be his big sister, and who could hardly speak English, beggars the imagination. But Ann Hammond was a witness at her son's wedding, and Caroline would in time become accepted as one of the family. She gave Hammond's mother a grandson two years after their marriage, though whether it was Charles' is impossible to establish.

Hammond, like Jack, grew up fascinated with whores. There were enough of them even in such a relatively small place as Gravesend, catering for the seamen who regularly embarked and disembarked there. Charles' father drowned when Charles was a boy, leaving him with a widowed mother, a dressmaking sister and an older brother. Charles worked as a shop boy but ten years later, he would be making his living in a far more dangerous but lucrative way.

Charles and Caroline were living at 25 Oxendon Street in the Haymarket when Jack became acquainted with them, and within two weeks he moved in as a lodger. Hammond was clearly taken with the pretty Irish boy. Jack possessed an irresistible combination of attributes, a rough edge hewn from his boyhood in the Dublin slums and the manners of a gentleman, acquired while in service as a valet.

At twenty-six Hammond was older, and Jack at first saw him as a kind of mentor, someone who could look after him in the big city, introduce him to people, but more than anything provide him with something he hadn't experienced since leaving Dublin – a home. The Haymarket was an area as rife with prostitution as one could find in London, and Oxendon Street was right in the centre of it.

A French prostitute made a poor substitute for a mother, but the Hammonds' union was no ordinary marriage, and Jack Saul was no ordinary lodger. Within no time at all, Jack and Hammond were both making their livings selling their bodies around the West End of London, Hammond showing Jack how he could make even more money if he put his mind to it, while Madame Caroline made her own living in her own way.

Charles Hammond had another string to his bow. He was also a pimp. He saw in Jack a perfect opportunity to line his own pocket and Jack soon found that he was giving most of what he earned to his 'landlord'. Out of this Jack would be given just enough money to live on and buy food. For Jack it wasn't the ideal arrangement. In Dublin, he had managed well on his own. But London wasn't Dublin. He needed to survive in the big city and for a few months he was content to let Charles and Caroline look after him.

Then in early December a communication arrived from Dublin. His father had died.

William Saul passed away on 7 December while living in Lemon Street, the house to which the Sauls had moved after Duke Lane. The cause of death was bronchitis. He was fifty-three.

Jack headed home, acutely conscious not only of the emotional state of his mother but the financial dilemma in which she would now find herself. The loss of the breadwinner was the worst thing that could happen to a family. There was no pension, no insurance. Widows were expected to work if their husbands died and that meant only one thing – charring or taking in laundry. There were no jobs better than that for a forty-year-old woman who could neither read nor write.

Eliza Saul welcomed her eldest son home, and hoped he would come back to stay. It was almost expected. Jack's younger brother Edward at the age of eighteen was thrust into the role of keeping the family. Their sister Annie helped their mother keep house. James was only five.

Edward was an accomplished horseman, he had learnt much about the hackney trade from their father, but he was still a teenager and the whole burden was now on his shoulders as he plied the streets of Dublin in his father's horse-drawn cab in all weathers for sixpence a trip.

Unless of course Jack stayed and got a job.

The funeral cortege left south Dublin for Glasnevin Cemetery where William Saul was interred in the same plot of ground in which he had buried his mother-in-law and two of Jack's siblings. He hadn't been able to afford a stone. It was a quiet place, by a path, and only a few feet from the wall which separated the cemetery from the Botanic Gardens. As Jack stood by the grave, his head befuddled with beer after the wake, watching his mother try to hold back the tears as she contemplated a bleak future, his mind would have wandered back to happier days when he strolled in the gardens on the other side of that wall with his Lieutenant in the Dublin Militia.

Dublin families were no strangers to death in their midst. Many died in the same room in which they had been born and in which they had lived most of their lives, and learned to accept the inevitable. The year before, Jack's sister Maria had lost her firstborn to her labourer husband William Donnelly from scarlet fever. One-year-old William Donnelly was already in the same family grave.

Priests thundered from the pulpit against wakes, regarding them as little better than bacchanalian orgies, but among the lower class of Catholics they were traditional. Family, friends, neighbours all gathered round, clay pipes were smoked, music was played and songs were sung. Round the corner, next door to the Sauls' old condemned home in Duke Lane, was Kehoe's pub. It had been there since the turn of the century and had seen its fair share of Irish wakes. It is still there today.

But when the heads cleared and the new day dawned, hard decisions had to be made. Jack would take until the following spring to make them, staying in Dublin with his family and renewing old acquaintances, such as Lieutenant Kirwan, Gustavus Cornwall and his young friend Bill Clarke. There was the opportunity to earn some money from prostitution to help his mother out, the source of which was no doubt passed off as 'odd jobs'.

Jack could no longer live in Dublin. He had partially torn up his roots and replanted them in London, where there was much more adventure and opportunity. He had outgrown the city of his birth and he wanted much more than it could offer.

Jack wasn't going to live in poverty. Like millions of boys before and after, he was going to make his way in the world and hopefully become rich. Edward could do the jarveying, but Jack would always be the apple of his mother's eye, making money abroad like a good Irish son and sending it home.

After five months back in Dublin, in April 1880 he set off for Kingstown and the steamer and returned to London, having missed one of the worst smogs in living memory. He renewed his acquaintance with the Hammonds and moved in with them at a new address, Frith Street in Soho. This time Hammond charged Jack thirty-five shillings a week for his lodgings, which Jack found excessive. Indeed it was, as three or four shillings a week could then get one a room. The thirty-five shillings (£1.75) was clearly not rent, but a cut from Jack's takings.

The first splits in his relationship with his newfound friend and landlord were beginning to appear. Jack didn't need to be pimped. He was perfectly capable of selling his own body, and didn't need anyone else to do his marketing for him.

The decision was half made for him as Hammond, who seemed to flit around as though always on the run from somebody or something, decided to go to Paris with Caroline but before he departed he sold his furniture to another prostitute called Madame Clemence who lived at 36 Lisle Street with her thirteen year old son Leon.

Jack moved into the same address, a very convenient one for Piccadilly Circus, which was just a short walk away, and Leicester Square, the real bustling heart of the West End of London and the centre of the sex trade. It was an address which would forever become associated – as would Jack – with one of the most notorious pornographic books ever written, a book in which he would become immortalised for all time.

Just how a boy from Dublin, after only two years in London, came to be the central character in a notorious pornographic memoir is one of the abiding mysteries of his whole life and indeed of the gay history of London in the late Victorian era.

* * * * * *

Chapter Notes

1. Although less fashionably inhabited than when it was first built for the Duke of Portland, Portland Place still numbered among its inhabitants several members of the upper classes including peers, baronets, judges and ambassadors. The Hundred Guineas Club would have been held in a private house. Its provenance is unknown though the first mention of it to the author's knowledge in any publication was in *The Sins of the Cities of the Plain* (1881), Jack's own memoir. A guinea was one pound one shilling, or £1.05p. Gentlemen dealt in guineas whereas pounds were for tradesmen and

the lower classes. In his biography of Prince Albert Victor Edward, *Clarence: The Life of H.R.H the Duke of Clarence and Avondale*, author Michael Harrison states that the Prince was a regular visitor to the Hundred Guineas Club where he adopted the name Victoria after his grandmother. Though it may well have been true, the evidence for it is as substantial as the claim that he visited 19 Cleveland Street.

CHAPTER SIX

THE SINS OF JACK SAUL

Hammond returned to London later in the year and invited Jack to spend Christmas with him and his friends. Jack accepted. The previous Christmas in Dublin, following the death of his father, had not been the happiest affair and all the conflicts between siblings at such times were there, under the surface if not simmering on top. Jack had left home, come back, now he had left home again at a time when he was sorely needed.

What Jack needed was a Christmas with somebody else's family where he felt under no pressure, and in which duty played no part. Hammond provided it. Though the most popular way to travel down to Gravesend was by river steamer, the train from Charing Cross took just an hour.

Gravesend, in spite of the name, was a lively town and being at the eastern boundary of the Port of London was the place where all vessels arriving from foreign countries collected on board the revenue officers before continuing up river. Troops embarked and landed at Gravesend, emigrant ships took passengers on board, collier ships discharged their cargoes, and a regular steam ferry put across to Tilbury on the Essex shore. The river was normally full of smaller craft too, those of the Thames watermen and lightermen, the former conveying passengers, and the latter, in their blue serge suits, stiff white collars and bowler hats, unloading the vessels which were too large to put in at the already crowded wharves and jetties.

Hammond's family had lived in the port all their lives and congregated around Windmill Hill, which climbed to a fine vantage point in what was then a splendidly rural location. It was a perfect stroll for a Christmas morning. The river could be seen stretching west towards London and eastwards out into the North Sea. The windmill, which gave the hill its name, boasted a camera obscura and there was also a popular tavern called the Belle Vue that in summer boasted a dancing platform.

Jack met Hammond's mother Ann, who had remarried three years after his father's death. As a widow she had been forced to take in washing, and like Jack's own mother had met hard times with fortitude. She was now a nurse, living with a family called Parker and was Mrs Ann Trigg, though she had separated now from her second husband, a gardener by trade. Jack liked her, and she took a shine to the pretty fair-haired youth who had befriended her wayward son, just as she liked all his rather bohemian friends.

Charles' life was far more exotic than that of his brother Ted, a plasterer by trade. Charles had made trips to Paris. His wife was French, albeit not a woman of unspotted chastity. Their son, little Charlie, was learning to talk French as well as English. There was nothing bohemian about Ann Trigg, a labourer's daughter from Tilbury on the Essex side of the Thames.

Just round the corner Jack saw the house in which Hammond had lived most of his boyhood and where he had lived when his father died, a tiny enclave of a few narrow terraced homes called Lydia Cottages, connected to the Wrotham Road by a stone archway. They are still there today, scarcely unchanged. Like Jack, Charles Hammond had left behind a family and an environment into which he no longer fitted. And in the same way that Jack would one day need his, Hammond would have to call on his own family for support when the going got rough. It would get very rough indeed.

Gravesend was not short of pubs. The oldest was the Three Daws, down by the cast-iron Town Pier, a hostelry with a rich history of smuggling and known to have secret tunnels along which men also escaped from the press gangs. Next door was the Amsterdam Tavern, outside which, Jack learned, Hammond's father had been found drowned.

It was a tragedy, the real cause of which had never been established. One Friday night he had left home about seven in the evening. He was never seen alive by his family again. He had walked down to the Amsterdam where he had spent a couple of hours drinking with friends, but then left by the back way without saying anything. That night he didn't come home. At half past six the following morning, a fisherman was standing on the bridge at the rear of the tavern and saw a body lying in the mud. It was that of Edward Hammond.

A coroner's jury heard that he had been in poor health for some time, and was sober when he left the pub. Ann Hammond also confirmed her husband was a very sober man, which for a waterman was remarkable. But it may well have been the truth. Edward Hammond seems never to have been in any trouble except in his twenties when he had been caught smuggling contraband goods close to Tilbury Fort. A coastguard vessel saw him throw a sack over the side, which contained silk, lace and ten boxes of cigars. He had been fined a hundred pounds, a stiff penalty in those days, and imprisoned briefly at Springfield Gaol. Smuggling was not uncommon among Thames watermen.

Suicide was suspected, for Hammond senior had drowned in just four feet of water. He had not cried out. A police sergeant helpfully suggested that he might have tripped owing to the heel-plate of one his boots sticking out, but Edward Hammond had been a waterman all his life, used to clambering in and out of boats, and would hardly fall from the back of a pub into four feet of water without creating a cry or a splash. The jury, in the absence of further evidence, returned a verdict of 'Found Drowned'.

Jack had been twenty-two when his father died. Hammond had been seventeen when he had lost his. It gave them a bond. Hammond had lost a sister too, Mary Ann, who died in the Gravesend workhouse of typhus fever.

Christmas Day 1880 was one of the few times that Jack felt a different kind of union with Hammond. They made their living as fellow sodomites, had been landlord and lodger, pimp and prostitute, but now Jack had met Hammond's family and friends, including brother Ted the plasterer and been accepted into their midst.

After the holiday, they returned to their London lives, Jack to 36 Lisle Street and to Madame Clemence, where Jack – perhaps unknown to Hammond – was already engaged in writing a memoir of his short life.

At least that is one word for it.

In the British library today resides the only known original copy of *The Sins of the Cities of the Plain*. It is kept under lock and key, and one has to read it under close supervision for reasons that most people would not question.

Though it was anonymously printed in London in 1881, the year Jack Saul moved to Lisle Street, the publisher is now known to have been a well-known purveyor of pornographic literature called William Lazenby. Only two hundred and fifty copies were ever issued, though it was reprinted by Oscar Wilde's publisher Leonard Smithers in 1902. According to Charles Hirsch, the proprietor of the *Libraire Parisienne* in Coventry Street, Oscar ordered a copy from him in 1890, nine years after its publication.

Jack may not have met Oscar, but Oscar would certainly know all about Jack Saul. For on page five of *Sins*, the hero of the book introduces himself with the immortal words 'Saul, Jack Saul, sir, of Lisle Street, Leicester Square, and ready for a lark with a free gentleman at any time.'

Lisle Street today is on the edge of the beating heart of Soho's gay village. The very garish and gay Ku Bar stands on the corner. In those days it was known as the Clock House, and just across the road was No 36, like all the others in the street a medium-sized building with a shop front below and two upper storeys. The census of that year provides a snapshot in time of the cosmopolitan nature of the inhabitants of the house, and indeed of the whole street. Unfortunately Jack Saul was not at home, or at least if he was Madame Clemence, who answered the census enumerator's questions, did not include him.

There were four separate 'families' – the others were all foreigners with English wives, an Italian cook called Carlo Gaverni and his English born wife from Hampshire, a domestic butler Francis Arnaud from France and his wife Alice from Finsbury, and Francis Raymond, a forty-eight-year-old wine merchant from Toulouse and his Westminster born wife Eliza. Clemence Roger Teker described herself as a lodger and housekeeper – a popular euphemism for prostitute – she was thirty-five years old, born in France, and her son Leon worked as a cook. No 'head of house' with whom she lodged, or indeed kept house for, is recorded.

Perhaps if the enumerator had done an unofficial census of the young men under the arches at Piccadilly, he might have encountered Jack.

But the greater mystery revolves around the person Jack met one day a few months earlier while strolling through Leicester Square in his patent leather boots, tight suit showing off the fork of his trousers and advertising his 'very extraordinary development of the male appendages'.

Many historians have tried to put a name to the man who encountered Jack on that day, and all the names will be considered here, but for the moment we shall call him simply by the name he gave himself.

Mr Cambon.

Mr Cambon was struck by Jack's 'fresh beardless face, with almost feminine features, and sparkling blue eyes'. Jack's appearance truly spoke to his senses. Mr Cambon realised immediately that the handsome youth must be one of the 'Mary-Anns' of London of whom he had heard were often to be seen sauntering in the neighbourhood of Regent Street and Leicester Square on fine afternoons or evenings.

The object of Mr Cambon's curiosity took off his hat, wiped his face with a white silk handkerchief, and commenced to tease the older gentleman by continually looking back at him.

Eventually, outside a picture shop down a small side street – picture shops were often used for sexual encounters between men – they made contact. Mr Cambon asked the young man to join him in a glass of wine. Jack was reticent to be seen drinking in a public place – or more likely he just had an eye to the speedier business opportunity. Mr Cambon duly relented.

'Would you mind if we take a cab to my chambers? I live in the Cornwall Mansions, close to Baker Street Station. Have a cigar and a chat with me, as I see you are a fast young chap, and can put me up to a thing or two.'

They hailed a cab and took it to Cornwall Mansions, a block of residences which backed onto the railway line out of Baker Street station, in earshot of the roaring steam engines of the Metropolitan Railway. The Victorian novelist George Gissing lived there and described them as 'quite aristocratic in character … there are carriages at the door all day long'. They were also occupied by many bohemian types including a fair number of stage performers.

Mr Cambon's housekeeper obligingly laid the table for two, where Mr Cambon and his delightful young pick-up did 'ample justice to a good rumpsteak and oyster sauce, topped up with a couple of bottles of champagne of an extra sec brand.'

Talk about the luck of the Irish.

It wasn't until after dinner that Mr Cambon was ultimately furnished with his guest's name, and his readiness for a lark with a free gentleman. At any time.

'What was it made you take a fancy to me? Did you observe any interesting points about your humble servant?' Jack asked, flirtatiously.

Mr Cambon referred to the prominence between his legs, and his fancy to satisfy his curiosity about it.

'It's as real as my face, sir, and a great deal prettier.' Jack said. 'Did you ever see a finer tosser in your life?'

Any music hall joke that might have followed swiftly evaporated as Jack opened his trousers.

'It's my only fortune, sir, but it really provides for all I want, and often introduces me to the best of society, ladies as well as gentlemen. There isn't a girl around Leicester Square but what would have me for her man, but I find it more to my interest not to waste my strength on women. The pederastic game (pederastic had a more general meaning then) pays so well, and is quite as enjoyable. I wouldn't have a woman unless well paid for it.'

Jack's subservience and openness impressed Mr Cambon.

What followed, in Mr Cambon's narrative, properly belongs in the field of pornography. But we might just pick one colourful bloom out of it. Jack's 'priapus' he described as ten inches long. He masturbated Jack until a jet of sperm went almost a yard high, and fizzled in the hot coals of the fire. Jack sat upon his knee and they indulged in love kisses.

Mr Cambon asked Jack where he got a taste for such activity, and how he had learned to do it so deliciously.

'That would be too long a tale to go into now.' Jack answered. 'Some other day, if you like to make it worth my while, I will give you the whole history.'

The whole history would have incorporated years of learning to survive poverty on the streets of Dublin but Mr Cambon didn't want that.

'Could you write it out?' Mr Cambon asked him. 'Or give me an outline so that I might put it into the shape of a tale?'

Jack wasn't going to offer his services – any services – for nothing.

'It would take me so much time that you would have to make me a present of at least twenty pounds. It would take three or four weeks, several hours a day'.

They eventually settled on a fiver a week for thirty or forty pages of foolscap notepaper a week. Tolerably well-written, Mr Cambon emphasised.

And so took place the genesis of a book which came to be known as *The Sins of the Cities of the Plain*, which Mr Cambon intended to subtitle *The Recollections of a Mary-Ann,* despite Jack telling him that was what the low girls of the neighbourhood called him. Jack didn't expect to be called a Mary-Ann by a respectable customer such as an occupant of Cornwall Mansions.

He had worked as a servant and if he didn't know much else about how to get on in polite society, he knew how to address people. He expected people to address him with respect too.

After some more shenanigans involving flagellation (which may have been a case of Mr Cambon gilding the lily somewhat in his description of the encounter) Jack was sent home with sheets of notepaper to effectively write the story of his sexual life.

Jack was in no doubt that this was for the pornography market. He wasn't going to be the next Charles Dickens or Jane Austen. The Victorians had a huge appetite for pornography, and much of it was for sale under the counter in London if you knew where to look for it. Jack had certainly come across some, even in his native Dublin, where certain places were well-known to Trinity College students searching for erotic literature.

Neither was Mr Cambon a respectable publisher. He was a pornographer, or at least he was in the employment of one. And Jack, with his pretty face and sparkling eyes and obliging manner, was the perfect subject for his latest enterprise. The fact that Jack was chosen says a great deal about him. There were scores of boys around Piccadilly, most of them very rough and disreputable trade, who could have told some equally salacious tales of their lives, but the one picked to do so was Jack Saul.

After just about a year in London, he had a reputation. He was twenty-four years old and had become known as Dublin Jack. It was a great name for a rent boy.

There was one other thing that Mr Cambon stressed, and it hardly needed telling. The pornography market, and particularly that catered for by the publisher of *Sins*, was very particular. Jack's new friend did not want a depressing tale of boys going hungry on the streets, selling their bodies in dark alleyways, encountering violence, catching disease, visiting hospitals for doses of mercury. It wasn't to be a story of raw survival and shortened lives.

Jack could have told that certainly, and in some ways it was a pity he didn't, for no candid autobiography of a Victorian rent boy exists. No, the publisher of *Sins* knew his readers and what they wanted was what he had given them before many times, chastisement and sex in high society between members of the aristocracy and the lower orders which included their servants. Sex between the classes was a great taboo in Victorian society, and so reading about it in heightened erotic prose provided a vicarious thrill.

Sins wasn't going to be the life he had led but the life he wanted to lead, the adventures of a libertine who crosses the class barrier and breaks every sexual norm in the book, a memoir of his alter-ego. He would create a past that would elevate him to the status of an athletic sexual adventurer. It wouldn't be the first work of prose-pornography. John Cleland produced that while sitting in a debtor's prison in 1748. That notorious work was *Fanny Hill, Memoir of a Woman of Pleasure*.

Jack might have preferred Memoir of a Boy of Pleasure to *The Recollections of a Mary-Ann*.

And if he fell down on the literary side, he would have plenty of professional guidance in the requirements of the pornography market from a true master in the field.

But who was Mr Cambon? While Jack was to rejoice in the memoir under his own name, Mr Cambon, who 'discovered him' that day in Leicester Square, was a pseudonym. His true identity remains a mystery to this day.

The world of Victorian pornographers is an esoteric field. It was also extremely small. Some who have made a study of it point to James Campbell Reddie as the possible co-author of *Sins*.

He was a well-known writer of pornographic books with titles such as *The Amatory Experiences of a Surgeon,* and was a friend of the Victorian erotica collector Henry Spencer Ashbee. Ashbee claimed that no obscene book of the time was unknown to Reddie who likewise amassed a formidable library. Unfortunately Reddie died in 1878 in Scotland, three years before Jack moved to Lisle Street, and a year before Jack even moved to London. Ashbee, however, was still around while Jack was living at Lisle Street. He is credited with three enormous bibliographies of erotic works, and is suspected of being the author of another 'anonymous' notorious book, *My Secret Life*. Ashbee, for all his interest in sex, was very against the excessive education of women.

Another pornographer of the time whose name has been dropped into the frame was William Simpson Potter, a friend of the erotica publisher William Lazenby, who was also a friend of Ashbee. It was certainly a cliquish world. Unfortunately Potter, aged 74, is believed to have died in Sicily where he had gone for his health, also before Jack came to be at Lisle Street. Potter *did* however live at Cornwall Mansions for two years prior to his death, so the real Mr Cambon undoubtedly knew him and used his address in the work.

Yet another contender is the artist Simeon Solomon. Solomon was a pre-Raphaelite painter who exhibited at the Royal Academy but fell from grace when he was arrested in a public urinal at Stratford Place Mews, off Oxford Street, with a man called George Roberts. Both were tried for an attempt to commit buggery. Roberts got eighteen months, Solomon appears to have got away with a short period of detention and a fine. He was not averse to the company of male prostitutes, having been further arrested with one in a urinal in Paris. Although known principally as an artist – one newspaper described his earlier paintings as of 'hideous wailing Jews' and a more recent homoerotic one of a melancholy winged male youth wearing nothing but a scarf as 'eccentric' – he also published literary works, one of which *A Mystery of Love in Sleep* was a prose poem illustrated by himself.

Solomon became an alcoholic, and also clearly more unhinged. He was arrested for breaking into the warehouse of a gold beater and dealer and stealing one hundred and seventy thousand gold, metal and aluminium leaves but was acquitted. In 1884, three years after the publication of *Sins*, he was admitted to a workhouse. He died in 1905 and was buried in Willesden Jewish Cemetery.

While two good reasons for suspecting Solomon will emerge later, it leaves us with the accredited 'anonymous' and notorious publisher of *The Sins of the Cities of the Plain,* William Lazenby.

Lazenby was responsible for a substantial canon of pornographic literature. His publication *The Pearl, A Magazine of Facetiae and Voluptuous Reading* was a collection of erotic tales and rhymes, which was banned for being rude and obscene. He undoubtedly wrote many of the contents himself, while the poems are believed to have been contributed by the poet Algernon Charles Swinburne, who had a penchant for sado-masochism. (Simeon Solomon knew Swinburne well and illustrated his scandalous Lesbia Brandon in 1865). To Lazenby is also attributed *Randiana or Excitable Tales*, *The Birchen Bouchet*, *The Romance of Chastisement*, *The Pleasures of Cruelty* and *The Romance of Lust* (itself written by William Simpson Potter).

Lazenby was arrested in 1871 for selling 'immoral prints', and in 1876 imprisoned for eighteen months for soliciting and inciting one Charles Drew Harris, who had answered Lazenby's advert promising money and a business opportunity, to print and circulate works of an 'obscene and indelicate character'. Lazenby's own predilections are, as far as I can ascertain, unknown, although he was married with a family. But *Sins* possesses all the hallmarks of his other works.

Jack would meet many gentleman down Piccadilly Circus and around the West End, and some of the names of the more high society ones would enter the public record, but in the case of Mr Cambon we must take our pick.

Jack spent much of the winter of 1880–81 putting together his memoir, while Madame Clemence entertained gentlemen off the street. Jack's first words gave little indication of what was to come.

> 'I need scarcely tell you that little cocks, and everything related to them, had a peculiar interest to me from the earliest time it is possible for my memory to carry me back to.'

Jack's memory carried him back to Ferns Court and Duke Lane. He told his readers that as soon as he could walk he would toddle up to anybody and ask them if they had a dilly, which sounds like the experience of many small boys growing up with sisters.

Of the slums of Dublin, however, there would no mention. The readership of *Sins* did not want to know about a boy whose father drove a hackney-cab and whose family was poor. Jack invented a new childhood, out in Suffolk, and conjured up a farm where his people were well off. His mother became a farmer's wife, and a brother much older than himself called Dick was created. Dick satisfied the craving he probably had for a brother who was older instead of younger than him and could take responsibility for his family.

One day at teatime (the phrase conjures up scones and jam and freshly patted butter as the Sauls' cows crop emerald green grass out on the pasture) Jack stared rudely at his cousin Jenny's disfiguring moustache and at last broke out with,

> 'What have you got girls' clothes on for? I don't believe you are a girl at all. My brother Dick has got a moustache like yours.'

He was cuffed and sent to bed for his rudeness. Jack had so many cousins any one of them might have been Jenny, and the incident may have been one of those minor childhood incidents which shaped his sexuality and gave him his cross-gender interest. Later on, when she grows up, he reminds her of it and she says he was such a tit in those days.

What develops between them and appears in the final book sets the tone for the rest of the memoir. Jenny has married a rich, old, ugly fellow and Jack decides to seduce her.

> 'She was one of those hairy lustful women one occa-
> sionally meets with, and when she had once tasted
> the fine root I introduced into her, she could scarcely
> ever be satisfied.'

It was clear that *Sins* was aiming for a wide readership,
if perhaps not those who read Dickens and Thackeray.
Sodomites were better catered for when Jack, whose
education had never come within miles of an English
boarding school, created one and used the name of
Ireland's most popular nationalist newspaper *Freemans
Journal* for the name of a boy.

> 'I was sent to a boarding school in Colchester when
> about ten years of age. Here the boys all slept by twos
> in bed. Well do I remember the first night. My bedfel-
> low, a big boy of about fifteen, his name was Freeman,
> at once began to fondle me as soon as the lights were
> out. His hands soon found my cock, which young as
> I then was, was a fine one for my age.'

After Jack has ejaculated for the first time, Freeman
says to him,

> 'Don't you know what that is, Jack? Perhaps you're
> not old enough to come like that; we call it spendings
> … it's so nice. We often put our cocks in each others'
> bottoms and spend there. Would you like to try that
> on me?'

Little Jack is introduced to all the other boys in the
dorm as a 'fit and proper chum' after which there is an
excessive amount of sexual activity (including a daisy
chain in which eight boys link up) that it seems Jack is
losing all touch with reality.

The fiction continues with a more dramatic cause of death of his father than from bronchitis, which would hardly have been titillating in a work of such prose, but here Jack's imagination starts to lose power as he tells us that his father died simply in an accident. His opportunity to invent and add a bit of drama to his family background passes.

His father's affairs turn out so badly, however, that Jack's poverty-stricken mother can no longer afford to pay for his schooling and takes him away from the school after only a fortnight, which is just as well really as he goes on to say that it 'prevented his constitution being ruined for life by such early precocity'.

Here he at least comes briefly back to ground with his mother being poverty-stricken after the death of his father, a matter which still pained him and made him want even more to send money home like a good Irish son. The money earned from Mr Cambon for his writings would contribute handsomely.

His narrative continues with life back on the farm, and a nod in the direction of the same readership that lusted after hairy Jenny. Their young eighteen-year-old dairymaid Sarah, whom Jack spies through a keyhole, is,

> 'a fine dark-eyed wench, very good-looking, a strapping, big strong young woman with rare plump arms and splendid full bosom, whilst as to her development of rump, to judge from the appearance outside her clothes … was something superb.'

Here is a character straight out of *Fanny Hill*. One thing leads to another, and after expending with Sarah what he describes as his 'juvenile tribute' Jack takes a fancy

to Master Joe the cowhand and milking boy and insti-
gates a threesome. Needless to say, Master Joe is a fine,
plump, good-looking, ruddy-faced boy of seventeen.
There is no hint of Irish famine here or potato blight.
Everyone in the farm of Jack's imagination is plump
and well fed and monstrously virile.

Even a gentle ruminant called Cowslip, which has
not yet been milked, is led into the menage.

Life on the farm, apparently, was a blast. Then,
almost disappointingly, he is sent away from the countryside by his mother who finds him a job as a draper's
assistant at a shop called Cygnet and Ego in London.

Here, *Sins* crashes from a highly unlikely bucolic
orgy into reality. Cygnet and Ego is a thinly veiled Swan
and Edgar, the long-established haberdashery store on
Piccadilly which catered for a very aristocratic clientele.
He knew it well. When it rained, or when business was
slack, he would wander its hallowed portals, the most
famous haberdashers in London. He had cast his eyes
many times on the faces of the young shop assistants.
Gracious and fawning, they were the epitome of service.
Young men would bow in solicitude to their customers,
and lady assistants would curtsey, forbidden to talk to
a customer unless they were addressed first.

Only yards from them, out on the pavement, Jack
too catered for an aristocratic trade. But in *Sins*, he
moves indoors and becomes one of them, an eager
young employee who knows perfectly well how to deal
with the Lords and Ladies. It is a perfect fiction for
Jack, and one would scarcely be surprised if he told
the folks back home that such was his job. (1)

The downside of his life there are the sleeping
arrangements. It was well-known that young drapers'

apprentices slept in strictly segregated dormitories on the premises. The contrast to boarding school in Colchester could not be more marked.

> 'Here morals were very strictly looked after, and it was quite impossible for the youths to indulge in any sensual amusements in the dormitories ... the sight of the many handsome girls and young fellows had a perfectly maddening effect upon me, especially as they were all forbidden fruit.'

Jack was never one to be deterred by forbidden fruit. His arrival in London brings adventures of an altogether more urban nature with very different types of people, Marquises, gentlemen in Chambers and other noblemen, just a few of the types of people who passed through Piccadilly Circus looking for rough trade. Only in *Sins*, he is doing it from a most respectable position, behind a counter.

Enter Mr Gooser, principal shopwalker, about as fictitious as the Marquis of Churton who lives in Churton House on Piccadilly, though Jack may well have had in mind one of the Rothschild Family who owned a number of mansions at the western end of the street.

He is required to take a cab-load of silks for selection by the sister of the Marquis, whom he learns is the Honourable Lady Diana Furbelow, a name that follows the pattern. Suggestive surnames were common in the pornography of the time. The portly flunkeys who usher Jack up to her Ladyship's boudoir are obsequious in their attentions to him and help him to carry up the parcels of silks, even though they know he is just a lowly 'counterjumper'.

Her Ladyship, reclining on an ottoman in a loose dressing gown, asks him his name.

'Mr Saul, at your ladyship's service, with a lot of silks for selection from Cygnet and Ego's. Will your Ladyship be pleased to have them brought up?'

How many ladies of this sort had passed by Jack at Piccadilly, having come out of Swan and Edgar with their servants in tow carrying parcels, stepped into hansom cabs and been whisked off to their fine mansions? This was the society Jack really wanted to belong to but never could. His position at Dr Cranny's had introduced him to some fine people, but then he remained forever below stairs, obliged to know his place.

In *Sins*, Jack no longer knows his place. He is now in charge, his good looks and sexual attributes allowing him to manipulate and control their sexual desires. It is not altogether a fantasy. Jack had met many members of the aristocracy around the West End of London, and so had his friends. Regulars were gossiped about. There was little discretion on the streets. A Lord who picked up a street arab and paid him for sex knew that he was not in control, and if he pretended to be he would soon be put in *his* place. The boys held all the cards, could give or withhold pleasure, demand money, exert black-mail, or be as sweet and obliging a companion as the Lord might desire for the right price.

At the Marquis of Churton's Piccadilly mansion, Jack soon seduces her Ladyship and reduces her to a quivering wreck just as her brother, the Marquis, enters. Jack being Jack, naturally the Marquis is tempted to join in, exclaiming,

'There's a lewd little bitch for you! To think of my sister the aristocratic Lady Diana, having a linendraper's assistant, but I'll punish you. You shall commit incest with me, your brother, and you, Mr Counterjumper, shall look on'.

Jack does more than look on. Such inventive encounters say more about Jack than any truthful description of a sordid encounter in a gents urinal could ever do. He becomes their favourite and keeps up contact with the Marquis and his sister for a couple of years, pleasuring them in the same way and receiving ten pounds for his and their pleasure, until Lady Diana's health fails and the Marquis whisks her off to Naples.

Their place is taken by another rich gentleman, Mr Ferdinand, who showers Jack with presents and keeps him out all night. Jack is promptly given the sack from Cygnet and Ego, but not before Mr Ferdinand has introduced him to the Hundred Guineas Club where he meets Fred Jones, the soldier from the Foot Guards who tells Jack of places where gentlemen can go to sleep with soldiers.

Here, Jack takes a sharp swerve back into reality, and gives us glimpses of the real world he inhabited.

'Young fellows are just as much after us as older men (says Jones), I have often been fucked by a young gentleman of sixteen or seventeen, and at Windsor lots of the Eton boys come after us. I know two men in the Blues who are regularly kept by gentlemen, and one has an allowance of £200 a year ... there are lots of houses for it. I will give you a list some day, where only soldiers are received and where gentlemen can sleep with them. The best known is now closed. It was the tobacconist's shop next door to the Albany

Street Barracks, and was kept by a Mrs Truman. The old lady would receive orders from gentlemen and then let us know. That is all over now, but there are still six houses in London that I know of. Inslip's club, however, pays me best.'

So it should have done at a hundred guineas a membership. Albany Street Barracks were in Regents Park and had been built to accommodate the Life Guards and Royal Artillery. Mrs Truman, if that was her real name, was on to a good thing. Jack then hands over the narrative briefly to his nice friend George Brown, the reformed star pupil of Red Hill Reformatory whose line of business it was to pick up a swell and ride about with in a cab, get him drunk and rob him.

Brown tells Jack of a particular encounter, some of which may be Jack's invention and part of which hints at his possible collaborator on *Sins*.

'I had a rare lark with a Jew the other day. I knew he belonged to some City financial firm. He was too fly to get drunk; but he took me down to the Star and Garter at Richmond on a Saturday afternoon (no doubt he had been to his synagogue in the morning). Well, we had a first-rate dinner, and by way of dessert I handled and sucked his rather worn-out prick till he spent, and he did the same to me ... at length when he ordered a last bottle of fizz, and took out his purse to pay the bill. I could see he had very little more than a tenner left, which no doubt was intended for me; and so it was.'

Young George appears to have been a very expensive lunch. The tenner to him is a mere 'flimsy' and he complains bitterly. The following dialogue ensues.

'I could wipe my arse on that! I mean to have a cool hundred; as I know it's nothing to you, who can swindle more than that any day in the City. Shall I call at your Cornhill Office for it on Monday, or will you give me an I.O.U.? "You bugger! You shan't have a damn'd penny more!" he growled out, putting on his hat. "I'm going!" Not till you square me, Mr Simeon Moses!' I said, speaking as loudly as possible. 'You know you have been acting indecently towards me, and showing me a volume of the *Romance of Lust!* Would you like a bobby to find that book on you?'

The name Simeon Moses sounds more than suspiciously like a disguised Simeon Solomon, one of Jack's possible collaborators on Sins, and the *Romance of Lust* was a real pornographic work by William Lazenby the publisher, who was well acquainted with Solomon the artist. It all begins to sound rather self-serving and incestuous, as though Jack is sharing a joke with his collaborator and publisher.

George Brown, Jack tells us, ends up arranging to collect the money at a house near Harley Street kept by a great big bully called Bill Johnson who had once been a soldier, who had been told by Moses to give him a tenner and nothing more. Brown brings a life preserver with him, a weighted club that people carried for self-defence, and becomes violent, but walks away in the end with ninety pounds while the ex-soldier, after sharing a celebratory bottle, takes ten as a commission.

More disturbing revelations are to come about the life of Jack's friend. He narrates how Brown tells him of his seduction of a pretty thirteen-year-old shoe-black straight out of the Ragged School whom he ends up taking to Paris and selling for a hundred pounds.

Coming over as an increasingly evil youngster, Brown informs Jack of a very select club in Paris 'where they practise every kind of cruelty and even kill their victims'.

Current historic child abuse scares are nothing new, it seems.

Jack drifted in and out of reality in his writing of *Sins*. But his ultimate contribution was the most audacious of all. He was partly responsible for the first published account ever of the private and intimate lives of the two Victorian transvestites, whose names were already known to the public and whose trial ten years earlier had both shocked and titillated Victorian society.

While the bustle of Leicester Square went on outside, Jack picked up his pen in the confines of 36 Lisle Street and made up his mind that he would tell the world of his meeting with Ernest Boulton and Frederick William Park.

He had no idea what he was starting.

* * * * * *

Chapter Notes

1. Cygnet and Ego/Swan and Edgar. Jack's intimate knowledge of the lives of shop assistants at the famous store is a curious addition to a work of pornography. One could speculate that Jack did actually work there as a shop assistant for a short while on his arrival in London, as he maintains in *Sins*.

CHAPTER SEVEN

JACK THE LAD

'You remember the Boulton and Park case? Well I was present at the ball given at Haxell's Hotel in the Strand. No doubt the proprietor was quite innocent of any idea what our fun really was. But there were two or three dressing rooms into which the company could retire at pleasure. Boulton was superbly got up as a beautiful lady, and I observed Lord Arthur was very spooney upon her.'

Lord Arthur Pelham-Clinton was the Member of Parliament for Newark, while Boulton, a shipbroker's son who was known as Stella, was his 'wife'. He had cards printed for the young man in the name of Lady Arthur Clinton, though Boulton was enamoured of two other young gentlemen, an old boyhood friend called Louis Hurt who worked as a telegraph inspector for the General Post Office in Edinburgh, and a dashing, ambitious American consul from the same city called John Safford Fiske.

Fourteen men dressed as women were known to have attended the ball at Haxell's, which is now part of the

Strand Hotel. We know the name of at least two others. One was Park, Boulton's 'sister' and assumed co-conspirator in the trial that followed, a judge's son and legal clerk who took the name of Fanny. The other was another legal gentleman called Amos Westrop Gibbings, who when not in chambers enjoyed dressing as a woman and appearing in dramatic performances. It was he who had organised the ball.

In fact most of them enjoyed theatrical drama as much as the dramatic risk of being seen in public in womens' clothes. Stella and Fanny were young hands at amateur theatricals, though Stella was undoubtedly the prettier and more talented. He had appeared at the Egyptian Hall in London with Lord Arthur Pelham-Clinton in a comedietta called *A Morning Call* by Charles Dance. Wherever Boulton went as Stella, he was taken for a beautiful woman.

This was the observation of Jack too, whose interest in amateur theatre with Bill Clarke in Dublin was stirred sufficiently for him to recount his experiences with Boulton and Park, true soul mates if ever there were.

Jack, who must have looked splendid in womens' clothes too and who called himself Eveline for the event, recounts watching Boulton and Lord Arthur sneak away to a private room, not one of those put aside as dressing rooms, but one taken by Lord Arthur for his own private use. Jack is thwarted as they lock the door behind them, but he creeps into an adjoining room and looks through the keyhole of a connecting door. The lovemaking he observes in front of a large mirror reminds him of the 'scene between two youths which Fanny Hill relates to have seen through a peephole at a roadside inn'.

Park, he relates, was dancing with a gentleman from the city, a very handsome Greek merchant, but he did not care for Park as much as he did for Boulton. Afterwards, Lord Arthur introduces Jack in turn to the true object of his desire.

Boulton immediately took to Jack. Then who couldn't? After a little conversation, Boulton gives Jack his card and asks him to call on them at their rooms the next day, saying, 'I know I shall love you, but there is no chance of it here. We must amuse our customers tonight.'

Stella and Fanny worked as male prostitutes too, providing services for the considerable number of gentlemen who thrilled at the prospect of lifting a fine petticoat and discovering a male appendage, and inevitably those who took them for real women and were, to put it mildly, unpleasantly surprised.

Their customers were well catered for. A guidebook to London back in the middle of the century warned about 'pooffs' who could be easily recognised by their effeminate air and fashionable dress. They operated, the guide book helpfully advised, in Fleet Street, The Strand and Charing Cross, while south of the river – God forbid that anyone should want to go there for sex – was the stamping ground of working class queens.

Jack didn't wait until the next day however. That night Boulton and Park both took him home to their rooms near Eaton Square, a very fashionable part of London. Boulton offers him a sip of his invigorating cordial and tells Jack about much of his own sexual adventuring, before the inevitable takes place. Jack offers a rare glimpse into the sexual side of two of gay history's most famous protagonists. Boulton, calling himself Laura for the occasion, and Park, Selina, think that Jack deserves considerable punishment, and our hero is not averse to receiving it.

> 'It was useless for me to remonstrate against being tied up, as they were too strong for me, and I was soon secured by both wrists to the foot of my bed; then my skirts were pinned up and my drawers opened and let down to the knees. "Ha, we have her now, the rude little slut!" exclaimed Laura. "Let me just pick out a proper little swishtail, and I'll take all that out of her naughty impudent bum".

On a future occasion, before Boulton and Parks' world exploded and they were arrested for importuning at the Strand Theatre, an event which swept up Lord Arthur, Louis Hurt and the American Consul John Safford Fiske too into the arms of the law, Lord Arthur, who had also obviously taken a fancy to Jack, dressed him up as a midshipman and took him to a garden party at a house by the Thames, 'not a million miles' from Richmond.

The party, given in honour of the Prince of Wales, culminated in the crowning moment of Jack's life. The boy from the slums, Dublin Jack, Piccadilly rent, one time butler, son of a hackney-cab driver was introduced by Lord Arthur Pelham-Clinton to the Prince himself. He could not remember the name he was introduced by, but we may put that down to the excitement of the moment. Furthermore, Jack is introduced to another Lord who requests to kiss his 'darling jewel' while seated in an arbour. After rejoining the Royal company, one of the retinue of the Prince begs for an introduction and tells Jack that he could make his fortune in Berlin and Vienna, where he would receive introductions to many of the highest personages in Germany.

Jack, however, has his feet on the ground – at least in one way – and resists the opportunity to become a European male courtesan. The pretty youth in the midshipman uniform does not want to leave dear old England.

And dear old England (and Ireland) is much the better for it.

Jack laid down his pen and took great satisfaction at that part of his recollections.

The only trouble was, none of it was true.

The ball at Haxell's Hotel did happen, but it took place on an April evening in 1870, at which time Jack was a twelve-year-old boy living in Dublin. But would anyone care? Would anyone really know how old he was? Did it matter that he never met the Prince of Wales, or Lord Arthur Pelham-Clinton, or Ernest Boulton, or Frederick Park? This was pornography, not biography.

If Oscar Wilde had been well-known at the same time, he too would have ended up in *Sins* rather than having to buy a copy of it years later.

It may not have been entirely Jack's idea. One person who was quite obsessed with the trial of Boulton and Park was Simeon Solomon. At the time it was going on, he exchanged numerous letters with Algernon Swinburne the poet avidly discussing the case. What finer mischief than to encourage Jack to incorporate it into his writing?

In the end it was Jack's penultimate trick, to inject himself into a historical episode in which he played no part. Though it was far from his intention, he set about confounding researchers and fooling a number of authors in trying to guess his real age. For Jack, the most important thing was that in the febrile world of his imagination, he had arrived in high society. *Sins* was the life he would like to have led. Boulton and Park were the real life characters he would like to have known. The Jack of *Sins* was the person he wanted to be.

For as long as it remained in print he would be that person.

Jack had one other bit of fun up his sleeve. In a later orgiastic episode with Boulton and Park at the home of an Earl, they play a game called the Slap-Bum Polka, in which they take the Earl's three pages across their laps and smack their bottoms. One of the pages is French, and is called Leon.

Jack was not the first author and would not be the last to use the name of someone close to him. Thus young Leon Teker, the French son of Madame Clemence, the prostitute with whom Jack lived in Lisle Street and who had bought Charles Hammond's furniture, found his way into *The Sins of the Cities of the Plain*.

Jack delivered his pages of foolscap and the book duly went into print in two volumes. Just as the book was going to press, the description of a criminal case in the Daily Telegraph of 8 July 1881 was inserted. *Sins* omitted the names, but it involved a Corporal in the 2nd Battalion of the Scots Guards called John Cameron alias Sutherland, who was charged with a Count Guido zu Lynar, Secretary to the German Embassy, with the commission of an 'atrocious offence' at a coffee house situated in Lower Sloane Street, Chelsea, where the two men were apprehended.

All of the two hundred and fifty copies have now vanished with the exception of the one in the British Library. A copy at the time would have sold for four guineas (£4.40) so only the rich could afford it. It is now regarded as a lost book.

If Jack had a few tricks up his sleeve, William Lazenby had a cracker. Two years later he brought out another work about Jack Saul's 'life' called *Letters from Laura and Eveline* which explored the totally fictitious obscene correspondence between Jack's persona as Eveline in *Sins* and Ernest Boulton's Laura. Jack isn't even mentioned in the subsequent work though it was published as an appendix to the original book.

It is a much cruder publication than *Sins*. Even Henry Spencer Ashbee, the erotica expert and collector, condemned it, claiming that it possessed no literary merit whatsoever. Compared to Jack's dulcet prose and steamy descriptions of creamy spendings and virgin tributes, it is pretty appalling stuff and well deserves its reputation. What it did however was further the myth – one that lasted well over a century – that Jack had been old enough to have known Boulton and Park.

The subsequent history of Jack's original 'memoir' is worth recounting.

In 1992, the cover of a new edition from Masquerade Books boasted that, after a century, it was finally back in print. The title was slightly different: *Anonymous, Sins of the Cities of the Plain*. The text turned out to be heavily bowdlerised, with lots of additions, and female characters turned into male ones. Sarah, the young strapping dairymaid with a taste for cow's milk, had become Klaus, an elderly farm servant, a rugged and dark-eyed man of 'expansive and well-proportioned dimension'. Hairy Jenny, the cousin, had turned into Jerry. Ages were changed too. In the original, Jack said he had enjoyed his first sexual experience at the age of fourteen. In the 1992 edition, he is eighteen. Linguistic modernisation was another sin that the new edition of *Sins* committed.

Whoever the ghostwriter of what swiftly became known as the Badboy version was, is just as much a mystery as the identity of the Victorian Mr Cambon.

In 2006, the Olympia Press brought out a further edition, in which Jack was actually named as author on the front cover. It would not necessarily have pleased him. Although inside it stated 'First Published 1881' it turned out to the Badboy text from 1992.

Finally, one hundred and thirty years after Jack put his name to his notorious memoir in the house in Lisle Street, an American company called Valancourt Books which specialises in rare and lost texts had the original in the British Library microfilmed, and published in a genuinely new and accurate edition.

People will debate endlessly on what is true and what is not in *Sins*. But Jack was flattered to have a work published in his name, and vain enough to want to write it himself, though he needed a collaborator. In the end, it created a legend around him that would only have given him the last laugh.

Three years later he was not laughing. The good days of *Sins* would be over, and the law would start taking its toll of many people he really had known.

* * * * * *

CHAPTER EIGHT

THE DUCHESS GOES
TO COURT

Jack did not stay at 36 Lisle Street. Like his newfound friend Charles Hammond, he moved addresses as it suited, living with various prostitutes male and female in an assortment of disreputable houses and managing to keep one step ahead of the law.

While he was writing *Sins*, Charles and Caroline Hammond had found lodgings in an infamous house of their own at 14 Church Street (now Romilly Street) in Soho. It was the residence of the elderly Mrs Sarah Hack and her daughter Harriet Wright. Charles described himself as a 'military braiding tailor', and Caroline as a dressmaker, but they weren't at Church Street to make clothes. Harriet Wright was a brothel keeper who preferred to keep one step ahead of the law herself and project a respectable image as landlady, and the fact that Charles and Caroline were a married couple, even though the two of them were regularly bringing back gentlemen to the house, aided her no end in furnishing that image.

Why, the Hammonds even had a three-year-old son called Charlie who was learning to speak French like his mother. Now just how respectable could that be?

Eight years earlier, it hadn't been so easy for Harriet Wright to appear respectable. She was landlady then at 12 Great Coram Street, yet another notorious address and one now forever associated with the unsolved murder of a young prostitute called Harriet Buswell. Mrs Wright angrily denied at the inquest into the girl's murder that she was a brothel keeper, even though she had known her tenant was kept by a gentleman when she gave her a room. Mrs Wright may well have believed that living in that twilight world where one knowingly rented rooms to prostitutes did not actually make one a brothel keeper, but the jury had other ideas. It was Mrs Wright and her young son George who had found the body, on the previous Christmas Eve. Harriet was lying in her room with her throat cut. A German clergyman was arrested but later released.

Mrs Wright moved in with her mother Sarah Hack at nearby 14 Church Street. No sooner had she done so than there was another death, this time at the new address, that of a twenty-three-year-old French artist and lodger called George Manduit. There were no marks of violence on his body, but suspicions were voiced he had died of poison, though none could be traced. The cause of death was given as heart disease. Inspector Harnett, who was investigating the Coram Street murder, realised Manduit resembled the description given of the murderer. But neither Mrs Wright nor her mother could give any account of where Manduit had been on the night of Harriet Buswell's murder.

Oscar Wilde might have put it thus. To lose one lodger may be considered a misfortune, to lose another sounds like carelessness. And he would probably have been right.

Charles and Caroline Hammond knew of the reputation of their landlady, but an unsolved murder going back eight years was of little interest to them. What Charles most desired was to run his own brothel, but not some cheap back-street affair masquerading as a house full of seamstresses, housekeepers, charwomen and milliners, the most common 'professions' given by women who sold sex. Charles wanted to run a brothel for people like himself, where boys and men would be on offer, a discreet establishment that only those 'in the know' would find.

That there was a ready clientele out there, he was in no doubt. He had met quite a number already in the course of his profession. He was getting on a bit himself, twenty-eight now, and was not as desirable as he had been. It suited him, the prospect of being a male madame. Male brothels were nothing new, though they were better hidden. His would be something more like those he had come across in Paris. It would be comfortable, welcoming, and above all safe. Caroline and he would truly make a great team. It would be the best house in London.

Hammond was an animal lover and also wanted somewhere he could keep pets without the restrictions of lodgings and landladies. He didn't just want his own latchkey, he wanted his own front door.

But how to afford such an establishment? There were gentlemen he felt sure would put a little money into the scheme, if a 'dividend' or two was promised in return.

And if money wasn't forthcoming in that way, then there was always blackmail.

As for the boys who would work there, they would not be lodgers, picking up customers themselves to pay him the rent, but boys who worked for him, for whom he would find the paying customers.

Jack was *la creme de la creme,* for the moment anyway. Still only in his early twenties, he had the soft feminine looks, the cheeky Irish personality, the gift of the gab, a winning smile, not to mention his sexual prowess. And Charles had heard he was a *writer.* There was no end to the boy's talents. It didn't matter that like so many other renters in London he could be mundanely described as a valet currently out of a situation. There were hundreds of those, but only one Jack. If Jack would play his game, and he could find other boys like him, Charles would make a fortune.

In the meantime, Jack had his eye on political events across the sea that, unknown to him, were shaping his own destiny in a different way.

On 6 May 1882, the people of Dublin were out enjoying the bright Saturday noonday sunshine in Phoenix Park. The event was a pageant, the likes of which they had not seen in years. Trumpets brayed, banners glittered, many who favoured Home Rule briefly put aside their convictions and marvelled at how the English could *do* ceremony. In the cortege, occupying an open carriage, was the new Chief Secretary, Lord Frederick Cavendish. He had been sent over to aid in the new policy of concession (so it was said), to initiate new and happy relations between England and Ireland.

The sun had not set before he was dead. That evening Lord Cavendish went for a walk in the park with Thomas Burke, the Under-Secretary for Ireland. Four assassins rushed at them with daggers, and in a well-orchestrated ambush, stabbed them both to death. The Phoenix Park murders, committed by a band called The Irish National Invincibles, caused shockwaves throughout the British Isles.

There had been a fermenting of Irish nationalist sympathies in the years leading up to the assassinations, and they only increased after the hanging of five members of the gang at Kilmainham Jail. One, Tim Kelly, was only eighteen and still looked like a child. It took three juries to eventually convict him.

Feelings were running at fever pitch on both sides of the Irish Sea. Dublin Castle was a symbol of all that the Irish Nationalists hated, and any opportunity to strike a blow at those within its walls was eagerly seized. It was not a good time to be a member of the British administration with an Achilles heel.

One such man was James Ellis French of the CID. Another was Gustavus Cornwall.

The past was about to catch up with Jack. The names that had recently arisen in the press he recognised instantly. It was catching up too with Martin Oranmore Kirwan, who had been promoted to a Captain and was now in the Royal Dublin Fusiliers, which had been formed out of the old Dublin Militia. In the face of growing accusations about his relationships with other men, notably his old friend Gustavus Cornwall, Kirwan had resigned his commission.

There was much talk of the Dublin Castle scandals. Strictly speaking, the scandals had very little to do with

Dublin Castle, but the name stuck, to the detriment and annoyance of the British administration who were the main targets. The only person who had any real link to the castle was James Ellis French. That was enough. That the head of the CID should be secretly taking part in 'abominable practices', while operating at the very seat of the administration in Dublin, was something that had to be exposed.

The political dimension of what the press also termed the Dublin scandals or the Dublin felonies – but which are better termed the Dublin tragedies – cannot be underestimated.

Sex and politics in Ireland make an explosive mix.

Cornwall, Kirwan, French and their friends provided the sex. The politics were provided by William O'Brien, newspaper publisher, Irish Nationalist and associate of Charles Stewart Parnell who started the ball rolling early in 1884 by rushing into print in his organ *United Ireland* to accuse James Ellis French of being a sodomite. French, as Oscar Wilde would later do so unwisely, began libel proceedings. O'Brien however was not through by any means. He still had his guns loaded. The next in his sights was none other than Cornwall who, at sixty-two years old, was still Secretary to the General Post Office.

Cornwall too started proceedings for libel, but only Cornwall's came to fruition in open court. If he had ignored the insinuations, and just carried on with his life, for he was near to retirement, the slings and arrows of *United Ireland* might have landed and been quickly forgotten. The libel trial, just as Oscar Wilde's would do, turned out to be disastrous for him, and led to a series of prosecutions for conspiracy and sodomy involving, it seemed at the time, half of Dublin. The cases exploded into one of the most sensational scandals of the Victorian era, dragging in Irish officials of high office, clergymen, army officers, young men of dubious reputation which included Jack, a corrupt ex-Scotland Yard detective, and accusations of sexual goings-on in one of the hothouses of the botanic gardens at Glasnevin. And if that wasn't enough, there were revelations regarding two male brothels practically in the shadow of Dublin Castle, one in Golden Lane and the other near the military barracks in Ship Street.

Jack had no doubt they would come for him at some point. If he did not gather what was going on from the newspapers, he got it all from his friend Bill Clarke, the young cooper with whom he had been arrested in Dublin. In January 1884, Clarke came to London with another rent boy called Michael McGrane. (1)

Back in Dublin, Clarke had been as generous as Jack with his sexual favours, working in the two brothels and building up a regular clientele. He knew almost everyone. Cornwall, French, the two brothel keepers Robert Fowler and Daniel Considine, and an elderly Quaker who was a tea and wine merchant from Rathmines called James Pillar, known as Papa to his like-minded friends.

A Dublin firm of solicitors, Chance and Miley, working on O'Brien's defence on the libel charge, employed a bizarre individual called John Meiklejohn, an ex-Scotland Yard detective now working as a private inquiry agent, to run to ground as many young men as he could, by fair means or foul, to give evidence which supported the charges that French and Cornwall were sodomites. He was in London with fifteen subpoenas, which he intended to serve.

Jack's name had been mentioned, and was undoubtedly on one of the subpoenas.

Jack had no intentions of being taken back to Dublin to testify against anybody or for anyone. He knew the way the law operated. For a number of years he had occupied a very good educational vantage point on Piccadilly. It was always younger men who were sought to give evidence against older men. They could be easily manipulated.

As were Clark and McGrane, who had been brought over to London by Meiklejohn, presumably to stop them being got at in Dublin. Clarke had made a full statement incriminating French, and French still had powerful friends in the police force, though his activities had been an open secret for many a year. French had a reputation for dishonesty and corruption that may not have been undeserved, and it was said that he had sent innocent men to the gallows. (2) Meiklejohn had found the youths lodgings and was paying each of them twenty-five shillings a week pocket money. They were being watched by the police. They were too valuable.

Both Clarke and McGrane had committed buggery with Cornwall. Clarke had also made a statement against the tea and wine merchant James Pillar. The young men were under no misapprehensions that if they did not play the game and give evidence at the libel trial, they could themselves be charged. The maximum sentence, as they well knew, was life imprisonment. It did not matter who buggered who.

Meiklejohn was the worst person imaginable to act in such a capacity. He was a convicted felon, one of three top Scotland Yard detectives who had been imprisoned for two years for involvement in bribery and turf frauds. He was a scoundrel, a trickster, a blackmailer and a crook whose labyrinthine dealings in the fraud case also branded him as a money launderer. (3)

With a solicitor called Fowler (unrelated to the Dublin brothel keeper) Meiklejohn attempted to serve his subpoenas. But the cat was already out of the bag and those named had scattered.

One should have been in barracks but had fled to France, another could 'not be found' at his club. The others were in various residences or rather *had been* in various residences.

Jack lay low. He had been given fair warning.

It would be stated at the libel trial, to the astonishment of the judge, that not one of the fifteen subpoenas had been served. Meiklejohn hoped that his failure would be alleviated by his taking care of Clarke and McGrane and persuading them to give evidence in court. Clarke admitted to being terrified by Meiklejohn, who was a drunkard and a bully and a 'big fat man' who for reasons that hardly seem suprising given his own criminal background operated under the pseudonym of 'Mr Brown'.

Another detective working with Meiklejohn, called Molloy, struck Clarke and cut his head open. He and McGrane hadn't money to escape back to Dublin (or to France), and besides Meiklejohn wouldn't let them leave. But the two boys had a trick up their sleeve.

They went to a Dublin clergyman they knew, a Mr Dolling, who was working in the East End of London helping the poor of Mile End and begged him to give them the money to go home. Mr Dolling knew nothing of their circumstances. He gave them the money and they escaped briefly from the clutches of

Meiklejohn, but in Dublin they were no safer. The net was closing in on not only them, but other young men, similarly persuaded to give evidence.

Jack now watched nervously the fate of his friends from across the Irish Sea. The chief witness against Cornwall was to be someone Jack knew very well indeed, Captain Martin Oranmore Kirwan. It was all getting too close for comfort.

The libel trial, Cornwall versus O'Brien, opened at the Four Courts building overlooking the River Liffey on 2 July 1884. It was a trial of three O'Briens, Mr Justice James O'Brien the presiding judge, his nephew the prosecutor Mr Sergeant Peter O'Brien, known as Peter the Packer for his skill in 'packing' juries to get the right verdict, and the defendant William O'Brien.

Chance and Miley, aided by the indefatigable and hard-drinking Meiklejohn, had acquired the services of three other Dublin witnesses, McKiernan the bank clerk who had fallen out with Cornwall, a former medical student, and Malcolm Johnstone, the wealthy miller's son. At the last minute they dragged over from London a young man, Cecil Graham, who lived in Brewer street (one of Charles Hammond's addresses), the allegations in O'Brien's defence being that Cornwall had been sexually involved with all of them and that the libel in *United Ireland* was essentially true and therefore justified.

Cornwall, the plaintiff in the case, opened his evidence with an 'iron nerve' and was a man of 'imposing stature' who appeared to fascinate the court. But he had also opened himself up to a searing cross-examination. A host of names, including that of Clarke, were put to him, most of whom he said he knew slightly though he had never heard of Clarke. They came at him like a hail of bullets, each one of which he attempted to parry. A lot of the names were those of soldiers, one of whom he had dined with recently in the Ship Street barracks. Another was Captain George Joy, formerly of the Dublin Militia, with whom he had lodged on a recent trip to London. He said he had been acquainted with Joy for about twenty-five years, which was the same period of time he had known Kirwan. Captain Joy was a man of about forty. It didn't take much for the court to work out that Joy had been a boy of fifteen at the time Cornwall got to know him.

It was stated that, at Chance and Miley the solicitors, over twenty names of soldiers had been put to the poor Secretary of the General Post Office. If he had enjoyed sexual relations with only half of them, Cornwall had been having a rare old time.

Wit and cruelty at Cornwall's expense abounded. After it became known to the court that he was nick-named 'The Duchess' he was asked if he had ever sent music to anyone. In the course of the trial, sending music, playing music, being played music, and simply just being musical became synonymous with indulging in abominable practices. Cornwall said Joy had played him music in his rooms. Dr Boyd, William O'Brien's defence counsel, passed him the score of an opera, which he suggested he had given to Cecil Graham in his rooms in Brewer Street when on a trip to London.

'Take this. What is it?' he asked.

'The score of an opera.' Cornwall replied.

'Which opera?'

Mr Sergeant O'Brien the prosecutor interjected.

'One of Mr Brown's compositions, conducted by Meiklejohn.' he said to howls of laughter.

'You will find Mr Brown's compositions are always true to the score.' parried Boyd.

He then asked the question again of Cornwall. What was the opera?

'Madam Flavart.' Cornwall answered.

'It might have been "The Grand Duchess" coming from The Duchess.' quipped Boyd to even more laughter.

The joke was on O'Brien's team on the second day of the trial. Disaster nearly struck when the witnesses refused to appear against Cornwall. They had spent evenings as a gang in a local hotel carousing and drinking with both Meiklejohn and Chance the solicitor, their hostility to their hosts numbed by alcohol, but in the cold light of day the danger they were putting themselves in suddenly became apparent. All of them were branding themselves criminals, regardless of the outcome.

Something akin to panic seized O'Brien's team. However, after a lengthy examination of a handwriting expert who attempted to prove that Cornwall had not written an incriminating letter (O'Brien referred to the expert in his paper *United Ireland* as the greatest impostor in Europe) the ice broke and the first witness, Malcolm Johnstone, strode confidently into court.

The fashionably dressed and wealthy recipient of the fortune left by the family firm of Johnstone and Company, for years purveyors of fine bread to the Dublin area, testified that Cornwall had put his hand on his knee in a cab on the way to the Botanic Gardens, though the rest of his evidence concerning Captain Kirwan, hothouses and an incident under a holly tree was 'unfit for publication'. The clerk with the Munster Bank, Malcolm McKiernan, said he had met Cornwall in 1876 and gone to his house for a drink. It was he who possessed the incriminating letter from that time, which he had kept in a locked drawer, an admission which has the strong odour of blackmail about it, but as with Johnstone most of his evidence about what happened between them at Cornwall's house – while Mrs Cornwall was away – was unfit to be published. Cornwall had fallen out with him after McKiernan had replied describing him as a 'superannuated old gentleman'.

The third Dublin witness, a well-brought up and good-looking youth called George Taylor, a one-time medical student now a clerk for the Dublin and Glasgow Steamship Company (though a representative of the company wrote to the paper afterwards to say he never was employed there) was equally gracious, saying he had obliged Cornwall reluctantly and was disgusted, though he had gone back to his house to be disgusted on two further occasions.

Cecil Graham, the young man from Brewer Street in London, who possessed a 'strong English accent', refused to give any self-incriminating evidence in spite of suggestions that Cornwall had given him a present of sheet music, though he did talk freely about singing and piano parties at the hotel the night before in Dublin with Meiklejohn. All of the witnesses seemed to be of a musical bent with good singing voices. They certainly used them.

If nobility had so far been lacking at the libel trial, it was restored in fine measure when Captain Kirwan stepped up to the table to rebut evidence that Cornwall had indulged in any inappropriate behaviour. Cornwall was an old friend and Kirwan wasn't going to betray him. He told the court how at the offices of Chance and Miley the solicitors it became apparent they were determined to drag Cornwall down, and a few others besides.

Meiklejohn, who was drunk and banging his fist on the table, shouted at him 'Will you row in the same boat as me, or Mr Cornwall?'

Kirwan replied 'Mr Cornwall.'

Meiklejohn then said they would sink or swim together.

'Then I would sink in good company or swim in good company', Captain Kirwan put him firmly in his place as an officer and a gentleman.

Kirwan's mother, who had been in bad health, had just died. Kirwan believed it was the shock of the trial that had killed her. He would find himself swimming in very deep water due to his decision to support his old friend.

Bill Clarke, despite having been taken to London, guarded then cajoled and bullied by Meiklejohn for weeks prior to the trial, was not called. The Crown discovered at the last minute that Cornwall had an alibi. Clarke put down in his statement that the first offence with Cornwall had taken place during a run of *Patience* at the Gaiety Theatre where they had met. Patience ran from Monday 17 September to Saturday 28 September. Cornwall could provide witnesses that for the whole of that time he was in Scotland.

The verdict nevertheless went for O'Brien and against Cornwall, who lost his case for libel. While the jury didn't particularly like the witnesses, they clearly believed their stories. The outcome of the trial was greeted with celebrations across the country.

O'Brien was cheered outside the court, with cries of 'Long Live United Ireland'. Several of the city bands turned out. In Dundalk, bonfires were lit. In Limerick and in Cork, local bands paraded the streets, while in Kingstown tar barrels were set alight. *Freemans Journal* reported that 'a great political as well as a moral triumph had been gained'. If further evidence were needed that the Dublin scandals were political rather than moral, that statement was surely it. Trials would inevitably follow, and many more people would have their lives broken on the anvil of Irish nationalism.

In London, Jack now knew it was only a matter of time. Captain Kirwan, having refused point-blank to row in the same boat as Meiklejohn, was to stand trial along with Cornwall. The police had woken up to the fact that there was, and had been for some time, a network of sodomites in Dublin and that the evil had to be rooted out and exposed. That men of high position and rank should mix freely with and write intimate letters to youths who were but lowly clerks was an abomination in itself. In what can best be described as a witch-hunt, they now sought information against a number of men, including Captain Kirwan. A political rout had become a moral crusade.

Some men fled Ireland. A wine merchant, Charles Fitzgerald, escaped when the police arrested his brother by mistake and only realised their error when they had him in custody. Neither were the police themselves immune from investigation. One of their number, Constable Esmond, a man so strong he once carried two thieves to the police station on his own, one tucked under each arm, fled when it was discovered he was involved in homosexual practices.

Courtroom hearings were held at which witnesses were examined so that the Crown could frame their indictments. The press were barred. But one name kept coming up time and time again by various people in connection with Captain Kirwan. That was Jack Saul. His ears must have burned as witness after witness spoke of the relationship he had enjoyed with the gallant soldier, then a Lieutenant of the Dublin Militia.

This time Jack would not be able to lay so low.

Chief Superintendent John Mallon from G Division – the Detective Division of the Dublin Metropolitan Police – came to London to find Jack. The DMP policed Dublin and was not a paramilitary force like the Royal Irish Constabulary, which covered the rest of the country. It was patterned on British forces with the same uniforms and ranks. That such a big name as Mallon should come across personally to find the young Irishman shows how seriously the police were taking their responsibility to find anyone who could help them nail Kirwan, Cornwall and the others. Mallon was a relentless copper who had led the search for the Phoenix Park murderers, ground down a whole series of informers and sent five men to the gallows. He wasn't an out-and-out rogue like Meiklejohn, but he was at that time under suspicion for bribing a man to give perjured evidence against a Fenian conspirator who had been hanged for murder.

At first he wasn't successful but with the combined forces of Scotland Yard, Mallon was soon on Jack's trail. Jack didn't stand a chance. London was full of secret policemen operating out of the Special (Irish) Branch of the Yard, then pursuing Fenian dynamite bombers from America who had created havoc in the capital. Only three months before, they had exploded a device in the public urinal immediately under the Yard itself, blowing a constable thirty feet into the air. Numerous London-Irish were being watched and tailed.

Minding his own business in Soho, Jack wasn't a threat to national security, but he was suddenly of interest in the great panic that had seized Dublin. He found himself arrested along with another young man called James Daly (who is difficult to identify but who also had evidence against one of the accused) and obliged to make a statement incriminating Captain Kirwan which went into considerable detail of how they had met and conducted their sexual relationship.

Jack had no choice, other than to refuse and be charged himself. It was the way the police worked. And after all, hadn't Jack's 'friends' in Dublin put the finger on him?

With the trials due to begin the following day, Jack arrived under police escort at Kingstown and was taken by cab to Dublin's Chancery Lane Police Station. It was announced in a number of newspapers that his evidence, now in writing, had been accepted by the Crown.

Jack wasn't alone at Chancery Lane. Bill Clarke was there too. Having escaped the pressure to give evidence at the libel trial, Clarke was not going to get away so lightly the second time, alibi or no alibi. On this occasion, his statement involving buggery with Cornwall was to be used regardless of trips to Scotland, along with new ones against the two brothel keepers, James Pillar the elderly Quaker, and Detective French.

It was the second time Jack and Clarke had been held in captivity together in Dublin. The first time they had been lucky. This time they were not suspects. They were informers who had to live with the consequences of what they were about to do, which involved sending other men to prison, possibly for life.

Chapter Notes

1. McGrane is referred to in some press reports also as Magrane. Magrane is the anglicised spelling of the Irish name McGrane. I have used the Irish spelling.

2. Thomas Murphy, ex-Detective Inspector, Royal Irish Constabulary, who was dismissed for drunkenness, claimed to have unmasked French, saying that for many years French was head of the Irish Secret Police, responsible for organising various 'horrible plots' some of which involved the conviction and execution of innocent men. *Startling Exposure of Dublin Castle Methods. Published 1894. Ir320. National Library of Ireland.*

3. The full case of Inspector John Meiklejohn can be found in *The Trial of the Detectives*, edited by George Dilnot, Charles Scribner's Sons, New York, 1928

CHAPTER NINE

THE DUBLIN FELONIES

The series of trials, which followed one upon the other, opened at Green Street Court House on Tuesday 19 August 1884 and ran for a week. The building with its grey columned frontage was very familiar to Jack and Clarke, for it was the very same place in which they had stood in the dock together six years earlier. As they entered, to be witnesses at whatever point they might be required, old painful memories must have been stirred.

The trials created a sensation. They were followed closely on the British mainland as well as in Ireland. From the outset the judge Baron Dowse, a self-made man known more for his oratorial wit than his law, made it clear that he expected the press to behave responsibly and more or less ordered them to print the details of the 'abominable acts' alleged. It would, he said, amount to a contempt of court. The newspapers obliged, and as a result no Irish or English newspaper – including the normally less than reticent and high-circulation *Reynolds News* – gave its readers any indication of what the men were actually on trial for.

The reader from another planet, assuming he had learned English, might have thought it was a criminal offence to ride around in cabs, visit botanic gardens, play music, buy presents, go to balls, write letters and act in amateur dramatics. He might have come to the conclusion that to wear a check suit was an indication of guilt. Thirteen years earlier, at the trial of Boulton and Park, while *The Times* duly told its readers that certain evidence was unfit to print, *Reynolds News* was not afraid to refer to dilated anuses and the insertion of foreign bodies into those orifices.

The Dublin trials would be reported very differently. (1)

With two members of the British Army indicted, and many more subpoenaed to come forward as witnesses, the War Office made sure there was an observer in court.

Jack and Clarke and Michael McGrane joined the other witnesses assembled by the crown, Malcolm Johnstone, George Taylor and Alfred McKiernan, all of whom had given evidence at the libel trial. This unholy alliance were now firmly in the bed of the prosecution, being put up in a hotel under the supervision of an officer from G Division. This would be the pattern for the week, all six waiting in the wings to make their entrances in what promised to be a series of courtroom dramas. No one would be disappointed.

For much of the day everyone had to sit and wait while a jury tried to decide if French was fit to plead. He had to be assisted into the dock where he wept loudly and attacked it with his fist. It was said that

THE SINS OF JACK SAUL

his mind had been failing for two years. He had been given electrical tests with a galvanic battery while being kept in Kilmainham Jail, and a surgeon from Mountjoy Prison who examined him believed that he was shamming. Other doctors disagreed.

The jury came back and like the doctors were in total disagreement. Baron Dowse said he couldn't discharge them until they were of one mind. They went back into the jury room, but still couldn't reach a consensus. They were sent back a second time. One juror became annoyed and said it was very inconvenient. For a third time they told the Judge that there was simply no hope of reaching agreement, at which they were finally discharged and told to come back in the morning.

It was not an auspicious start.

At half past three in the afternoon, James Pillar was put up. He was described as a thin man with a brown wig, and was over seventy years old. He belonged to the Society of Friends and had a large family in Rathmines where he ran a business as a tea and wine merchant. He had been a regular visitor at the two male brothels in Golden Lane and Ship Street at which Clarke had offered his own services many times.

Clarke's services were now to the Crown. He grew more and more nervous, expecting to be called to give his evidence at any moment. Then suddenly it was announced that Pillar was changing his plea to guilty of the chief offence, that of felony. The prosecution agreed not to proceed with the other charges, which involved conspiracy, and a 'much affected' elderly gentlemen was immediately taken down to be sentenced at a later date.

It would be said that the guilty plea was his own decision, and not something advised by his counsel, that being a Quaker he was sincerely actuated by a spirit of repentance. It may well have been, but it did him no good. Baron Dowse would sentence him to *twenty years* imprisonment. He reminded the court that a quarter of a century ago, the penalty was death. This was a clear indication that the stakes were very high indeed. A twenty-year sentence for a man of Pillar's age was effectively a death sentence.

At half past three in the afternoon, Gustavus Cornwall mounted the dock. Bearded and imposing, he pleaded not guilty to the same offence.

Sergeant Hemphill for the prosecution set the scene.

'The decadence of great empires might be dated from the time when such crimes were regarded with leniency. Your duty, gentlemen, is to do your part in endeavouring to extirpate from among you this dreadful crime, a crime which you know from the earliest recorded history draws down the wrathful power of Heaven.'

Jack was required only to give evidence against Captain Kirwan. It was Clarke who was now called to help bring down the wrathful power of Heaven on the Secretary to the General Post Office.

He had first met Cornwall about three years previously, and on as many occasions since, at his home and at the brothel in Golden Lane. He gave his evidence in a 'rapid and glib' manner but he was clearly nervous and suffering from something akin to stage fright. He told the court that not only had he and McGrane committed buggery with Cornwall on the same occasion, one committed the act while the other looked on, waiting to take his turn.

Under cross-examination, he said that he didn't actually *know* he was Cornwall. And he never gave Cornwall his name, which explained why Cornwall said at the libel trial he had never heard of anyone called Clarke.

It transpired that Clarke, along with McGrane, on their return to Dublin had been taken by Meiklejohn to Molesworth Street, where the Masonic Temple was, and asked to identify Cornwall as he left the premises.

This insight into how Meiklejohn had got up the original case ended the first day's proceedings. Jack and Clarke were taken back to Chancery Lane Police Station to spend another night, while the favoured three, whose evidence was well practised and rehearsed, spent another night at a hotel, as did the jury for whom rooms had been obtained at the Angel Hotel by the Liffey. The weather was hot and the Liffey stank, and a juror from Kingstown told the court that he could not put up with the smell for even one night. Baron Dowse was unsympathetic.

'For a man from Kingstown to tell me that he cannot put up with the smell of the Liffey for one night is preposterous.' he said.

The smell of the Liffey pervaded Chancery Lane Police Station, which was a very old decaying building in a street of slum properties. Jack's night there was neither comfortable nor pleasant.

In the morning, Jack and Bill Clarke were back at the courthouse where Michael McGrane gave evidence about the offence with Cornwall, to corroborate that given by Clarke the previous day. He wore a check tweed suit, which had been given to him to wear by Malcolm Johnstone, who being rich probably had a whole wardrobe of check tweed suits. Johnstone in fact had been left forty thousand pounds, a vast sum in those days. He was the most exquisitely dressed of them all. McGrane, by contrast, was out of work.

Like Jack and Clarke, McGrane had been involved in amateur theatricals, which clearly carried a stigma judging by the way such information was regularly teased out in examination. He had acted in a Temperance Hall. He thought it was the St Nicholas Society. They were not, he was forced to admit, all teetotallers.

In Cornwall's defence, Clarke and McGranes' evidence was denounced as a vile concoction, though as always in such cases it was never said why they should have put themselves in the frame by concocting it. Cornwall's trip to Scotland was presented as an alibi, for it spanned the whole period that *Patience* was on at the Gaiety Theatre, when Clarke said they first met. Clarke, recalled, said he was *sure* it was *Patience* but it may have been a different opera.

Would Captain Kirwan come up with a similar alibi, or simply deny that he had ever known Jack? Who was going to corroborate him? It was all so long ago, about nine years now. While Jack was confident Captain Kirwan – or Lieutenant Kirwan as he had been then – could never actually forget him (who could forget Jack?) he knew that Kirwan had to fight for his freedom.

Three doctors gave evidence, which 'proved' that Cornwall could not have taken part in such abominable practices. Medical examinations in such cases were fraught with controversy, and there were some very weird deeply held convictions. (A doctor in the Boulton and Park case had stated that abnormal penis size was indicative of sodomitical activities, and given evidence in court that their sphincters were much dilated – in Park's case it 'refused to act).

As none of the evidence in Cornwall's case was reported, we may justifiably use but not overstretch our imaginations.

Baron Dowse's summing up was highly favourable to the Secretary. The jury went out and came back after five minutes. Cornwall must have breathed a very deep sigh of relief. They had found him not guilty. There was rapturous applause in the court, but Cornwall showed no emotion.

Clarke and McGrane were therefore liars in the minds of the jury. For them, that too was very possibly a relief. Neither had wanted to give evidence, and especially evidence that might put someone away for life. They had done what the police asked, made statements, gone into the witness box, but in the end the jury hadn't believe them. What respectable citizen – and the jury was composed of such people – would take the word of a cooper and an unemployed actor in a borrowed check suit over that of a senior civil servant with her Majesty's Post Office service and three physicians?

Sadly for Cornwall it wasn't yet over. He was brought back to face other indictments, those for conspiracy with Captain Kirwan when it would be Jack's turn. Jack hoped the jury wouldn't believe him either. He was no fool. He knew what a jury would think of him. He knew what Kirwan's defence would throw at him. He was a renter. A Mary-Ann. He hadn't done an honest job in years. They would bring up his having had to leave Dr Cranny's employment after being charged with burglary. He couldn't be trusted. The effeminate manner he had adopted was part of him, he couldn't discard it. They would take one look at him and surely say 'who could believe a man like that?'

Jack could make it as unbelievable as he wanted. Then they'd let him go back to London to resume his life, the only one he knew. Or he could tell it straight, as it was. But how did you tell it straight when you were up against a cousin of Lord Oranmore whose father was a magistrate and who owned over four thousand acres of County Galway? Jack owned nothing, just the clothes he stood up in. Who were they trying to destroy?

Who indeed.

The third day was spent presenting evidence against the two brothel keepers. The brothels were little more than back drawing rooms of tenements where men gathered to drink, smoke and have sex away from prying eyes. The Crown hammered away at them relentlessly, for if they failed to put two low brothel keepers away what chance did they stand with the more well connected accused? It was a day in court when the gentleman from the War Office sat up and dared not blink.

A Lance Corporal Pearson strode up with a whip in his hand, laid it down on the table, and gave his evidence in a very grandiose manner. He had been taken to Robert Fowler's brothel in Golden Lane by James Pillar and there had seen another soldier, Lieutenant Villiers Sankey of the 5th Dragoon Guards, for whom an arrest warrant had been taken out and who had since left the army.

'No doubt in consequence of urgent private affairs' observed the judge.

The rest of Pearson's evidence was unfit for publication, though the court learned that Lieutenant Sankey was known as Baby, no doubt because of his youthful looks, and the keeper of the brothel Mother Fowler.

Malcolm Johnstone stepped up next, his first appearance at the trials. He was elaborately dressed in an overcoat with deep fur collar and cuffs and patent leather boots, with a waxed moustache and a diamond ring on his finger. He told the court that he was known as Lady Constance Clyde, or sometimes just plain Connie Clyde, after Clyde Street in which he lived. The name had been bestowed on him by a clergyman at Donnybrook called Thomas Dancer Hutchinson who like half the people mentioned in court was believed to have made himself scarce. (Actually he hadn't.) Another person of his acquaintance was known to everyone as the Marchioness of Dame Street, and he told the court that George Taylor was nicknamed the Maid of Athens.

'It appears we are not to wait for any change in the relations between Ireland and England.' observed Baron Dowse, producing one of his many shafts of humour into the proceedings. 'These young men are perfectly capable of creating their own titles here on their own account.'

Johnstone had visited the brothel and seen Pillar there, but he denied seeing any impropriety. There was smoking and drinking. That was all.

Asked by Baron Dowse why he went there, he said,

'For curiosity, for innocent purposes.'

'You swear that?'

'Yes.'

McGrane gave further evidence about the character of the room, then Fowler, asked if he had anything to say, denied he was guilty of the offence charged. The jury didn't even leave their seats. The accused before them was described as 'a wretched old man, badly attired'. He was sentenced to two years with hard labour for keeping a disorderly house. Baron Dowse expressed a wish that he could have given him more.

Daniel Considine kept the brothel in Ship Street. He was a female impersonator of a theatrical bent who on a number of occasions had appeared by special invitation at Dublin Castle for the amusement of small parties. He was, he said in his defence, 'well known in the City of Dublin'. Considine was now blind and made a legitimate living as a basket maker.

Bill Clarke once again stepped up to the table to give his damning evidence. The cooper was a regular at Considine's. He saw Pillar in Considine's rooms, also a sailor, a Captain Traynor and others. Considine's defence was that as he was blind he couldn't see what was going on in front of him, but Clarke caused much merriment when he spoke about Considine speedily picking up a half sovereign that someone had dropped.

Angry and protesting, Considine was likewise taken away to begin serving two years with hard labour.

If Jack needed an example to match his own of selling one's soul to the devil (or to the British Crown) it was provided in the afternoon by Malcolm Johnstone. For Captain Kirwan wasn't the only army officer accused in the trials. Another was Spanish-born Juan Albert Fernandez, Surgeon Major to the third battalion of the Grenadier Guards, a soldier of middle age and long medical and military experience, who had clearly been in love with Johnstone. Because of Johnstone's wealth, this was not a case, it was pointed out, where the temptation of money was an issue. Johnstone, it became quite apparent, had also been in love with Fernandez, though the word love could scarcely be mentioned.

The miller's son had met him on the bridge over the pond in St Stephen's Green when Fernandez had approached him and discovered they had a mutual liking for fish. This was viewed at the trial as quite remarkable, as officers did not approach young strangers in parks. Their joint interest in fish developed into something more passionate. Fernandez bought Johnstone a gold ring inscribed *In Memoriam Mally from Juan*, and they enjoyed a night of intimacy at the Victoria Hotel in Killarney.

Fernandez became a regular guest at Johnstone's father's house, and when he fell ill Johnstone visited him regularly at his barracks.

The judge betrayed his sympathies by telling the jury before they deliberated that there was enough vice in the whole business without finding a man of Fernandez' military service and impeccable credentials guilty. Besides, where was the corroboration? The prosecution tried to make out that the ring was the corroboration. Baron Dowse said it was no corroboration at all.

In spite of Johnstone's evidence and that of an employee at the Killarney hotel where they had stayed, Fernandez was acquitted.

The twenty-one-year-old Johnstone's readiness to send to prison for life his older lover was matched by his offering to give similar evidence against his own twenty-year-old cousin, Johnstone Lyttle, the son of a Protestant clergyman, who worked for Jameson's Distillery and had attended Malcolm Johnstone's balls dressed as a woman. Lyttle had already been disowned by his widowed mother. The Crown took it out of Johnstone's hands in the wake of the Fernandez verdict by discharging Lyttle. In Lyttle's case, they knew, there wasn't even a ring to corroborate his cousin's testimony.

Jack wondered what was going on. He wasn't stupid. Why were they bringing forward cases for which there was no corroboration? Buggery was a crime committed between two people. It wasn't enough for one to 'accuse' the other. Such a case without any corroboration was bound to be thrown out.

But he wasn't a lawyer. The police had done their bit by arresting him and dragging him to court. The Crown were a law, so to speak, unto themselves.

Friday 22 August was the day he was ready to be called. He had been a guest of Chancery Lane police station since the Monday, it being doubtful that they would have let him return to see his family, though members of his family may have visited him. Johnstone, Taylor and McKiernan had been obliged to leave the Prince of Wales hotel where they were staying when commercial travellers complained to the hotelkeeper about the class of guest with whom they had to share accommodation.

Captain Kirwan and Gustavus Cornwall stepped into the dock, Kirwan for the first time and Cornwall for the second, charged jointly with conspiracy to corrupt public morals and public decency by introducing men to others with the intention of bringing about acts of immorality, a misdemeanour at common law. This was the charge that Boulton and Park had faced, and which totally failed to convince a jury. In the present case, a *nolle prosequi* – a decision not to prosecute – had been entered in all other counts of the indictment.

Kirwan was not to be tried for felony, i.e. the act of buggery, but just conspiring with Cornwall, who had already been found not guilty of the felony for which he was now to be tried for conspiring to bring about. The Crown were going to have a second shot at him.

It was their first at Captain Kirwan who, it turned out, had been a busy man since the days of his relationship with Jack.

Malcolm Johnstone, reported as being dressed not quite so loud as before, stepped up to the table once more and gave evidence about how *he* had met the young officer. Johnstone had left Trinity College at the age of fourteen – one finished one's education at a much younger age then – and visited Homburg, a spa town in Germany. There he met an English Member of Parliament, Sir James Tynte Agg-Gardner, Conservative MP for Cheltenham, who knew Captain Kirwan well. Agg-Gardner, who lived most of his life in hotels with their endless supply of liftboys and waiters, would stand down at a later election because of his homosexuality. He wrote the teenage boy a letter of introduction to him.

On his return to Dublin, Johnstone used this letter of introduction to meet Kirwan at the exclusive Kildare Street Club, the heart of the Anglo-Irish Protestant Ascendancy, famous for 'aristocracy, claret and whist' and reputed to be the only place in Ireland where one could enjoy decent caviar. The two had then gone to the Gaiety Theatre where 'misconduct' took place.

When Johnstone was a little older, Kirwan introduced him to Cornwall at the Post Office, just as he had done with Jack. The three of them, the middle-aged secretary, the handsome soldier and the fresh-faced lad drove in a cab to the Botanic Gardens. Once again, no newspaper reported the 'loathsome details', which earned the repetitive refrain 'unfit for publication', but

Johnstone repeated his story of sexual activity in the back of the cab, which involved the Secretary putting his hand on his knee, and the more steamy activity in the hothouse.

The importance of class in all aspects of Victorian life was exemplified in comments made by the prosecution as to the conspiracy to ensnare Malcolm Johnstone, described as a 'a mere youth'. What was the explanation for the intimacy between Cornwall and the miller's son? The latter, though respectable, had a father engaged in *trade*. Shock, horror.

Never mind that the trade was a business which had set up the horribly spoilt youth with a fortune of forty thousand pounds, check tweed suits and a fistful of diamond rings. Trade was trade. And tradesmens' sons certainly did not mix with gentlemen.

Never mind that the innocent youth had written a letter home from London to James Pillar, addressed 'Dear Pa' about his homosexual life in the English capital which the Judge described as an 'emanation from Hell'.

Never mind that he had held balls at his father's house where men dressed as ladies and at which the Reverend Thomas Dancer Hutchinson, who had given him the name Connie, had danced with Father Paul Keogh, a Catholic priest who lived opposite the court. This unorthodox contribution to inter-dominational relations counted for nothing, especially when Johnstone admitted he had not received any religious education from either of them.

Conspiracy was conspiracy, and Captain Kirwan had introduced the young man to a gentleman who had put his hand on his knee in a cab. That was, if one wanted to look at it that way, quite definitely a conspiracy. Conspiracies didn't always happen in smoke-filled rooms.

Johnstone completed his evidence with the unbelievable and risible admission that he had only been woken to a sense of morality by Detective Meiklejohn.

Jack was beginning to wonder if he would ever be called at all. The tension was unbearable. Surely they wouldn't drag him all the way from London, force him to make a statement, accept the statement and then leave him sitting in the wings? Would they?

Next it was the turn of pretty young George Taylor, the 'Maid of Athens', the former medical student who had by now spent so many hours getting legless with Meiklejohn that he had been terrified out of his wits with the threat of prosecution. Taylor testified that Kirwan had accosted him in the street when he was sixteen and that they had spent an hour together, the details of what they did in that hour once more unreported by the press. Taylor afterwards went to Cornwall's house on several occasions for sex, where as we saw in the libel trial he was 'disgusted', though not so disgusted as to return and accept from Cornwall tickets to the Horticultural Show.

Cornwall was a member of the Horticultural Society and had claimed that he and the youth were united simply by a taste for music and flowers, much as the affair between Mally and Juan began with a love of fish.

It transpired that the disreputable Meiklejohn had even incited Taylor to write a letter to Detective French with the intention of trapping and compromising the head of the CID who had clearly also enjoyed Taylor's company on a number of occasions.

123

Like Johnstone, Taylor confessed he had no idea that what he was doing was wrong.

'Did you too then get your religious education from the Right Reverend Mr Meiklejohn?' asked defence counsel to roars of laughter.

The answer was not forthcoming. Then the prosecution case closed.

Jack was angry, but relieved. He had indeed been dragged back to Dublin for no reason. He had waited around a week to give the evidence that was in his statement, every moment of each day dreading the time when he would have to stand up and face his old friend and describe their relationship, to tell the court of indecent acts that might have sent Kirwan to prison.

Now they had abandoned him and his evidence.

The reason that Jack was not called soon became apparent. It was the same reason that the ex-Munster Bank clerk Alfred McKiernan was not called against Cornwall, though he sat through the trials like Jack waiting to give evidence. His went back to 1876 when he had fallen out with Cornwall. The acts he maintained took place were all prior to the date of the conspiracy as laid down by the Crown in the indictment, namely December 1881.

Jack's evidence also went back to the 1870s. Neither could testify about a conspiracy that took place when they weren't there.

One might legitimately ask why Jack was taken to Dublin in the first place. Baron Dowse provided the answer very succinctly in his summing up when he recapped on the history of the cases.

'Once the verdict had gone against Cornwall in the libel trial, in walked the police, our industrious, active, intelligent constabulary!' he said sarcastically. Meiklejohn along with Chance and Miley the solicitors, he told the court, had rounded up everybody against whom a charge had been made and given them the alternative of working with them against Cornwall, French *et al*, or having the guns turned against themselves.

The first extraordinary statement is revealing. Baron Dowse obviously regarded the police in the case with the same scorn he reserved for some of the witnesses. Johnstone was an exquisite young man who 'knew nothing'. Clarke was a youth of tainted life and habits. (What Jack would have been we can only guess) Nevertheless, 'in walked the police' and assembled all the witnesses they could, fair and foul, including Jack. It was up to the Crown to decide what charges to bring, what indictments to frame. In the case of Kirwan and Cornwall, they had narrowed the case considerably and given both men a fighting chance.

Why had Kirwan been charged only with conspiracy, which was much harder to prove? They had Jack's evidence, they had Johnstone's, and they had Taylor's. Four thousand three hundred and five acres of County Galway, being cousin to a Lord and son of a Protestant magistrate, both of whom had put up surety for the young Captain, were matters, of course, of no little consideration.

The jury wanted to finish the case that night, but Baron Dowse made everyone wait until the Saturday morning when he completed his summing up and sent the jury out. They came back after forty minutes, unable to agree.

There was a tortuous discussion about finding one prisoner guilty but not the other. Baron Dowse reminded them that this was a conspiracy charge. They had to find both guilty, or acquit both.

'You can't conspire with yourself,' he said testily.

Their problem, they answered, was in believing the witnesses.

At the end of the day, unable to agree, they were discharged and the case put over to the next Commission in October.

It was the worst possible verdict for everybody, except perhaps Jack who was allowed to visit his family and go back home to London, most likely at his own expense. He had not seen them for a few years. His brother James was thirteen, old enough to earn money to bring in to the family. Edward at twenty-three was now the main breadwinner. The family were still living in poverty, Annie helping their mother around the house. Things were difficult and would remain so for some years.

James was not quite old enough to make sense of the exotic, effeminate Jack with his theatrical airs who had disgraced the family by ending up in court twice and who admitted to being a sodomite and a criminal, who moved within outlawed circles in London, who slept with soldiers and sold his body for money. Brother Jack was truly beyond the pale.

Edward was old enough. The money Jack sent home in regular postal orders was tainted, and he knew it.

As for Eliza Saul, mothers are, after all, mothers and Jack was possibly still the good Irish son who had just fallen in with the wrong people. He would find a good job in London, another position as a valet in a nice respectable house, mend his ways and get married.

Perhaps this nasty affair in Dublin would teach him a lesson.

The nasty affair in Dublin went on without Jack. At the October Commission, Kirwan and Cornwall were put up again for conspiracy. The same witnesses, Johnstone and Taylor, gave evidence against them. Since the last trial they had been living in the north of Ireland, with a detective, moving around as and when people became aware of their identities. They had changed their names. Johnstone had got a girl into trouble. They were pilloried, hated, despised.

The second jury took the same view of them. They acquitted Kirwan and Cornwall of conspiracy on the grounds that the evidence of the Crown was not considered sufficient.

Neither, one is tempted to say, was it ever supposed to be, but the law had to be seen to take its course, and where sodomy was concerned even more so. The crime 'not to be talked about among Christians' had to be aired among Christians, and then put away. For good. The Crown simply didn't have the stomach to see eminent, respectable citizens and army officers given life sentences for such unmentionable crimes.

In the end, an elderly grocer and two lowly brothel keepers had received prison sentences while the more eminently respectable Captain Kirwan, Gustavus Cornwall and Surgeon Major Fernandez walked free.

The Nationalists got their pound of flesh with Detective French, whose case dragged on through a number of hearings to decide on the question of his sanity. He suffered a mental breakdown, and it was stated in court that two of his relatives had died in a lunatic asylum. French was finally sentenced to two years, much on the evidence of Bill Clarke and George Taylor.

United Ireland thundered about the acquittals, how the police had done very little to advance the prosecution case, how the crimes would never have come to light in the first place had O'Brien and Meiklejohn and their cohorts not started the whole ball rolling. The role of the Crown, the newspaper said, had been feeble-hearted to say the least in securing convictions.

The Dublin trials were over. Lives were ruined. Kirwan's career in the army was ended, and Cornwall lost his Post Office pension, a cruel snub if ever there was one. The consequences were tragic for all of the accused, particularly James Pillar who would be in his nineties by the end of his twenty-year sentence. Kilmainham Gaol was one of the most horrific prisons in the country and was a symbol of oppression to the Irish. Heat and light came from a single candle. Most of the time prisoners just sat in the cold and dark. A visit to Kilmainham Gaol today is a sobering experience that makes one feel almost ashamed to be British.

Pillar – Papa to the friends who had betrayed him – would survive ten years before being released from his suffering. If it was his Quaker faith that woke in him the conviction to plead guilty, one hopes the same faith sustained him to the end.

Gustavus Cornwall returned to live in Scotland and died of syphilis at his brother's estate in Linlithgow. He never recovered from his ordeal initiated by *United Ireland*.

The reverberations of the trials spread across the sea to England, giving rise to the belief that homosexual 'vice' was rampant in official circles in Ireland, and doing much to discredit Gladstone's Liberal administration at the time.

Jack returned to London and his old life, and to his friends the Hammonds. Five years later, at another trial, he would not be left sitting in the wings but would instead become a star witness. He would bring a courtroom to a state of hushed anticipation and breathless excitement as he stepped into the dock. In Dublin his family would shake their heads and despair that an Irish son could sink so low in a pit of vice.

It all had to do with yet another male brothel. Not a back street affair full of men smoking and drinking and having sex behind makeshift curtains but an altogether grander and classier place of business. And one rumoured to have entertained a Royal visitor.

* * * * * *

Chapter Notes

1. Most of the information about the Dublin trials and the Cornwall libel case is taken from contemporary reports in *Freeman's Journal*. Though partisan, it covered both in great detail. One mystery remains. What *was* in Jack Saul's statement that was so readily accepted by the Crown, and then not used? It has been said that agents of the government later destroyed all of the court documents on the Dublin scandals. Then, on 30 June 1922, an explosion in the occupied Four Courts on the north bank of the Liffey, a direct result of the civil war raging between opposing groups of Irish republicans over the Anglo-Irish Treaty, sent up in smoke the National

Archives of Ireland which were stored there, destroying a thousand years of Irish history, including mediaeval documents and the records of government and most criminal trials. Given, however, that we have the evidence of Kirwan's other young men, it takes little imagination to reconstruct Jack's statement.

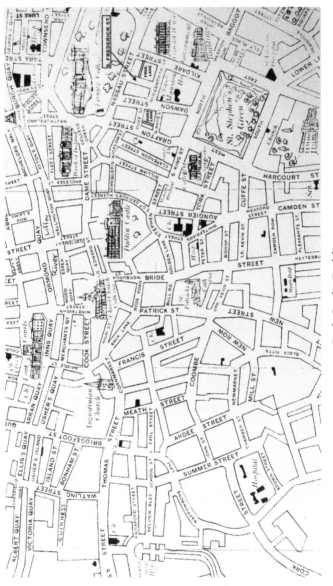

Jack Saul's Dublin

Martin Oranmore Kirwan
of the Dublin Militia

Gustavus Cornwall, courtesy
of the National Library
of Ireland

Cregg Castle, ancestral home of the Kirwans

Edward Saul, portrait, and with carriage at the
Dublin Horse Show, courtesy of Maura Harvey

133

Grafton Street at the turn of the century

Duke Lane as it is today, showing Kehoe's Pub.
The house in which Jack grew up has been
replaced by the modern block at the end

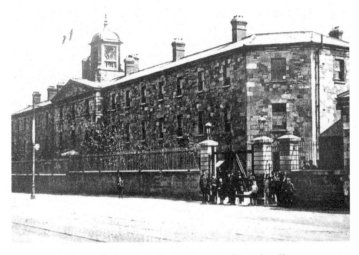

Griffith Barracks, where Jack and Bill
Clarke were locked up before their trial

The Kingstown steamer, a sight that would
become very familiar to Jack

Simeon Solomon, who may have been Jack's collaborator
on Sins. Courtesy www.simeonsolomon.com

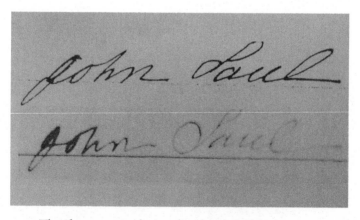

The 'footsteps in the sand'. Above, Jack's signature
on his police statement. Below, Jack's signature on the
1901 Irish Census return

Baron Dowse, who
presided over the
Dublin Felony trials

Mr William O'Brien M.P.,
whose attack against Gustavus
Cornwall in United Ireland led
to his trial for libel

Green Street Courthouse, where the
Dublin Felony trials were held

John Meiklejohn, the ex-
Scotland Yard detective,
'a bully and a big fat man'.

John Mallon, Chief
Superintendent of the
Dublin Metropolitan
Police, who arrested
Jack in London.

Piccadilly Circus. The corner of Swan and Edgar is at the
far left - note the famous arches opposite

Charles Hammond, the
male madame of 19
Cleveland Street

Lord Euston, from a
sketch in court

George Cavendish-
Bentinck, MP, from a
cartoon in Vanity Fair

Lord Arthur Somerset,
'Podge', from a cartoon
in Vanity Fair

Ernest Parke, editor of the
North London Press

The house in Cleveland
Street from a contemporary
newspaper

Prince Eddy, who was
reputed to have visited
19 Cleveland Street

Martin Kirwan's grave in
Mount Jerome Cemetery

The Sins of the Cities
of the Plain

Lisle Street today, where Jack
wrote his infamous memoir

15 Old Compton Street,
where Jack was living when
Ashley came to beg for help

Our Lady's Hospice, Harold's Cross, where Jack Saul died

Jack Saul's unmarked grave in Glasnevin Cemetery
is the space between the front stones

CHAPTER TEN

THE BLACKMAILER'S CHARTER

The Dublin scandals were a watershed. Jack realised he couldn't take anything for granted. Neither freedom nor immunity from arrest. Back on his beat at Piccadilly Circus and around the West End, he found that he was still left alone by the police. How long that would go on for he had no idea. He was twenty-seven now and had been a male prostitute in London for five years. Five years was a long time to be a rent boy on the streets of the capital. 'Dublin Jack' was no longer the little fresh-faced lad with the cheeky grin and the gift of the gab. He still had the grin and the gab, but he was older and wiser. Worse, he was now too well-known. Nothing aged you more than a life on the streets.

Not that he couldn't still pull a punter. The golden days of *The Sins of the Cities of the Plain* might be over, but though he was an old kid on the block, he knew the ropes, and had a regular clientele that came back for more. Trading sex with strangers every night was hard work and dangerous. No pornographic publisher came past these days to admire his manhood and invite him to write about it, but it was there for the taking.

He was still ready for a lark with a free gentleman. At any time.

The money didn't set you up. It stopped you being hungry and allowed you to buy new clothes. Rags were a handicap at Piccadilly.

Unless you were a newcomer. There were lots of them, some in their early teens, runaways from homes and ragged schools and orphanages. Jack did what every prostitute did who saw time catching up. He became a pimp, not just of young men but of women too. You want a girl? You want a nice boy? Fresh-faced from the countryside? Jack knew where, and Jack could take you there.

As long as there was something in it for Jack.

It wasn't a pretty life but it was the only one he knew. The streets he walked were full of grooms, valets and unemployed barmen doing exactly the same as he. The Circus stood at the centre of his universe and he knew all the performers. There was Mr Percy E. Davis. Just a young man, but the 'Mr' on his card gave him a gentlemanly air. A gentleman to gentleman. No address but retain the card please. In the days before one could pluck a rent boy off the Internet – or male escort as they call themselves now – and have him in bed within the hour, these young men needed a way of advertising themselves. Everyone carried a card. Jack had a card.

So did a youth called Carrington, who became a friend of Jack's, though it wouldn't stop Jack later giving his name to the police. His card, in fine Gothic script, identified him as P.H. Carrington of 15 Hugh Street, Ecclestone Square, a private address just to the south of Victoria Station. For a time, it was also used between engagements by an Edinburgh-born homosexual actor called Charles Maitland Hallard. He was to be seen in small parts in West End theatres, and would get his break five years later when he appeared in *Trilby* with Herbert Beerbohm Tree at the Haymarket Theatre. Carrington and Hallard may have been lovers. (1)

P.H. Carrington wasn't his real name. Known by the boys as 'Lively Poll' he was very possibly a young man called Paul Harry Ferdinando, born 1867, a well-educated East End office boy who changed his surname. By the age of sixteen, Ferdinando was selling books out of a barrow in Farringdon Market. The enterprising lad would eventually change his name to Charles Carrington and go on to become, in his early thirties, a major publisher of pornography, moving to Paris where he sold largely to English buyers. He also printed legitimate works and translations as a cover for his less savoury business, much of which would bear a striking similarity to *Sins*. (2)

Back in 1881 Ferdinando was far too young to have collaborated with Jack on *Sins* (he would have been just fourteen at the time), but it is not a long shot to suggest that the fledgling bookseller, publisher and East End barrow-boy, while learning the ropes of his ultimate career, was involved somewhere in facilitating Jack's delivery of his manuscript. Nowadays we would call him a street-smart kid. Jack's 'Mr Cambon' may well have been an associate of them both.

As for Jack, did his card state on the back 'ready for a lark with a free gentleman'? Definitely not. Cards had to be business-like. You never knew whose hands they were going to fall into.

Mr John Saul at your service.

Jack kept up his semi-nomadic existence, moving from address to address, helping out the 'gay ladies' (a term used to describe female prostitutes). One such address was in Nassau Street near the Tottenham Court Road and the Middlesex Hospital, just a short walk from where the Hammonds were now living at 19 Cleveland Street, a cut above their usual abode he thought.

The brothel in Nassau Street was operated by a widowed labourer called Frederick Dye, a friend of Hammonds, and a madame in her seventies Emma Collins. The women working there, at one stage a 'housekeeper' of forty-four, a 'charwoman' of fifty-five and a 'laundress' of fifty-three were no spring chickens and probably driven to the occupation by necessity. There is no evidence this operated as a male brothel, though Jack would later be accused of living in a house in Nassau Street where 'vicious practices' went on, a euphemism for sodomy. Perhaps there was another one. You didn't need to walk far in London to find a brothel of the type that suited you.

Then one night – it was 14 August 1885 – Jack went to bed wherever he was living at the time. When he woke up in the morning his world had altered. It was nothing perceptible, and as he wandered through the West End in the days afterwards, perhaps to stroll among the painted male faces who congregated at the Dilly or for a change at one of the Promenade Concerts at Her Majesty's Theatre, it is doubtful whether anyone he met had noticed it either.

What had occurred was momentous, and it would affect thousands like himself. Quite simply, the law had changed.

For years the government had been concerned about prostitution in the metropolis, particularly that practised by women, and even more particularly child prostitution which was rife.

The Eliza Armstrong case had alerted the nation to the horrors of it at great cost to one particular man. W.T. Stead, editor of the *Pall Mall Gazette* and a campaigner against what he saw as a 'Modern Babylon', joined forces with Bramwell Booth of the Salvation Army and together they 'purchased' a girl of thirteen and took her away from her parents. The girl was looked after, but Stead wrote about it in the Gazette as an example of how easy it was to spirit away a child in London for nefarious purposes. For the crime of child abduction, he was sent to prison. He later died on the Titanic, a fitting death for a man who in his professional life had battled an evil he regarded as only the tip of an iceberg.

The government of the day – the Prime Minister was now Lord Salisbury, whose brother-in-law, the Earl of Galloway, was fond of picking up little girls around the railway station in Dumfries – listened and acted, and the result was the Criminal Law Amendment Act of 1885, an act to 'make further provision for Women and Girls, the suppression of brothels, and other purposes'.

When it was finally passed it raised the age of consent from thirteen to sixteen, made it an offence to abduct a girl under eighteen for carnal purposes, provided for summary proceedings to be taken against brothels, and extended the buggery laws so that any kind of sexual activity whatsoever between males was criminalised.

The last of these was not its initial purpose. At the final minute the Liberal MP for Northamptonshire, Henry Labouchere, tabled an amendment which began with the words 'Any male person who in *public or private* ...' and rushed it through in the early hours of the morning. It made gross indecency, an expression that had no legal definition whatsoever, a crime in the United Kingdom, so that putting your hand on another man's knee in a cab on the way to the Botanic Gardens to look at flowers could just possibly earn you two years with hard labour.

For homosexual men, Britain had become a dangerous country overnight. The Labouchere Amendment or the 'Blackmailer's Charter', as it came to be known, would not be repealed for another eighty-two years. There were many who wished that Henry Labouchere had gone down in the Titanic.

One young man who was ahead of the game, almost as though he saw it coming, was Herbert Coulton, a nineteen-year-old grocer's assistant from Brighton. He was sentenced in June 1884 at Lambeth Police Court to eighteen months for demanding money with menaces from a draper called Edwin Fancourt, by sending him a letter threatening to accuse him of an 'infamous crime'. If he had waited two years, he might just as easily have accused him of a careless kiss.

Jack would know of Coulton because Coulton learned fast, not unfortunately to be a model citizen but how easily homosexual men could be blackmailed into paying large sums of money.

Jack by that time had become acquainted with a twenty-year-old Scotsman called Andrew Grant, another boy who saw the potential in the new law. Andrew Grant was nicknamed Queen Anne and would live not only with Jack but also for a time at the Hammonds' new domicile at 19 Cleveland Street.

Grant was dangerous. A newcomer at the Dilly, he would become one of a vicious gang of blackmailers. He would befriend Coulton when the shop boy got out of prison and they would join forces. For the moment he was raw and inexperienced and just another pretty face with blue eyes being led on by other boys on the streets.

No less dangerous was another youth that Jack got to know. Tom Wells was known as Clifton – his personal card was handwritten or rather scrawled with just the one name and an address. He would take gentleman back to his lodgings in Upper Marsh, Lambeth. Just as they were performing on his bed, two or three men would jump out from underneath and bounce money out of the unsuspecting victim by threats.

It was an ugly world, and Mr Labouchere had made it even more ugly.

In May 1887, Jack made the decision to return to stay with the Hammonds for a while. He never stayed anywhere with anyone for very long, and Charles Hammond was a bizarre choice as on two occasions the older man had happily seen him short of money. Perhaps Jack was desperate, or perhaps he just needed the companionship of people he knew. The Hammonds were the first people he really got to know in London, and there was a bond between them.

Besides, he had heard about the reputation that 19 Cleveland Street had already earned, and Jack wanted to see for himself if it was justified.

Jack went and stayed there for a few weeks, but it quickly became apparent to him that it was Charles Hammond who had truly arrived.

* * * * * *

Chapter Notes

1. By the 1891 census, Charles Maitland Hallard had moved across the road to number 16 Hugh Street where he lived with a professional singer called Harry Yeo. Sometimes known as Charles M. Hallard, he was born in 1865. He went on to become a film actor. His first silent movie *Convict 99* was made in 1919. He survived the advent of the talkies and went on to make movies up until 1938 with *The Sky's The Limit*. He also acted on Broadway. He died unmarried in Farnham, Surrey, on 21 April, 1942.

2. I am indebted to Jerry Dunlop of Las Vegas, another Cleveland Street researcher, for putting me on the trail of Paul Harry Ferdinando, aka Carrington. He married a Frenchwoman but was widowed after a few years, and died of syphilis (like so many) in 1921. He points out that Ferdinando is thought to have been the courier of the other notorious work, *My Secret Life* by 'Walter', to a publisher in Belgium. As we have seen, Walter is strongly reckoned to have been Henry Spencer Ashbee. Compared to *Sins*, it is a massive work of eleven volumes and was banned for a hundred years. Mr Dunlop entertains the possibility that Jack might have been responsible for it too. My own feeling is that Jack was far too busy!

CHAPTER ELEVEN

THE BEST HOUSE IN LONDON

As Jack turned into Cleveland Street, in what was then called north Soho (it would only become known much later as 'Fitzrovia'), he could not help but be struck by the extensive 130-year-old Middlesex Hospital which practically took up the west side of the block. It had been constructed when the area was just green fields and lanes, though it had long been absorbed by the march of bricks and mortar. On the eastern side of the street was the grim, heavy bulk of the former Strand Union Workhouse, believed to have been Charles Dickens' inspiration for the workhouse in *Oliver Twist* when the author lived at what was now No 22. By the time Hammond took up residence, the old workhouse was being used as the Central London Sick Asylum Infirmary. The rest of the road was taken up by business premises and terraced Georgian housing, the majority of which, like the hospital, was structurally unsound. Like many of the less fashionable parts of London, it was an area of furnished and unfurnished lodgings in garrets and attics and sometimes cellars.

No 19 Cleveland Street, Jack's destination, was to all appearances in the grounds of the hospital itself which extended practically to Hammond's door. The two houses formerly used as the nurses' institute on one side had been pulled down, the house on the other was used by the hospital to accommodate nurses, and a whole stretch of six houses beyond that had recently been demolished. While much rebuilding work went on, three properties stood side by side, one empty, one housing nurses, the third a very well-appointed male brothel.

Jack's first impressions of the interior of 19 Cleveland Street can scarcely be imagined.

Hammond, like Jack, had been making his living from prostitution for years, but unlike Jack he had apparently turned it to a much greater advantage. The wily Hammond, now thirty-four years old, his black hair thinning to a very obvious bald patch, but still with a luxuriant handlebar moustache, had achieved his ambition and set himself up as a male madame. Jack had met a number of the female variety, in Dublin and in London, but never in his life – one supposes – had he encountered the Hammond variety. The Gravesend waterman's son had clearly prospered. In the two years since they had moved in, they had transformed the place from an ordinary lodging house into what Hammond had always desired – the best 'house' in London.

It hadn't happened overnight. The Hammonds had taken up residence as lodgers themselves, when the building had contained around twenty people. Hammond clearly saw the potential. The evidence from the rates books suggests that a year or so later the owner and ratepayer was Michael Loughlin, a prosperous rag dealer who lived two hundred yards away in Upper Rathbone Place, and who also owned No 102 Cleveland Street. Small merchants and businessmen often speculated in local property, and Loughlin had done a lot of that. By the time of Jack's arrival, all the old tenants had left and Hammond had taken over the tenancy. (1)

There were caged birds, and pet dogs running about. Some of the animals were, he was informed, gifts from appreciative clients. On the mantelpiece were a number of Dresden vases, on the wall more Dresden in the way of plates and a number of oil paintings. The curtains were velvet and in the bedrooms were silk sheets and yellow silk pillows. Hammond had acquired not just one piano, but two. The Hammonds' son, Charlie, was now a boy of six or seven years old. He had a bent for music and practised regularly. Hammond boasted a watch chain with a gold seal on it and looked more like a bank manager who had just come home from his job in the city than a brothel keeper. Landlord was the way he preferred to describe himself.

Downstairs there was a tray of cards for guests as one entered the sitting room. Discreet, as they had to be. Hammond, 19 Cleveland Street in fine lithograph lettering. Take one sir, pass it on to your friends. All are welcome here. For a certain class of customer, there was champagne. Then you were shown into a room to meet a youth. Or, if you wanted, you could bring one with you and rent a room. For a charge of course. There was always the chance the boy might come back and work there. Or if you liked, you could bring a soldier for the night. This was quite definitely one of these houses where, if uniforms were your bag, you could spend the night under silk sheets with a handsome guardsman.

He had even brought his last prostitute lover back to the house, Emily Barker, to act as a sort of secretary, making appointments and writing them in a book, many of which arrived by telegram, for Hammond's literary skills were as poor as Caroline's. What Caroline thought of a rival living in the same house isn't known.

Jack must have wondered how Hammond had been able to afford all this. The oil paintings, the Dresden china, the silk bedlinen. This was a posh bordello, catering, though not exclusively, for the aristocracy. Hammond made no secret of that. Gentlemen of a certain class, of a position in society, did not want to take risks at Piccadilly Circus with a shady young blackmailer. (Though a number of them ended up working at 19 Cleveland Street!) Many of the clients were married. A number had well-known names. Some were politicians, others were in the military. What they wanted was a safe house, a discreet establishment where they could indulge themselves without fear of discovery, or the threat of villains jumping out from underneath a bed as soon as they took their clothes off.

Many extremely wealthy men visited 19 Cleveland Street, and they helped pay for it too. Hammond was too clever a man to try and extort money but it was definitely their fortunes that had set Hammond up in his domain and were keeping him there like a king on his throne. Hammond knew who they were and many had obviously come to trust him. They were willing to pay well for his discretion.

The gold seal on Hammond's watch chain had been given to him by Major Moet, a brother of the firm of wine merchants who had brought the famous champagne brand Moet and Chandon across the channel. It was quite possible he supplied the champagne at cost price, which Hammond provided. It was in everyone's interest to stay on the right side of Hammond. Many clients of the house used false names but a number, lulled into a sense of security, dispensed with caution and were known to the boys who worked there.

Boys like young Frank Hewitt, a seventeen-year-old carpenter's son from the Hampstead Road who worked during the day at a stained glass window makers in Brewer Street and whose 'hours' at 19 Cleveland Street were from eight in the evening until one o'clock in the morning, at which he time he clocked off.

Hammond was not one to keep his hands off the goods. Hewitt had become his 'spooney boy' as Jack observed. Hewitt, in spite of his young age, had become adept at procuring for Hammond, finding other boys who would like to work there. One of those was a well educated youth called Henry Horace Newlove who lived with his mother in Camden Town and had a very good job as a 3rd class clerk in the Secretary's office of the General Post Office at St Martin Le Grand in London.

There was definitely a culture within the General Post Office. Gustavus Cornwall had been Secretary to the GPO in Dublin. Henry Newlove was well placed in the London Secretary's office to launch himself forth into the basement toilets of the building where his penchant for sodomising telegraph boys was well satisfied.

Jack was at 19 Cleveland Street to stay for a while, and that meant he was there to work. Whatever drove him back into Hammond's clutches, it must have included the need for support and money, because Hammond was still a pimp regardless of the airs and graces he had given himself. Jack would have to pay his landlord a proportion of his earnings. In return Hammond would give him accommodation and food (so Jack hoped) and a share of the Hammond network of posh toffs who regularly visited the establishment.

Jack was already beginning to feel jealous of the competition. Pushing thirty, he knew he was no match for teenage lads like Hewitt and Newlove who were new on the game. It was galling to watch Hammond also 'spooning' with Newlove.

He needn't have worried. His looks and his formidable talent were still there and if one wanted the more mature experience rather than the fumblings of a mere beginner, nobody could touch him.

Jack was still ready for a lark with a free gentleman. At any time. And they would come.

On 4 May, 1888, a meeting was held at London Bridge Station of the Submarine Continental Railway Company to pass a bill authorising experimental work for a tunnel beneath the Straits of Dover. It would not be built – not then – but the great and burgeoning spirit of Victorian enterprise was alive and well in the hall. The approval of the bill was seconded by George Cavendish-Bentinck MP, a member of the board and Conservative Member of Parliament for Whitehaven in Cumbria.

A long communication was submitted by Colonel Hozier, Secretary of Lloyds, dealing very comprehensively with the advantages of such an undertaking.

It was Colonel Hozier's considered opinion that the benefits to business and commerce and the huge profits to be made by shareholders far outweighed the risks of the scheme. For that was Colonel Hozier's job. To assess the technicalities and weigh up risk. He was very good at it. A keen technophile, in the days when he had been a Royal Artillery Officer he had created a network of coastal signal stations, all equipped with telegraphs, to improve shipping safety.

George Cavendish-Bentinck and Colonel Hozier however were linked by more than a dream of seeing a tunnel under the Channel built in their lifetimes. Both names would be given by Jack as regular visitors to No 19.

George Cavendish-Bentinck MP, or 'Little Ben' as he was known in Parliament, was descended from the Dukes of Portland. He was married with two sons and two daughters. A barrister, a racing man and a first class cricketer, he had served as Secretary to the Board of Trade under Benjamin Disraeli. One of his daughters, Mary Venetia Cavendish-Bentinck, would be Godmother to Queen Elizabeth the Queen Mother. He lived at 3 Grafton Street with his family, but the address which Jack would supply was that of his son whose residence was 5 Richmond Terrace in Whitehall, so close to the Houses of Parliament that one could almost hear the order papers being shaken. His son, William George Cavendish Bentinck, was Conservative MP for Falmouth and unmarried.

For Jack to have known such a prestigious address, it is likely he was taken there. Father and son would have both used the Whitehall residence in the event of late sittings, and it was perhaps while young William was away at his constituency in the west country that his father took the calculated risk of entertaining Jack, which he couldn't do at home. Jack may have seen it as a way of depriving Hammond of his commission, something he was eager to do whenever possible.

It was an experience straight out of *The Sins of the Cities of the Plain*. A highly respected Member of Parliament, with a wife and family, entertaining Jack well within the sound of Big Ben, Jack demonstrating that he too could give service to his country.

George Cavendish-Bentinck would not be able to use his son's residence for very much longer. Shortly after his initial encounter with Jack, William got married and took his bride Ruth Mary St Maur, the illegitimate daughter of Lord Edward Adolphus Ferdinand St Maur, across the threshold. Thereafter his father probably needed the sanctuary of 19 Cleveland Street, away from the constraints of the marital nest, to carry on his illicit pleasures.

Jack even possessed Colonel Hozier's card. Jack never revealed his address, only his name, though he would later tell the police he could find it if they wanted. They didn't.

Colonel Hozier of Lloyds was the most well-known man of that name and rank in London. Otherwise known as Sir Henry Montague Hozier, he was not only Secretary to Lloyds of London but a Liberal Member of Parliament, Secretary to the Liberal Unionist Association and had a family seat at Maudslie Castle in Lanarkshire. His army record was exemplary. Educated at Rugby and trained at the Royal Military Academy in Woolwich, he served as attaché with German headquarters in the Franco-German war where he was made a Knight of the

Iron Cross. Giving up the sabre for the much mightier and more profitable pen, he had been Secretary of Lloyds for twelve years.

His wife, Lady Blanche Ogilvy Hozier, was the mother of a one-year-old child named Clementine Hozier who would grow up to become famous as the wife of Sir Winston Churchill. It is generally accepted that Clementine was not Colonel Hozier's biological daughter. Her mother maintained that the real father was Captain William George Middleton, a famous horseman. In fact, it has been suggested that none of Lady Blanche's children were the genuine progeny of Colonel Hozier. Lady Blanche was somewhat free with her favours. They would eventually divorce.

It would not, therefore, be surprising if Colonel Hozier was free with his. Colonel Hozier's job with Lloyds of London was to assess risk. Visiting a brothel and giving one's card to a male prostitute, no matter how much one trusted him, was a simple matter of calculating risk. Hammond's house was discreet and one couldn't just walk in, unless one's face was well-known. What did it matter that one of his cards had found its way into the hands of a London rent boy? There were many ways he could explain that, if the need ever arose. He was an old soldier – he had served in the 2nd Life Guards, the Royal Artillery and the 3rd Dragoon Guards. The possibility of blackmail was something that rich and powerful men took in their stride as the price of illicit and illegal pleasure. Some men even got a vicarious thrill out of the danger. Oscar Wilde would be one of many who enjoyed playing with fire.

A number of students of the Cleveland Street case have satisfied themselves that Henry Montague Hozier was Jack's visitor at the brothel. But Colonel Hozier had a brother. In fact he had *two*. And both were Lieutenant Colonels.

Lieutenant Colonel William Wallace Hozier, 1st Baron Newlands, was the eldest. In London he resided in Grosvenor Square, when in Scotland he stayed at the family seat in Lanarkshire. The other was not spoken of much, with very good reason.

Lieutenant Colonel John Wallace Hozier of the Royal Scots Greys had retired in 1882. He was now fifty-three, unmarried, homosexual and with a penchant for young soldiers. Four years after the Cleveland Street scandal broke, he created a scandal all of his own. He walked into the shop of a second-hand clothes dealer in Westminster with a twenty-year-old private, Hans Blomfield Hamilton of the Dorset Regiment, and said that his 'young friend from the country' wanted to change his uniform for a suit of private clothes, as being an officer he did not want to be seen walking about the streets with a common soldier. The dealer obliged, but amazingly – at least to our way of thinking now – called the police as soon as they had gone. A few days later, Colonel Hozier returned, this time with a Sergeant Aitken in the uniform of the Scots Guards and made the same request. They were just about to leave in a cab when the police pounced.

Hamilton and Aitken were charged with desertion and disposing of their uniforms, Hozier with assisting and inciting them. Hozier had befriended Hamilton at Charing Cross Station and taken him to Windsor, presumably to a hotel for the night. Hamilton was sent to prison for three weeks, while Sergeant Aitken and John Wallace Hozier were discharged. The newspapers said that it was no business of theirs to speculate on how or why the Colonel had befriended two private soldiers. He had merely acted 'foolishly'.

So foolishly that a few months later his brother, Henry Montague of Lloyds, an expert in matters of risk, had him locked up in a private lunatic asylum, the Flower House in Catford, where he could no longer disgrace the family. It wasn't the first time they had branded him a lunatic. Two years earlier they had put him in the private care of a surgeon in deepest Cumberland, an action typical of well-connected families who had a member they wished to conceal. It is entirely possible they suspected him of involvement in the Cleveland Street case. John Wallace Hozier died in 1905.

Jack knew who he was. Hammond knew who he was. Madame Caroline, the little French prostitute who sat smoking cigarettes, knew who he was. And the tinkling of the ivories in the next room as the Hammonds' young son practised his scales was a comforting sound that made Colonel John Wallace Hozier think of any number of respectable drawing rooms. A few glasses of champagne, a relaxing chat afterwards on the chaise longue, a bit of banter with the proprietor and with the young man who had satisfied his urges, what man would not be encouraged to tempt providence?

And 19 Cleveland Street was most definitely the kind of place that might endear itself to John Wallace Hozier, the sort of establishment, which Jack described so vividly in *Sins* as one of those houses in which, for a fee, you could sleep with soldiers.

In his later police statement, Jack provided most of the names of the gentlemen who visited the Cleveland

Street house in the Queen's Jubilee year of 1887. The same names would be provided by some of the other boys who worked there, plus a few more. False names like Green, Brown and Black abounded. Some customers only visited once or twice. About twenty became firm regulars, like Major Moet, and became well-known not only to the Hammonds and to Jack but also the other lads who drifted in and out of the premises. The hard core came mainly from the political sphere, the banking world and the higher echelons of the military.

The landed gentry and the upper classes covered themselves liberally in names. Jack only needed two. They were his passport into society. With them he crossed borders and traversed classes. Those were honeyed days for Jack. More members of the aristocracy and the ruling class passed across his lap – or within sitting distance of it – than at any time in his career.

Jack was now making considerably more than the eight or nine pounds a week (which calculates at about £300 in spending power today) he had made after his arrival in London. The cost of a boy in Hammond's brothel was a sovereign, or a pound. Gentlemen who came to sleep with boys or soldiers obviously paid a great deal more. Of his takings, Jack had to give Hammond his share. It didn't please Jack, but at the very least he had a safe and comfortable place in which to meet and take clients. And that counted. Every rent boy knew the danger of picking up a client who might refuse to pay at the end of the session, or become violent, or commit rape.

Also, at 19 Cleveland Street he was among friends, old and new. Hammond and his wife Caroline were seasoned whores who brooked no nonsense. Hewitt

THE SINS OF JACK SAUL

and Newlove were regulars there and became friends of Jack.

Jack liked Henry Newlove. In a way, they had both risen by their own efforts. It wasn't every telegraph messenger boy who was clever enough to achieve the coveted position of clerk in the Secretary's office. Newlove abused his position, though the telegraph messengers he sodomised in the toilets of the General Post Office seemed none the worse for it and carried on having sex between themselves.

One of the more bizarre characters who drifted in and out of the house was The 'Reverend' George Daniel Veck, forty years old and the son of a publican from Alverstoke in Hampshire. Veck was not there to give the boys religious instruction. Far from it. He had been a telegraph clerk with the Eastern District Post Office until he was sacked for improper conduct with messengers. He had then become a student of theology, or at least professed to have been one, though the description may well have been as fanciful as the title Reverend. As far as anyone knew, he had never taken holy orders.

Dressing as a man of the cloth gave him power, and limitless opportunities to pick wayward youths off the street to give them a bed for the night. He anticipated the notorious Roger Deakes, the self-styled Bishop of Rochester, who decades later in the 'sixties was part of a gang who collected runaway boys at railway stations, recounted in the book *Johnny Come Home*.

There was always a room for Mr Veck and a youth at 19 Cleveland Street.

Hammond had met Veck in Gravesend where the latter had run a hotel and tavern, the Terrace, just a few yards up the hill from the pub outside which Hammond's father had drowned. Veck's charm had worked on Hammond's mother and brother Ted, where he was a welcome guest. Who would not welcome a man of such religious convictions? Unfortunately his convictions did not run to paying what he owed. His house in south London had been repossessed after The Midland Railway Company who owned the property threw him out and took him to court for arrears of rent. He also absconded from Gravesend, for non-payment of rates.

But the Lord looked after those who looked after themselves.

At Cleveland Street, Veck became inordinately fond of the young GPO clerk Henry Newlove and charmed his way into his home to meet his mother. It might not be an exaggeration to say that he fell madly in love with him.

Mrs Newlove was delighted that her son, already in a coveted position with the Post Office, should be keeping company with a man of the church. What could possibly go wrong with such a friendship? It could only be to Henry's good. The boy had been without a father almost since the time he was born, and she had worried about the influences on his life. She need not have. Veck became such a regular caller at the house that Mrs Newlove began to recognise his knock and would answer the door instantly before immediately putting the kettle on.

Meanwhile, Jack was working his own charms down Piccadilly, looking for another client to go back home with, or if that wasn't convenient, take back to 19 Cleveland Street.

Jack would remember it as a day in May, 1887, shortly after he moved to the house. London was in festive mood, gearing up for the Queen's Jubilee week in the middle of June. Bunting was going up and the shops had souvenirs on sale. There was an outpouring of patriotic fervour that hadn't been seen since the Crimean War more than thirty years earlier.

Jack was on his usual beat down at Piccadilly Circus, still largely unmolested by the police except for the occasional instruction to move on. The gentleman who smiled and winked at him was tall, six-foot-four inches in height, and of aristocratic bearing. Jack was immediately struck by his big white teeth and full whiskers. He was no stranger to the place and was known as the 'Duke' though at that time Jack had no idea of his real identity.

Jack started walking into Sackville Street, just round the corner, and the gentleman followed. They fell into conversation.

'Where are you going?' asked the Duke.

'Home.' said Jack.

The next question was a furtive way of establishing if home was somewhere that they might enjoy an assignation.

'I see, and what is going on there?' the Duke enquired.

'You'd better come and see.' answered Jack.

'Is it quiet?

'Very quiet.' Jack assured him. 'And comfortable.'

'And safe?'

'Very safe.'

The ceremonials concluded, they hailed a cab and took it to Cleveland Street. Doubtless in the cab, financial arrangements were discussed. They got out at the Middlesex Hospital and approached No 19, where Jack let them in with his own latchkey.

In the reception room, before things began, Hammond bustled in with a tray of cards and handed one to the guest. Hammond knew a toff when he saw one. As was usual with this class of visitor, he proffered a glass of champagne which was readily accepted.

The Duke was impressed. This was not the kind of brothel he had imagined he was being taken too. This place had *class*. He had picked up Jack – or rather Jack had picked him up – but there were other youths present, a lot younger and very pretty too. The Duke wasn't exclusively into young men but they made a pleasant diversion. He had quite a thing for actresses and enjoyed the bohemian world in which they moved. In fact, he had quite a reputation as a stage door Johnny. But Jack knew nothing of that then.

He pocketed Hammond's card and had already decided that he would return. Though perhaps not to see Jack.

'Perhaps,' said Hammond, 'you would both like to retire?'

Jack and the Duke went to a bedroom. There was the preliminary discussion of what the customer was looking for. The Duke made it clear that he did not indulge in sodomy, at least with young men. That was no problem. Not everyone was a sodomite, as Jack from experience well knew, though the popular conception regarding men who had sex with other men was that they were. The same misconception holds true today.

What the Duke wanted was foreplay. Jack undressed, lay on the silk sheets, and duly obliged. It was nothing like the encounters he had written about in *The Sins of the Cities of the Plain*. Those were mainly, though not entirely, fantasy and born of his febrile imagination.

This was pretty ordinary stuff, of which Jack did plenty. He had seen everything, done everything, nothing surprised him.

The Duke masturbated Jack then explained that to ejaculate himself he would like to bend across Jack and spend on his belly. No problem. The tall aristocratic man with the huge white teeth and the full moustache lay across the body of the five-foot-five working-class Irishman and spent his tribute, as Jack might well have put it in *Sins*.

As they dressed, the Duke made a request.

'Should you see me in the street, I would be greatly obliged if you did not speak to me. I may be with someone and it could very awkward for me.'

'I understand.' said Jack. 'Don't worry.'

Discretion, he might have said, was his middle name. It wasn't, but he would see the Duke a number of times in the street and abide by the letter.

They returned downstairs, the Duke put a sovereign on the sideboard, donned the top hat which he had left in the hall, felt Hammond's card inside his pocket and left, departing, or so he thought, into obscurity.

Hammond took the sovereign and his cut, and gave Jack his. Jack was not too pleased. He had done all the work. What had Hammond done other than sit downstairs and dispense champagne and largesse? It was the reason they had fallen out before. Jack didn't enjoy being pimped and even less being kept short of money. But times were hard. Hammond fed him, gave him a room. The other boys were younger, taken in by Hammond, happy to do his bidding and to 'spoon' with their landlord. They would learn.

Four or five days later Jack saw the same gentleman again at the house, but the Duke had not come to see him. He did not know who entertained him that time but it may have been Newlove. On a third occasion, the tall gentleman was entertained by Frank Hewitt, the seventeen-year-old carpenter's son. Jack heard that he had also come to the house with his friend Carrington and with Tom Wells or 'Clifton', the youth who made a living inviting men back to his room where his fellow blackmailers would lay hidden under the bed.

Hammond was taking a big risk allowing boys like Tom Wells to work from 19 Cleveland Street. Such lads could jeopardise the whole operation. Hammond was motivated more by greed than anything else however and seemed willing to take risks. Character assessment was not one of his talents, though to be fair it was not easy to get a character reference from a male prostitute, or a female one for that matter.

It was not until a few weeks later that the Duke was pointed out to Jack in the West End by Carrington. He and Jack shared their experiences of him.

'Do you know who that is, Jack?' Carrington said. 'That is Lord Euston.'

Henry James Fitzroy, Earl of Euston, was the eldest son of the 7th Duke of Grafton, a title that had been created in the seventeenth century by Charles the Second. He had residences at Grosvenor Square in London and at Euston Hall, Thetford, and was in his forties. The ladies' man and stage door Johnny had been embroiled in scandal over a Variety Theatre actress called Kate Cook whom he had married, only to discover that she already had a husband who in turn already had another wife. This somewhat complicated matrimonial adventure might have ended in a charge of bigamy were it not for the fact that Miss Cook, although she believed that she was, was not legitimately married to her first husband. Lord Euston was a man-about-town (that much is obvious), a Freemason, and a Provincial Grand Master.

Then, Jack had little reason to remember his aristocratic client, who was just one of many.

Right now, Hammond's little operation was coining it in. His cards were passed around discreetly and surreptitiously in the corridors of power and in the higher echelons of the military. 19 Cleveland Street was the place to go. The boys were young (mostly) and the proprietor was a man to be trusted. A white card with the name Hammond combined with word of mouth were enough to ensure that he enjoyed a ready stream of aristocratic gentlemen and army officers. The boys would get younger, the stream would flow on, and for a time it seemed that nothing could go wrong.

Would not the establishment always shield a man like Hammond who had provided that very establishment with such an oasis of joy?

As Jack worked at the house to earn his bread and Hammond counted the sovereigns, white cards and whispered words made their way into banking halls, gentlemen's clubs, barracks, and legal chambers.

One even climbed its way into the immediate circle of the Royal Family.

* * * * * *

Chapter Notes

1. *Westminster City Archives Rates Books*. Before Hammond's arrival, the occupier and ratepayer was William

Jones, a packer. In 1887 the house is recorded for a time as 'Empty', though it certainly wasn't. Michael Loughlin is then recorded as the 'occupier' and ratepayer in 1888. However, in the rates books, owners and occupiers are all listed under occupiers whether they occupied the property or not, so it does not mean that he lived at No 19 or at any address other than his own, or had anything to do with Hammond's operation. Hammond's name does not appear in the rates books as a tenant until 1889, long after he began operating the house as a brothel. His name appears alongside that of Ephraim Tysall, a silversmith and publican, who lived with his family in Poland Street and ran the Kings Arms Pub (now a popular gay hangout). Tysall, whose name crops up nowhere else in the scandal, might have been a friend of Hammond's who helped pay the rent and rates in return for certain 'services'.

Michael Harrison, in his biography of Prince Albert Victor Edward, confuses Michael Loughlin the rag dealer, property speculator and ratepayer of 19 Cleveland Street with the Michael O'Loughlin, the son of a coal dealer, who later gave evidence alongside Jack at the libel trial involving the Earl of Euston. This error is also compounded in *The Cleveland Street Affair*. While the two may be related, they are not the same person.

CHAPTER TWELVE

BANKING TOWARDS DISASTER

The ebullient Mary Adelaide, Duchess of Teck and mother to the future Queen Mary, was fond of taking tea with Mrs Maria Bevan, the third wife of Mr Francis Augustus Bevan. He was one of the firm of Bevan Barclay Tritton and Co., which would eventually become Barclays Bank. The banker's wife and the Duchess would discuss all manner of good causes, for like her philanthropist husband and his family, Mrs Bevan liked to involve herself in organisations such as the Watercress and Flowers girls Mission and the Rescue of Homeless Waif Children.

On 11 October 1887 the Duchess wrote to Mrs Bevan kindly accepting an invitation to tea the next day. (1) There was a gentility about invitations to tea among the upper classes. On this occasion the Duchess brought her daughter with her, Princess Victoria of Teck, more popularly known as Princess May. The fair princess was the favourite cousin of Prince Albert Victor

Edward, the Duke of Clarence, son of the Prince of Wales and grandson to the Queen, and it was hoped that one day they would marry. Indeed, the rumours would begin very soon, to the delight of government and the Royal Family.

In time those same institutions would move to quash the more unpleasant ones circulating that Prince Eddy had once visited a certain house in Cleveland Street.

As the two ladies and the young princess delicately sipped their tea and munched on wafer-thin cucumber sandwiches, none of them knew of the existence of such a house.

But one close member of the Bevan family did.

Jack described him as 'Mr Bevan the banker from the corner of the Haymarket' and as a short man with a fair moustache.

The Bevans were immensely wealthy, liked to court Royalty and mix in the highest echelons of the aristocracy. The patriarch, Robert Cooper Lee Bevan, would on his death leave nearly a million pounds, plus properties in Wiltshire, London, Brighton and Cannes and an estate at Trent Park, New Barnet. His three sons were all in the banking business. Francis Augustus Bevan would become the first chairman of Barclays. He and his brother Wilfred Arthur Bevan worked at the Lombard Street branch in the city, while Roland Yorke Bevan was based at the bank premises at No 1 Pall Mall East, which was as near to the corner of the Haymarket as one could possibly get.

One of the greatest moments of Roland's life was when he had been presented to the Queen at Buckingham Palace by his father-in-law Lord Kinnaird. His wife Augusta had been presented to Her Majesty five years earlier on the occasion of their marriage. He was forty years old, the youngest of the family, Secretary of the Essex Hunt, and like his brothers a keen philanthropist. But charity, as they say, begins at home.

When the banking day was over at Pall Mall, Mr Roland Yorke Bevan would often hail a cab and take himself off in the direction of the Middlesex Hospital. There he would dismount and quickly step up to the door of 19 Cleveland Street where he would ring the bell and be instantly admitted, for he was a constant visitor and his face was well known there.

Not only to Jack and the occupants of the house, but to many other people in the street besides. A man like Bevan would have found it very difficult picking up a boy on Piccadilly, so near to his place of work where he might easily be recognised. That was why a house like Hammond's was such a Godsend to a man in his position.

A sovereign or more for a young man like Jack, depending on services, was a price Roland Bevan could well afford.

Bevan might have been one of the wealthiest visitors to the house but he wasn't the most extravagant. That laurel belonged to Hugh Weguelin, stockbroker, the son of a rubber merchant from Grosvenor Gardens. His dances at that address were incredibly lavish. For one he arranged a costermonger's cart laden with real canaries to be wheeled into the middle of the dance floor, and for a huge trophy of roses to be brought all the way from Cannes. Every lady was presented with a Watteau hat and a crook so that at five in the morning, a number of ladies spilled out onto the pavement with their husbands and admirers, looking like Little Bo-Peeps.

Weguelin was even younger than Jack, twenty-seven years old, giving the lie to the belief that only elderly men visited brothels. He was perfectly capable, like Jack, of turning a trick himself, which made his presence in the house as a client rather extraordinary. A reckless adventurer in sex, he sought youthful fun at any price with no responsibility. To a man like Weguelin, money bought love. And like Jack, and so many other visitors to the house, he was fond of a man in uniform.

The handsome and heroic William Alfred Ernest Lornegan, a lieutenant in the 66th Regiment of Foot, was one of his favourites. Lornegan had carried his injured captain out of the devastating battle of Malwand during the second of the Anglo-Afghan wars and was mentioned in dispatches. His heroics later extended to robbing his stockbroker friend of male jewellery worth a hundred pounds from his dressing room. That had happened six years ago. Lonergan was still wanted by the police but was wandering openly around London and Brighton, occasionally meeting with a desperate Weguelin who told him how he wished that the charges could be dropped. The police were less romantic than the love-struck stockbroker. He would eventually be given four months after giving himself up.

If Jack was wondering which grateful clients supplied Hammond's menagerie, he need not have looked much further than the likes of Hugh Weguelin, though according to one of the boys who worked there, Lord Euston brought him a dog called Rose. Weguelin shared his life with dogs and parrots. Saving the animals was the stockbroker's priority when, in bed one night with a male friend in his Windsor houseboat, he woke up to discover the boat on fire after a candle set fire to a curtain.

Colonel Hozier, Cavendish-Bentinck, Lord Euston, Roland Bevan and Hugh Weguelin were by no means the biggest fish to swim into Hammond's net. The largest catch, and by any standard the most well-connected, attempted to conceal his real identity by using the pseudonym 'Mr Brown', the name which Emily Barker religiously put in the appointments book. (Mr Brown was obviously a very popular pseudonym by those up to no good, for it was also the one employed by the corrupt ex-Scotland Yard detective Meiklejohn.)

Hammond knew who this Mr Brown was, and in time everyone would. He was Lord Henry Arthur George Somerset, Personal Equerry to the Prince of Wales himself, and the man who had charge of the Marlborough House stables. The network was growing.

The son of the eighth Duke of Beaufort, he began his military life as a cornet in the Blues, rose to become Major, and served with his regiment in Egypt and the Sudan. He had fought in the battle of Tel-el-Kebir, which led to the British occupation of Egypt. Two years later he was up the Nile helping to rescue General Gordon who was besieged by Sudanese tribal forces in Khartoum, and only two years before Jack went to stay at Cleveland Street he was fighting at Abu Klea with the Mahdi's troops, an engagement for which he won the campaign medal with two clasps and a bronze star.

In the same year that Jack took up residence, it was announced that Somerset had been appointed Extra Equerry to the Prince, an even more prestigious title. Because of his somewhat corpulent figure his brother regimental officers nicknamed him Podge.

Hugh Weguelin was his close friend, and so just as it may well have been Weguelin who introduced Lord Arthur Somerset to the brothel, Lord Arthur Somerset was, in turn, in a prime position to slip one of Hammond's cards into the hand of the Prince's son, though he would later deny he had ever done so. The disgrace of taking the father's money, while leading the son criminally astray in the West End, was not something an officer and a gentleman could ever admit to. Besides, the fey and very possibly homosexual Eddy had an equerry of his own, George Holforth, who was also rumoured at one point to have been the catalyst.

Historians have long argued whether Prince Eddy ever visited 19 Cleveland Street. None of the boys who worked there ever mentioned him, yet as we have seen and for other reasons to be stated later, he hangs tantalisingly over the affair.

It is doubly ironic that in *Sins*, written a few years before he came to No 19, Jack made up the tale of meeting Eddy's father, the Prince of Wales, at a garden party on the Thames while dressed up as a midshipman. If Jack had counted Prince Eddy among his followers, he would have been sure to say something in the police statement he would later give to Scotland Yard.

Assuming that the police would have dared to put it in writing.

Would Jack have recognised him? Would anyone?

If the majority of the population didn't know what George Cavendish-Bentinck looked like, or Colonel Hozier, or Mr Roland Bevan the banker, a great many people did know what their Royal Family looked like. Victorian family albums were full of *carte visites* of the Royals. Prince Eddy was distinctive. Fey, somewhat effeminate, with an oval face and gentle eyes, he was definitely not a man's man (in the popular sense of the expression). Neither did the man who would never be King have the makings of a soldier.

There were enough real soldiers other than Lord Arthur, however, ringing the bell of No 19 to fill a recruiting office. A lot of them were past their fighting days but their libido was undiminished.

Not all were, or are, easy to identify. Jack entertained a Colonel Jervoise. Newlove said that the same gentleman lived in Winchester Barracks, implying that he was a serving soldier. The police would do nothing to trace the officer. As with the case of Jack's 'Colonel Hozier' there were – somewhat incredibly – three Colonel Jervoises to choose from, none of whom appeared to live at Winchester Barracks. One, Lieutenant Colonel John Purefoy Ellis Jervoise of the 3rd Hussars was the only serving soldier among them and at the time was stationed at Hulme Barracks in Manchester. He was a bachelor and would remain one until the age of fifty-nine when in 1906, long after retirement, he married a tea-planter's daughter young enough to be his grand-daughter, no doubt to keep him company in his old-age.

The other two were already retired by the time Jack stepped over the portal of 19 Cleveland Street. Colonel John Gordon Jervois – a different spelling and pronunciation – was the son of General Jervois, a Knight of Hanover, who had commanded the 76th Foot. He had retired five years earlier after completing five years service commanding the Royal Engineers in Portsmouth, which at least in the Southern District. He had returned to his native Bath, where he lived with his wife and children and was President of the Royal Mineral Water Hospital.

The third and most likely contender also had Hampshire connections. Lieutenant Colonel Sir Henry Clark Jervoise was in his late fifties, his soldiering duties behind him. He now channelled most of his abilities into supporting the Havant Chrysanthemum Show, out-manouvring his opponents with military skill at the Havant Chess Club, and helping his father Sir Jervoise Clark Jervoise to prepare entertainments for officers at the annual Volunteer Review in Portsmouth. That plus the usual round of balls and regimental dinners was about the sum total of his life, a far cry from his younger days in the Royal Fusiliers and the Royal Highlanders and as an acting Colonel with the Coldstream Guards. A confirmed bachelor all his life – and no doubt the subject of gossip – he would have known Winchester Barracks. Old soldiers never really lost their passion for the military life, the camaraderie, the company of other men. He owned Idsworth House in the little village of Finchdean in Hampshire, which stood in a fine park of one hundred and fifty acres commanding views across to the Isle of Wight.

Military men saw risk as a challenge. Colonel Jervoise regularly took a risk by visiting 19 Cleveland Street. His guard down, his confidence raised, he allowed his name and rank to be known. At the very least he was just as careless as Lord Arthur Somerset.

Henry Newlove spoke of a Captain Montague Barber, who turned out to be Captain Charles Montague Barber, a slippery individual not only to pin down but in his private life as well.

He was the son of the vicar of Tyneham, who married him at St James Church on Piccadilly to an Annie

Brown of Bentinck Villa, Newcastle upon Tyne, without the consent of her father. They settled in Leicester from where he disappeared for four or five weeks at a time – for reasons not hard to imagine – finally deserting her two years after the marriage. She never saw him again. He cropped up in directorships of various companies, the laughingly named 'Invisible Trouser Stretcher Company Ltd' and the 'Automatic Match Supply Company Ltd' neither of which appear to have stretched many trousers or lit up a lot of lives. He was always in debt and had been declared bankrupt.

He was probably introduced to the house of Hammond by the roguish George Veck, who met him through a short-lived enterprise called the Metropolitan Coal Consumers Association. It was set up to benefit its members by breaking through the London 'coal ring', cutting out merchants and middlemen, though it became embroiled in legal and financial difficulties itself. Both Veck and Barber were involved in the company, and were men who left a certain amount of financial chaos in their own wakes.

At the time he was regularly visiting 19 Cleveland Street, he was living at the Ridgeway in Wimbledon. Hammond's business was probably one he would happily have become involved with, after stretching trousers and supplying matches. A brothel could be a successful operation that benefited everyone con-cerned, as Hammond was proving.

Except, to Jack's mind, himself.

With so many of the upper and upper-middle classes coming to the house and spreading the word, Hammond needed fresh blood. Frank Hewitt and Henry Newlove were his main procurers and could always be relied upon to find a fresh face or two. Tom Wells and Carrington from Piccadilly would bring men back. The boys were ever changing, circulating between 19 Cleveland Street, the Dilly and their own lodgings around the West End.

Jack was beginning to resent the competition. His was probably the oldest face in the place, next to Hammond, Caroline, Veck and the clients, with the exception of the youthful stockbroker Weguelin. That was galling. The ancient tensions between him and Hammond were never far from the surface. While he needed money and Cleveland Street was a very good place for meeting clients, and for bringing them back, it wasn't his house and he saw just a fraction of what he earned. He couldn't afford oil paintings, Dresden vases and yellow silk pillows, thank you very much. Back in Dublin, his family couldn't afford such things either.

Jack was in the same position as many female prostitutes he had known, working for madames who took a large part of their earnings. Hammond, the male madame of Cleveland Street, didn't exactly put him on a cart and take him up to the West End, like the brothel owners in the Monto did down Sackville Street in Dublin, but he might as well have.

Jack was getting past his sell-by-date anyway. If Hammond had a cart, it wouldn't be Jack he would put in it.

Top hats and overcoats piled up in the hall, men arrived, men left, men returned. Emily Barker had a row with Hammond and walked out, never to return. She disappeared into the Seven Dials district, a notorious area for criminality and prostitution through which policemen walked in pairs, if they walked at all.

Hammond acquired a young lad from Shoreditch called Herbert Ames, the son of a warehouseman, who was fairly well educated and could read and write. Ames as well as acting as Hammond's 'secretary' would entertain gentlemen at the house. He was fifteen.

The final confrontation between Jack and Charles Hammond took place in the summer of 1887, according to Jack, though it was almost certainly later than that as we shall see for he maintained a very good link with the house and knew exactly what was going on there.

One cause of the row was money, another was Jack taking the side of Hammond's mother, who must have suspected that her son was running some sort of bordello, as might Hammond's brother Ted and his sister-in-law. There seemed to be few secrets back in Gravesend. From the moment Hammond brought home a French prostitute and married her, the Hammond clan appear to have supported their errant relative even if they didn't entirely approve of his lifestyle. They were working class, but they were not narrow-minded by any means. Hammond was very possibly supporting his mother just like Jack. A mother's love was omnipotent.

A third cause of Jack's disgruntlement was the age and type of boy that Hammond was beginning to court. No longer was Hammond content to present his aristocratic benefactors with old faces from down the Dilly, among which Jack's was the most well-known. He wanted youths who had not yet turned eighteen, not runaways, not street arabs, not budding criminals like Tom Wells and Andrew Grant, but neat respectable boys from good homes who unlike himself could read and write and if need be hold a decent conversation.

Henry Newlove had the answer. The telegraph messenger boys at the GPO.

* * * * * *

Chapter Notes

1. The dealings between Maria Bevan and the Duchess of Teck is taken from private correspondence seen by the author.

CHAPTER THIRTEEN

A VERY FINE COLLECTION OF TELEGRAPH BOYS

There were about three thousand telegraph messenger boys in London, as young as thirteen and as old as seventeen, the age after which many aspired to be postmen. In their handsome blue uniforms with red piping and peaked caps, they were a particular delight to a certain type of gentleman, many of whom patronised 19 Cleveland Street. They had to be well educated, at least up to the 5th standard at Board School. The Post Office overseers also made a point of visiting their homes to assess the respectability of their backgrounds.

Parents did not like the idea of their sons being out on the streets all day where anything could happen and everything did, though many regarded it as a necessary risk if the boy was to have job prospects. In London especially, it had become well-known that a boy's character could be ruined by being a telegraph messenger. The pay was low, about eleven shillings a week – they were paid by results for each telegram delivered – and it was kept that way purposefully because the job was regarded as a privilege. So to supplement their income the boys often resorted to petty-crime, becoming involved with hardened street criminals in the process, which was naturally something the Post Office was desperate to eradicate as it posed a risk not only to the boys but to the security of Her Majesty's mail.

It was well-known in Post Office circles (and by Hammond too who had been round the block a few times) that there had been for quite a number of years a problem, at least in the eyes of the Post Office, with telegraph boy messengers indulging in prostitution. Hammond's good friend the Reverend George Veck, having been a telegraph boy himself, was even more of an authority on the subject.

Because of this danger – it was even known for gentlemen of that persuasion to send each other telegrams so a pretty youth in uniform would deliver it – a number of plainclothes inspectors and investigators had been added to the small General Post Office police department known as the Missing Letter Branch, later the Confidential Inquiry Branch, with the intention of increasing vigilance over such vulnerable young men. The GPO's problem however was Hammond's opportunity and he took full advantage of it.

This was the real crunch for Jack. How could he compete? Was it time to get out of his profession? Find a proper job? *Could* he get out? Without references could he ever go back into service? Next time he wouldn't mess it up. He would valet for a fine gentleman in a Georgian house, a gentleman who wore silk pyjamas, which Jack would fold neatly in the morning and put away in his portmanteau before laying out his clothes for the day.

"Will you be home for lunch, sir?"

"No Jack, I'll be taking lunch at my club today. Tell the servants not to prepare anything. Why don't you take the afternoon off?"

Dreams.

Confronted by a stream of much younger lads, many of whom he considered still wet behind the ears, and some of whom had the nerve to stop by in their uniforms on their way to and from delivering telegrams, Jack stormed out of 19 Cleveland Street. Hammond was, in Jack's own words, 'forming a very fine collection of telegraph boys'. The statement, which would be made in court a few years later would be laced with vitriol, and make his old friend sound like he was collecting them to put on the wall like his Dresden plates.

Jack moved back into his other world, the world of rooms in lodging houses, meeting men down Piccadilly, sussing out the competition, and trying to make enough money to feed and clothe himself and pay the rent. At least, all the money he made he was able to keep, though that was lessening by the year. Back at Hammond's, the telegraph boys, handpicked and tested by the ever vigilant Newlove, continued to move in.

Jack moved into Church Street close to where Hammond had lived with Harriet Wright, the lady who had had the misfortune to preside over the death of her prostitute lodger. Mrs Wright was still there, and renting more of her rooms to male lodgers. Perhaps she decided that they were less likely to be murdered than female ones.

For a period, Andrew Grant, the Scot known as Queen Anne, moved in with Jack. It is not clear whether they had separate rooms or whether they shared.

However, it was not a wise arrangement. Grant was well into his blackmailing routine. Other members of his gang would include Robert Cliburn, a one time butcher's boy and telegraph messenger, and William Allen *alias* Pea, a well-educated and gentlemanly valet, both of whom would one day be involved in blackmailing Oscar Wilde.

If the whole world in which Jack moved wasn't small enough, almost opposite the address in Church Street was Kettner's Restaurant, which Oscar frequented.

It was the nature of the gang to share out a few shillings among their friends when money came their way from a victim. As stated before, Jack was no angel. He inhabited a world of sex, violence and blackmail in which it was difficult to escape from your friends, even more difficult to choose new ones. It would be many years before the law caught up with Andrew Grant, but at some point in his illustrious criminal career he lost an eye, which was presumably put out by somebody. For the rest of his life, he wore an artificial eye in the right socket and a scar on the right side of his nose. It couldn't have happened to a more deserving person.

At Hammond's, another young thief and blackmailer took up residence for an extended period. This time he came with excellent credentials, provided by none other than Lord Arthur Somerset, who had written to Hammond asking if he would take the youth in. Hammond being Hammond, and flattered by the fact that the Prince of Wales' Extra Equerry should ask him to accommodate a young man, immediately said yes.

It was another disastrous move, for Somerset as well as Hammond.

Algernon Allies had once been employed at the Marlborough Club in Pall Mall, where Lord Arthur was a member, first as a hall boy and then as a bar boy and it was there that Lord Arthur had taken a fancy to him and struck up a financial relationship. A few months after leaving the club's employment, he broke in during the early hours of a Saturday morning and stole £16 8s (£16.40) from a cupboard in the bar. He was seen by a policeman leaving the club and took the train back to his home in Isleworth, where he lived with his coachman brother. There, a detective called Holder later arrested him and found the money hidden in the stable.

Or at least those were the reported facts, and the grounds on which he was committed for trial. But there is a thick fog of conspiracy about the case.

When the trial took place a few weeks later, on 14 September 1887, the crime alleged, to which he pled guilty, was rather different. He had broken into the house of Charles Colville, 1st Viscount Colville of Culross, who served as Lord Chamberlain to the Princess of Wales, at 42 Eaton Square and there had stolen the £16 8s. Lord Colville was also a member of the Marlborough Club and knew Lord Arthur well. This extremely odd state of affairs was rendered even stranger by the fact that judgement was held over until Lord Arthur put up surety for the lad, who was then given just *one* day in Pentonville prison without hard labour.

The trial was not reported. Most likely it was held and quickly dispensed with at the end of a day when reporters had gone. Lord Arthur was taking a terrible risk, but then Allies did possess letters of his signed

'Brown', the name under which he visited Hammond's. After his release, Lord Arthur took the boy to live with him at his grandmother's house in Hill Street until Hammond came to the rescue.

At Cleveland Street, Allies, a good-looking curly haired boy of seventeen, stayed for many months, going to bed with Lord Arthur and receiving from him the regular sum of fifteen shillings a week.

Something had to go wrong and it did, in the summer of 1889, by which time Jack had turned thirty-one and was realising that his days as a rent boy were soon coming to an end. All those youngsters turning up at Hammond's, making their shillings, it would all come to no good. Hammond had been playing with fire for years and it was coming dangerously close to burning him. When it did, as with the Dublin scandals, it would be events completely out of Jack's control that would drag him back into the limelight.

* * * * * *

CHAPTER FOURTEEN

THE UNRAVELLING

Charles Thomas Swinscow was fifteen years old when he stepped over the threshold of 19 Cleveland Street with Henry Newlove and was ushered into a parlour where he met 'the proprietor', Charles Hammond.

'Good evening, I'm very glad you have come.' Hammond shook his hand. Then after a little while, during which the telegraph messenger boy sat nervously, a second gentlemen came in.

'This is the gentleman I would like you to go with this evening.' said Hammond.

The fifteen-year-old and the gentleman to whom he was assigned, whose name he did not know, went into a back parlour on the same floor where there was a bed. They both stripped naked and got in. The whole business took about half an hour. The gentleman gave Swinscow a sovereign, which Swinscow on instruction gave to Hammond. Hammond gave him four shillings, pocketing the remaining sixteen shillings, and sent Swinscow on his way. Swinscow never saw the gentleman again, at least not at 19 Cleveland Street. Four shillings was about a third of what Swinscow normally made in a week, and he had made it in thirty minutes.

Swinscow had been appointed a telegraph boy on 2 January 1888. His family were lower middle class people from Islington. His father had run a newsagent's shop but eventually become a dock steward. The Swinscows like most parents whose sons got jobs with the GPO saw it as a step up the ladder for their son, though in common with many others they were concerned that he might come into contact with criminality. Their concerns were fully justified.

It wasn't Swinscow's first sexual experience by any means. Those had taken place in a water closet in the basement lavatory of the Post Office building with the boy clerk Newlove, Hammond's chief procurer, on a number of occasions. It was Newlove who had persuaded Swinscow to go to the house. Swinscow had been at first reticent, but said he would give it a try.

Boy messengers were not allowed to carry money. There had been a series of thefts involving small amounts of cash from the office of the Receiver and Accountant General to which the boys had access, and so a messenger with any amount of money on him was bound to be questioned if found out. Swinscow was. On 4 July, he was caught and interrogated by Police Constable Luke Hanks, an officer attached to the Post Office, and discovered to have at least fourteen shillings in his pocket.

'Where did you get it?' Hanks asked.

'For doing some private work away from the office.'

'For whom?'

'For a gentleman named Hammond. He lives at 19 Cleveland Street.'

'What did you do for him?'

Swinscow told him. He initially admitted going to the house just twice where he saw two different gentleman, but no more than that. It was a lie. He would later confess that he had been to the house not twice, but five times.

And so began the unravelling of Hammond's little operation.

Hanks, who had something of a drink problem that often got him into trouble, reported the matter to his superior officer, John Phillips. The Post Office investigators had no idea what was about to hit them. Swinscow was not alone. There was a boy prostitution racket going on at St Martin Le Grand, one of the very things they feared most. A boy called George Alma Wright and another with the highly comical name of Ernest Thickbroom were involved and had visited the house. Newlove had procured them too. All four were quickly suspended from service.

Hanks was most anxious to know if any of the boys had performed these disgusting acts *in their uniforms*. It was, after all, the Queen's uniform. Thickbroom admitted that he had done it with his trousers on, in the basement lavatory of the Post Office, though they had been round his ankles at the time.

The matter was passed up to the Postmaster General himself, then to the head of the Metropolitan Police, Commissioner James Monro, a Scotsman who had only been in the job a few months. Monro quickly assigned one of the best of his inspectors, Frederick Abberline.

Abberline was a Dorset man who had started life as an apprentice clockmaker in his hometown of Blandford Forum. At the age of twenty, in 1863, he enlisted with the Metropolitan Police, rising to Sergeant and then Inspector attached to H Division in Whitechapel, an area about which he gathered extensive local knowledge. Abberline's name is best associated with the failed hunt for Jack the Ripper, but what is less well-known is his solving of the various Irish Fenian bombing cases in the 1880s, including one at the Tower of London and the bomb in the public urinal underneath Scotland Yard.

Abberline arranged a special sitting of Marlborough Street Police Court on the Saturday morning. Wright, Swinscow and Thickbroom were arraigned. Wright came from the East End, his middle name of Alma given in commemoration of one of the famous battles of the Crimean War. Thickbroom was the eldest, seventeen years old, also from Islington and the son of a carpenter, Zephenia Thickbroom, a name that belonged firmly in the novel that Dickens never wrote.

By the end of the sitting, Abberline had what he wanted, warrants for the arrests of Henry Newlove and Charles Hammond.

Newlove was fair game, but Hammond was ahead of it. Like Jack the Ripper, he was about to slip frustratingly through Abberline's fingers. Newlove sought out his fellow procurer Frank Hewitt, and together they fled to Hammond's and warned him. Hammond, who must have been expecting something like this to happen at some point, made a getaway, which in its speed was almost obscene. Leaving his wife Caroline and son Charlie, he fled to his brother's house at Gravesend, then escaped by steamer across the Channel to France, the favoured route of Englishmen on the run from potential sex charges, accompanied by his new boy-secretary Herbert Ames.

He would never return to England.

Henry Newlove was arrested the next day at his mother's house in Bayham Street. On his way to the police station he said,

'I think it very hard that I should get into trouble while men in high position are allowed to walk about free.'

Newlove then told the police about the visits to the house by Lord Arthur Somerset, Colonel Jervoise and Lord Euston, the last of which Jack had brought back to the house personally.

Abberline at this point must have realised that this was a case which could elevate his reputation after the drubbing it had got during the hunt for Jack the Ripper. For here were real names, real identities, no fleeting chimeras around the back alleys of Whitechapel but men of flesh and blood who had addresses. And pretty respectable addresses too.

Constable Hanks' drink problem was not helped by the adrenalin that now coursed through his veins at the prospect of being involved in an investigation like few others to which he had been assigned. With Newlove in prison, singing for all he was worth, Hanks went back to Newlove's mother's house to see if could get more information. He was lucky. He was learning from the widowed Mrs Newlove about the excellent character of her son, who had never known his father, having been only a baby when he had died. While they were talking, there was a knock on the door.

'That sounds like Mr Veck's knock.' said Henry's mother.

Hanks' version of what occurred is somewhat dramatic and casts him in the role of master detective.

Upon the entrance of the Reverend George Daniel Veck he hid in a passageway while Veck told Mrs Newlove how he had discovered that Hammond had fled abroad.

'Don't worry,' Veck said, 'if you need any money just let me know. I will instruct a solicitor to defend Henry in the morning.'

Veck left, and the GPO's greatest detective stepped out of the passageway having heard everything. If he did not know who Veck was then, he soon did. Veck was the kind of stain the GPO wanted to eradicate. He was no clergyman. He was a sodomite who had molested telegraph boys in Gravesend and been sacked from the GPO in 1880. Now he was back. And Hanks had caught him single-handed. Almost.

Hanks excitedly reported the information to Abberline, who was now in the process of putting 19 Cleveland Street under observation, and particularly the keen eyes of one Police Constable Jack Sladden. It was a bit like watching the stable door after the horse had bolted. But Abberline reckoned that people, not knowing Hammond had gone, would still turn up at the house. He was right.

Lord Arthur Somerset turned up with a Corporal of the 2nd Battalion Life Guards but was turned away at the door. He came back a second time and was seen to shake hands with a common soldier. For a man of Lord Arthur's position to shake hands with a common soldier was simply not done.

Veck went in. Having come over from Paris, Hammond's wife's sister Florence followed, obviously to help with arrangements prior to the removal of the furniture. On the third day of observation, a van belonging to Saunders Brothers of 7 Southampton Street turned up, the contents of the house were loaded into it, and taken away to Hammond's brother Ted's house in Gravesend, including the velvet curtains, silk pillows, oil paintings, Dresden china and pianos. Ted was a working class plasterer. What he made of his brother's possessions one would like to know.

The dogs and birds went to Frederick Dye, the brothel keeper in Nassau Street, which demonstrates to some extent a support network among the male madames of the district.

Algernon Allies, when arrested, would state that he took one of Hammond's dogs to Wimbledon. To Colonel Montague Barber perhaps on the Ridgeway?

Caroline went to stay at Hammond's mother's house in Gravesend. Under English law, a wife could not testify against her husband who in this case was now staying with a Madame de Foissard at 8 Passage des Abbesses in Paris, in the heart of the red light district. Hammond wrote home to her, telling her he was distrustful of Veck and what the man might say if arrested. He wanted Veck to get money for him, and in the first sinister hint that he was about to call in his dues, he wrote 'If he has not got what I asked for, *I will write to our friends.*'

The clients of 19 Cleveland Street had enjoyed the plentiful harvest. Now it was time to pay up. One of those friends was Lord Arthur Somerset, who now began to pull strings with the help of his father, the Duke of Beaufort, to get Hammond from France to America. The Duke, who possessed a well-known penchant for young mistresses, was eager to help his son in any way he could to avoid any more besmirching of the family name. A solicitor called Arthur Newton, a charming and highly persuasive young attorney who sailed rather close to the wind in his professional life, was employed as the conduit by which money could be got to Hammond, and also to defend Henry Newlove.

Events were moving quickly. The two telegraph boys Swinscow and Thickbroom were taken to Piccadilly Circus where they identified Lord Arthur Somerset coming out of the Savile Club, and Swinscow stated he was one of the men he had had sex with at the brothel. Somerset was speedily traced to the cavalry barracks at Knightsbridge. With the clan Hammond in Gravesend staked out, 19 Cleveland Street under observation, and Commissioner Monro compiling a file on the whole case requesting that extradition proceedings be taken out against Hammond and charges made against Newlove and Lord Arthur, it seemed that arrests were imminent.

Abberline even went to Paris to see if the French police were willing to help. And as had happened in Dublin, the more the police made enquiries at home, the more Jack Saul's name came up time and again.

Then somebody put on the brakes.

Not just somebody, but quite a lot of people. Sir Augustus Stephenson, the Treasury Solicitor and the Director of Public Prosecutions, returned the file suggesting that perhaps the police would like to handle the matter themselves to avoid unnecessary publicity. Frustrated, Monro sent it to the Home Secretary, Henry Matthews, who said it should really be handled by Sir Augustus, though he endorsed the extradition warrant for Hammond. So far so good until it attracted the attention of the Prime Minister, Lord Salisbury. Such a matter wouldn't normally bother the head of state, but with names like Lord Arthur Somerset and his links to the Royal Family, one couldn't be too careful. Lord Salisbury did not think it a case where application should be made to the French government. Nobody further up the ladder from the police really wanted Hammond brought back. Like Jack, he knew too much.

Furthermore, the French police weren't too willing to help either.

Hammond, who skipped to Belgium, and was now being watched closely by the Belgian police, wrote to Caroline's sister Florence to whom his wife was very close and who was still in London helping her sister. Florence had fallen out with Veck and they were frequently rowing, the strain beginning to show on everybody. In the letter, penned by his new secretarial assistant Ames, Hammond expressed compassion for his son Charlie whose musical studies at 19 Cleveland Street had been sadly and rudely interrupted.

'Now my Dear Charlie, be kind and good to your mother and likewise to everybody. Try and learn all you can for you will perhaps help your mother. Stick to your music for that will be useful by and by so goodbye and God bless you.

Dear Florence, try and do all you can to make Caroline as happy as she can be. You must stick to one another and do all you can for each other. For things may soon come to the worst and I may be turned away at a minute's notice and I have but very little money left and traveling (sic) is so expensive I wish Mr Newton would send someone over with money at once … I remain, your most Unhappy Brother, Charlie.'

Delay followed delay in the police case until eventually, seven weeks after young Swinscow had been found with all that money in his pocket, Sir Augustus Stephenson finally took charge of the poisoned chalice that was the Cleveland Street case.

That was when Inspector Abberline decided it was time to interview Jack to see what he could tell him about the house and its occupants. One of those who had mentioned Jack's name was undoubtedly Newlove who, while on remand, was singing very sweetly for his supper.

Jack was not difficult to trace this time. He never wandered far from the West End, except to go back to Dublin. Nobody was helping Jack find money to flee the country. And why should he? And what would he do if he got there? He didn't have Hammond's contacts and although he was a survivor, he wasn't wily and manipulative like his friend.

He had moved but was still in Soho, now living at 15 Old Compton Street, in the heart of what is now London's gay village, a street which then had its share of booksellers and printers of the kind who would not have been averse to discreetly selling *The Sins of the Cities of the Plain*. Jack's new abode was a room in a three-storey house on the corner of Old Compton and Dean Street. Whether he was living with anyone else isn't known but Andrew Grant wasn't far away. Nothing had yet appeared in the newspapers about Hammond's escape and the various high profile visitors to the brothel – it would stay suppressed until October – but it is likely that Jack had heard something on the grapevine. So many boys from Piccadilly had passed over the portal of that scandalous house. Frank Hewitt was laying low, and yet another messenger boy William Meech Perkins, who had been procured by Newlove, wasn't yet in the frame.

On Saturday 10 August they came face to face, the experienced male prostitute from Dublin and one of Scotland Yard's top detectives. Jack must have felt desperately uneasy. It was the second time in his life he had been sought out and asked to make an incriminating statement. The first time it hadn't been used, but once again it was made under the threat that if he didn't he would be charged himself. He had become, to use modern parlance, a copper's nark. He didn't like doing it – nobody did – but it was an accepted part of the life he and others led. If Jack didn't inform, others would on him. And Jack would have been well aware of the sentence recently passed on a clergyman from Hackney for the same kind of offences. That gentleman had been given penal servitude for life.

Abberline was no Meiklejohn but was a hard, tough-nosed detective with years of experience who, in the Fenian bombing cases, which he had handled, relied a lot on informers. None of them however had ever given him a statement so packed with names and sensational disclosures as Jack was about to do. This was dynamite of a very different kind.

Had Abberline ever come across *Sins*, a book in which his star witness-to-be to the goings on at Cleveland Street, described a life of unbridled debauchery? It is unlikely. Married but childless, Abberline would probably have dispensed with it in disgust before he even reached the page in which Jack Saul of Lisle Street announced his identity to the reader. Besides, such rampant invention would not do the credibility of his witness much good, even if it could be proved that the Jack who wrote *Sins* and the Jack in front of him were one and the same person. Which of course they were.

One of the few names Jack didn't mention, possibly because their paths hadn't crossed, was that of Lord Arthur Somerset, who only a few days before had taken part in a review to mark the state visit of Kaiser Wilhelm, the German Emperor.

Abberline already had him. He wanted the others.

As Jack's statement is one of the most important and revealing documents in the case, it is worth quoting in full, as written.

'I know Charles Hammond who lately lived at 19 Cleveland Street, Fitzroy Square. The photograph produced is a good likeness of him. I have known him since the 1st May 1879. He then lived at 25 Oxenden Street, Haymarket. I was on that day introduced to him by a man called Warrington, and two weeks afterwards I went to lodge with him at the above address. We both earned our livelihood as sodomites. I used to give him all the money I earned oftentimes as much as £8 and £9 a week, I lived with him till the early part of December 1879 when I left him and went to Dublin where I stayed till April 1880 when I returned to London.'

As we have seen, this was because his father had died. In the margin of the statement opposite the reference to Dublin either Abberline or his clerk scribbled that he was known as Dublin Jack and a mention of his involvement in the Dublin scandals.

'He was then living at 17 Frith Street Soho Square. I lodged with him again. We stayed there for about a month and then removed together to No 4 Frith Street. I stayed with him till the following July and then left him as he was charging me 35s per week for my lodgings which I considered too much, and when I was unable to earn any money he refused to give me food.'

This is a telling admission. It is the only indication, and
a not very surprising one, that Jack might have been suffering from some venereal disease or other 'ailment' that
made it difficult for him to pick up clients who wanted
a certain kind of activity.

> 'He sold his furniture to a prostitute named Madame
> Clements (sic) and went to Paris. I went to 36 Lisle
> Street. He returned to London about Christmas 1880.
> I met him on the Christmas morning and we went
> together to Gravesend where we spent the day with
> some of his friends. Shortly before I knew him he
> married a French prostitute named Madame Caroline
> with whom he has always lived since I have known
> him. In the early part of 1881, he went to live at No
> 14 Church Street where he stayed for several months.
> The landlady's name was Mrs Wright. He afterwards
> lived at 3 Wardour Street, 2 Brewer Street and 29
> Great Poultney Street also at 35 Newman Street and
> about the latter part of 1885 he went to 19 Cleveland
> Street. I lived with him at the last address for about
> 5 weeks and then had a row with him (about two years
> ago) and have not spoken to him since.'

If this was strictly true, Jack knew an awful lot about
what had gone on since.

> 'I know a lad named Frank Hewitt who I think lives at
> Cromwell Road, Hampstead Road. He used to work at
> a stained glass window place in Brewer Street. He used
> to procure boys for Hammond. He was Hammonds's
> 'spooney boy'. I mean that Hammond used to 'go' with
> him. I remember his having introduced a lad called
> Harry or Henry who used to live somewhere near him
> in the Hampstead Road. A gentleman named Captain
> Le Barber used to visit the house and bring boys with
> him. He used to get the boys situations in the Post
> Office service.'

There are enough mentions of Barbers in the Cleveland Street canon of names to form a barbershop quartet. The name sounds like an affectation, but there was a Captain Le Barber at his depot in Colchester. He rode with the Newmarket Drag Hounds and on steeplechase courses in France, and was a jockey too.

We have met Captain Montague Barber. Herbert Ames, Hammond's young secretary, would talk of a Captain Barberie, probably the same person. If that was not confusing enough, the so called Reverend George Veck was going around with a seventeen-year-old boy called George Barber whom he passed off as his son, and while on the run had decided to call himself George Barber too.

> 'Emily Barker, a prostitute, whose address I can find tonight lived with Hammond for 3 or 4 years. She used to write all his correspondence as he was a very bad scholar. She can give the names of all the gentlemen who used the house, as she used to write them in a book and make appointments for their visits. Hewitt introduced a boy who lived near him in the Hampstead Road. He was called Harry.'

This repeated snippet must have been a reference to Henry Newlove, who was also called Harry and whose address at Bayham Street was just up the top end of the Hampstead Road. One should remember that Jack wasn't just giving random bits of information. He was providing specific answers to specific questions.

> 'Major Moet – a brother of the firm of wine merchants – used to visit the house as a sodomite. Hammond wears a gold seal on his watch chain, which the major gave him. I identify the seal on his photograph.

Fred Dye lives at 13 Nassau Street. Hammond's dogs and birds were taken there by him after Hammond absconded. Colonel Hosier (sic) used to visit Hammond's house as a sodomite. I can give you his address as I have got his card at home. Mr George Cavendish-Bentinck of Richmond Terrace, Whitehall frequently visited the house and had to do with boys. Mr French, tailor in Jermyn Street two doors from Duke Street, his two sons Dick and? (sic) they used to take gentlemen to Hammonds home, they were both professional sodomites.'

The 'George' of George Cavendish-Bentinck was inserted above as an afterthought, Jack obviously being asked if it was the father or the son who had visited the house. William French was one half of the partnership of French and Muir, tailors of 50 Jermyn Street, Piccadilly, whose two sons, one of whom Jack couldn't recall the name of, prostituted themselves at Hammonds.

'Some people named Seavers who keep a public house almost opposite 19 Cleveland Street can say a good deal about Hammond if they like. Mr Bevan the banker at the corner of the Haymarket, a short gentleman with a fair moustache, was a constant visitor at the house.'

Jack was just building up to the big one.

'The young Duke of Grafton, I mean the brother of the present Duke was a constant visitor at Hammonds. He is a tall fine looking man with a fair moustache. I will meet you again at 3 o'clock on Monday afternoon and give you some more information.'

Jack had the rest of the weekend off, though it was unlikely Inspector Abberline had much of a relaxed

Sunday. Peers of the realm, Members of Parliament, high-ranking members of the military establishment – all were involved. Abberline was not too far off retirement. Would this make his career or break it? It was a serious consideration.

Jack returned as promised on the Monday morning. He had been sleuthing for Abberline and had discovered the address of Emily Barker, who appears now in the statement as Emily Parker. He also had three calling cards of his friends to hand over.

> 'I have not seen Emily Parker since I saw you on Saturday night but I have ascertained that she is living at Rockenham Court off Neale Street near Seven Dials. I hand you three visiting cards which are the cards of the Mary-Anns, Clifton and Carrington used frequently to go to Hammonds with the young Duke of Grafton, I mean, as I said before, the present Duke's brother. I saw him myself last night. I know him well.'

Jack was a walking Debrett's. Between the first part of his statement and the second, he had seen Lord Euston at Piccadilly Circus on the Sunday night. Then came his story of how he had taken Lord Euston, whose true identity he didn't know at the time, back to Cleveland Street. Presumably he hoped that Clifton and Carrington would back up his story that Lord Euston was a regular visitor.

> 'He went to Hammond's house with me on one occasion. He is not an actual sodomite. He likes to play with you and then 'spend' on your belly. Clifton's correct name is Tom Wells. Carrington is called 'Lively Poll'. A professional Mary Ann named Andrew Grant used to lodge with Hammond. He can tell you a lot

about him if he likes. I can point him out to you any night at Piccadilly. Clifton takes gentlemen home to his room where by arrangement two or three men are secreted under his bed, and just as they are performing the men suddenly come out and bounce money out of them by threats. I am sure that Emily Parker will tell you anything she knows as she hates Hammond because he was the cause of her being seduced at his own house.'

Which house Jack didn't elaborate on, though he must have been referring to the time prior to Miss Barker or Parker becoming a prostitute. He was coming to the end, probably a relief for Abberline.

'A solicitor who used to live at 14 Church Street Soho and who now calls there for his meals can also give you plenty of information. His name is Steadall. I am still a professional "Mary Ann". I have lost my character and cannot get on otherwise. I occasionally do odd jobs for different gay people.'

And with that sad admission, Jack was handed the statement to sign. *I have lost my character and cannot get on otherwise.* It was probably how he really felt. He was beyond getting a respectable job. He knew only one. Or thought he did.

As Jack walked home from Scotland Yard, all sorts of thoughts assailed him. Would Hammond be brought back and would he have to stand up in court and give evidence against him? Would Lord Euston be arrested and would he have to do the same? His statement was now in the files of Scotland Yard. There was no going back. This time they wouldn't keep him sitting in the wings. This wasn't old information about a lover. This was new material, recent, relevant. He had been spared from having to give evidence against Captain Kirwan, but how would he feel now about betraying so many other old friends?

He had to do it. He owed them nothing.

Jack be nimble, Jack be quick, Jack jump over the candlestick.

Jumping over the candlestick was said to be a way of telling your fortune. Good luck would surely follow if you cleared the flame without extinguishing it.

Or perhaps in Jack's case, getting burnt.

Inspector Abberline sat down and read Jack's statement a number of times. He believed it. There was absolutely nothing fanciful in it. Jack was a witness credible and true. The statement was a conglomeration of facts about people. Who some of them were he had as yet no idea. Henry Newlove had already mentioned Lord Euston independently. It was unlikely that the two young men would tell lies about the same person individually.

He even now had some of the calling cards of the boys who sold sex on the streets. Those of Carrington, Percy Davis and Tom Wells, though he probably didn't know the real names of the first two.

He contemplated his next move. He considered getting Jack and the boys Carrington and Wells to identify Lord Euston. Perhaps there was some way he could get Henry Newlove out of prison to also identify him. That would be four eyewitness accounts.

He already had witnesses against Lord Arthur Somerset, who, it had now been decided, should appear to answer a charge under the Criminal Law Amendment

Act 1885. Yet only that weekend, Lord Salisbury had urged yet another delay.

Delay, delay. When were those above him going to take some action? Abberline had never been a detective to play things absolutely by the book. He didn't know any detective who did. But those above him not only appeared to have shut the book, they had put it back on the shelf and were not inclined to read it. They didn't want Hammond brought back. They didn't want anyone put on trial, especially not the Equerry to the Prince of Wales. Nobody knew where *that* might lead.

Neither did anyone in authority want a re-run of the Dublin scandals, with one public figure after another being put into the dock. They had learnt their lesson. The police had to be stopped from rushing in. A little less duty, a little more caution. If the whole affair could be swept quietly and unobtrusively under the carpet before the newspapers got hold of it, they would be very satisfied indeed and anyone who helped them to achieve that aim would be forever in their debt.

Anyone who didn't should look over their shoulder.

Abberline looked once more at Jack's statement. In the end, he did nothing. He filed it away. It wouldn't be seen for quite a few months, and then after that for a hundred years.

* * * * * * *

CHAPTER FIFTEEN

ARRESTS AND ESCAPES

On 19 August the police burst into a house at 2 Howland Street just off the Tottenham Court Road, hoping to find George Daniel Veck. The self-proclaimed Reverend gentleman was not at home, but his 'secretary', seventeen-year-old George Barber, was lying in bed. (1) Interrogated, Barber said that his employer was in Portsmouth, where Veck had probably been visiting his family. The police went to Waterloo Station and arrested Veck when he came off the train.

In his possession were various documents including letters from Algernon Allies, asking for money and mentioning a 'Mr Brown'. This was the youth whom Lord Arthur Somerset had taken under his wing after the burglary at his club (or at the residence of Lord Colville of Culross, whichever one prefers) and put up at 19 Cleveland Street. Allies was much addicted to writing letters asking for money. From the time he left his employment at the Marlborough Club, he had bombarded his benefactor with requests for financial support. There was a very thin, almost invisible, line between that and blackmail. Abberline had never heard of Allies, who was now living back with his parents in Sudbury where his father, like his brother, was a coachman. But he knew that Mr Brown almost certainly referred to the Prince of Wales' Equerry.

If Abberline could have Brown, or Lord Arthur Somerset, it would take the heat off him to act on Jack's statement incriminating so many others. Allies was arrested, brought to London and kept under police supervision at a room above a coffee house in Houndsditch. His elderly parents and brother complained, believing he was being held under duress. They didn't want him mixed up in all this, preferring their errant son to go abroad where he could start a new life. Abberline was having none of it. Next to Jack, Allies was his star witness. The boy was cunning. He had possessed numerous love letters from Lord Arthur, which he had burnt after receiving an anonymous letter tipping him off about his imminent arrest, probably from Veck. He had cashed three postal orders sent to him by Lord Arthur, no doubt in response to more letters begging for help.

Inspector Abberline comes across, at least in the later stages of his career, as one of the unluckiest policemen in the force. From this moment on, nothing went his way. Constable Hanks, on one of his visits to Sudbury to talk to Allies' family, became drunk and started creating problems, and Abberline had to travel to Sudbury to sort the matter out personally. A colleague with a drink problem antagonising the families of witnesses was not what he needed.

Then Lord Arthur Somerset skipped the country. Unknown to the police, his flight was aided and abetted financially by his good friend Hugh Weguelin, the stock-broker, who was acutely conscious of the potential discovery of his own dealings at Cleveland Street. Abberline was furious. Commissioner Monro, the only superior who really supported him in his efforts, was at a loss. It had been almost two months since Swinscow had been found with that cash. Warrants had been delayed, extradition orders weren't worth the paper they weren't written on, and now the second prime suspect had been allowed to leave the country.

Where would it end?

The dark forces operating from above were amply matched by efforts from others to get Allies and the tele-graph boys Swinscow, Thickbroom, Wright and Perkins out of the country as well. Allies was practically whipped away from under Abberline's nose by a clerk working for the solicitor Arthur Newton, who was still hard at work trying to get Hammond on a ship to America. Allies was promised a fresh start in the same country, and fifteen pounds to start him on his way. Allies said he wanted under linen, two suits, a pair of boots and hat. His demands were not met – at least not at that time – because Abberline and Hanks, who observed the conversation in a pub near Newton's office, snatched him back.

As with Allies, the telegraph boys were offered passages abroad, this time to Australia, by Newton's team of conspirators, which comprised his clerk Frederick Taylorson and an inquiry agent Adolphe De Gallo. How were their escapes to be financed? The Duke of Beaufort, Lord Arthur's father, was very anxious that anyone who could give evidence against his son should be helped to make a new life. In the event, the telegraph boys didn't go. Australia's loss was, for a while, Abberline's gain.

In the meantime, Jack found himself a job in the theatre. It may have been fatherly advice from Abberline to do something better with his life, or it may just have been that he was so unnerved by having to implicate himself in another statement to the police that he felt a period of respectable employment might improve his chances in any courtroom.

Not that the theatre was considered terribly respectable, but it was easier than getting a job as a valet. He was not without some experience of the stage, having been involved in amateur dramatics in Dublin. The theatre he went to work in was none other than Drury Lane in Covent Garden, and the production, which had just opened was *The Royal Oak*, written by Augustus Harris who was the lessee and manager, in collaboration with Henry Hamilton.

The Royal Oak was billed as a grand historical drama set during the English Civil War, and required a large crowd of stage extras to play the parts of Roundheads, tenants and citizens. Jack was taken on as one of those.

The production had its teething problems throughout September. The hammering of carpenters trying desperately to get the set ready in time for the opening night, plus the all too audible voice of the prompter, were unfortunate distractions.

But when the play finally opened on 23 September, two days late, it was a great success though it had mixed reviews. A critic complained that there were altogether too many people on the stage for all the good that was made of them, though the costumes were mostly effective. Plays at Drury Lane were frequently spectacular, with volcanic eruptions, houses on fire, storms at sea and naval battles all being rendered by vast armies of designers and technicians. *The Royal Oak* had none of those, being described by the *Morning Post* as a pleasant sympathetic love story interwoven with the escape of Charles the Second after the Battle of Worcester. The scenery and stage effects were described as 'remarkable', particularly a scene where the historic oak itself appeared in the middle of Boscobel Wood, something that the reviewer credited with never having been seen on any other stage. On the opening night Mr Augustus Harris came on stage and asked the audience if they were satisfied. There was a thunderous applause.

It was Jack's fortune to be associated with a success rather than a failure. Sadly it didn't last very long. The play ran until December, when it was replaced with the Christmas pantomime *Beauty and the Beast*. By Christmas he was out of a job again.

Another show in town opened just a few days before *The Royal Oak*. It was just as successful, though in a different way, success being measured in this case by the almost complete lack of an audience and the total absence of any publicity. It was the trial of George Daniel Veck and Henry Newlove and it took place at the Old Bailey on 18 September, 1889. It wasn't entered on the court calendar for the day and was held virtually in secret at the end of the afternoon when the press had gone home, just as in Allies' case. When it suited the authorities, justice did not always have to be seen to be done.

Since the committal proceedings earlier that month, Sir Augustus Stephenson the Treasury Solicitor and those above him had been concerned about Veck and Newlove mentioning names. The magistrate had also expressed qualms, but of a different sort. He wanted to know why they *couldn't* mention names. It was highly irregular. Sir Augustus quietly put him back on the straight and narrow.

What really upped the game was the rumour, believed to have been started by the solicitor Newton, that if the search for names went on, the case not closed and certain people not allowed to flee the country with impunity, one other visitor to the house would turn out to be a very distinguished person indeed. Newton was not naming more names, but the initials PAV might be of interest.

It fell to the Assistant Prosecutor, Hamilton Cuffe, who apparently had the honour of being the first to hear the spectacular rumour at his club, to write about the matter to his boss Sir Augustus. He said that he didn't credit the rumour but, 'in such circumstances as this, one never knows what may be said, concocted or true.' He realised of course that PAV stood for Prince Albert Victor.

The letter still exists in the Cleveland Street files at the National Archives. This passage is scored with double lines down the left hand side of the page. It was clear that the Assistant Prosecutor took it to be of considerable importance in making any decision to prosecute. (2)

Newton of course had a vested interest in putting a stop to the investigation. He was wily and disreputable enough to pull such a stunt. His main client was – or rather had been – the Equerry to the young prince. What more likely situation could there be than that Lord Arthur had tipped off his employer's son about a house where his sexual peccadilloes could be explored in safety?

It was a brilliant move. Whether the story came to Newton in confidence via Lord Arthur Somerset, or from Newton's fertile and scheming brain, it worked. Lord Arthur in his numerous letters home to his friend Reginald Brett MP, expressed voluminous amounts of regret that he had got the Royal Family into such a mess. This is not the place to examine whether Eddy did or he didn't. Other authors have done much on that front, and many more will do so, as they have tried to suggest he was Jack the Ripper (which he most certainly wasn't). Suffice to say, Newton would later be put on trial and sent to prison for conspiracy to pervert the course of justice by trying to get Allies and the telegraph boys out of the country.

It was in this fevered climate that Newlove and Veck were hurried through the justice system without fuss or fanfare. The Crown did a deal. Some of the boys would give their evidence, and both of the accused would plead guilty to certain counts in the indictment, but not all. Lenient sentences were undoubtedly hinted at if not promised outright. Newlove pleaded guilty to procuring the commission by George Barber, George Alma Wright, Charles Thomas Swinscow, Charles Ernest Thickbroom, William Meech Perkins and Algernon Edward Allies to commit acts of gross indecency. For that he received four months.

Veck, who was indicted for conspiring with the absent Charles Hammond to incite and procure the same boys to commit an abominable crime – which might have earned him a life sentence – pled guilty to gross indecency only and received nine months. They were taken below to start their sentences and many people who knew the full story breathed a collective sigh of relief.

It was a monumental cover-up and a complete travesty of justice, based on the laws of the time, though for Newlove and Veck it was the best they could have expected.

Jack, anticipating any day to be taken to numerous locations, where he would be asked to identify those people he had accused in his statement, waited but heard nothing. There was no mention in the newspapers of Lord Euston, Colonel Hozier, Mr Bevan the banker, Cavendish-Bentinck, Major Moet or any of the others.

There was nothing about the Newlove and Veck trial, bar one short paragraph in *The Times*. Frank Hewitt had gone on the run and was nowhere to be found. Jack would later come to believe that he had been spirited out of the country. Hammond too was on the run. Was he still in France? Jack didn't know. Hammond wasn't writing to him. Andrew Grant and Tom Wells were still working their beat, unaware that Jack had pointed the finger at them. Had they known, Jack might well have been advised to go back to Dublin or flee to France himself. Grant and Wells might be pretty boys but they could be tough and violent.

The telegraph boys Swinscow, Thickbroom, Wright and Perkins were not in custody. They would be officially given their notice from the GPO on 6 December, a full five months on from the discovery of the money in

Swinscow's pocket. They were free to tell, and knew everything that had happened in court.

What blew the case wide open and brought Jack to a most important decision – probably the most important of his life – were the actions of a young newspaper proprietor Ernest Parke. Had it not been for Parke's intrepid journalism in the face of Government silence and the frustrations of the police, Jack would more than likely have gone the same way as his statement. Folded, filed and forgotten.

Parke was the editor of the low circulation *North London Press,* which reported local news from Hackney and Bethnal Green as well as covering events of major importance. Parke, who looked more like a poet than an editor with his lion's mane of rich auburn hair, was a radical and at every opportunity stuck up for the working man and his rights. He supported the dockers during their strike, agitated for bakers, railway workers, the coalies (the coal whippers at the docks) and even the poor old badly-done-by photographic cabinet makers. He was one of the first newspapermen to come out against the forced silencing of whistleblowers. His support of a union for the eleven thousand postal workers was accompanied in one issue by a cartoon showing a gagged GPO worker alongside a top-hatted pistol-drawing highwayman against a poster which read in large letters,

ANY POSTMAN WRITING TO THE
PAPERS WILL BE DISMISSED.

Parke was also an advocate of Irish Home Rule, something that would have been dear to Jack's heart.

Parke made his first tentative foray into the Cleveland Street case on 28 September with a criticism of the lenient sentences passed on Veck and Newlove, obviously based on police sources. He more than hinted at those who had been allowed to go free, mentioning 'the heir of a Duke, the younger son of another Duke, and an officer holding command in the southern district.' Euston, Somerset and Jervoise by any other name.

On 16 November he pulled his journalistic rabbit out of the hat and named Lord Arthur Somerset and the Lord Euston outright, both of whom had been 'allowed' to leave the country, the latter for distant Peru. It was a direct challenge to the police and the Government. The criminals, he said, were not just limited to those two individuals but 'were to be counted by the score'. The press in those days was far more compliant than it is now, but a new journalism was invading the Fourth Estate. Parke was one of those at its helm.

He was no liberal in the broader sense of the word. He described the whole affair as a 'hideous and foetid gangrene on the social life of London' and challenged other newspapers to take up the cudgel.

By this time, Hammond had succeeded in reaching America. He had demanded £800 from Newton to take Caroline, his son Charlie and his wife's sister Florence with him. Newton had come up with the money courtesy of Lord Arthur's father. Hammond sailed on 5 October by first class passage from Antwerp to New York on the Red Star liner *Pennland* under the name Charles Boulton, with young Herbert Ames his boy-secretary – whom he had abducted, according to the press, without the permission of his respectable working-class father – as young master Arthur Boulton.

The choice of surname, that of one of the famous pair of transvestites Boulton and Park whom Jack had dragged outrageously into *Sins*, was not lost on Newton's clerk Taylorson who sailed with them. Caroline, Florence and Charlie were to follow as Saloon passengers.

Their destination was Seattle, Washington State, where he was to lodge with a French prostitute called Adele Gayet, care of one John Stricker. (3) It was far from the last that the world or Jack would hear of Charles Hammond.

Ernest Parke's exposé was well timed. On the same day that Hammond set sail for the New World, Lord Arthur Somerset returned to England, in full view of anyone who cared, for his grandmother's funeral. Abberline was helpless. The hard-drinking Hanks, had he possessed a warrant, would have had no qualms about arresting him at the graveside. Somerset promptly left the country again, and ten days later Prince Eddy embarked on a most conveniently planned voyage, accompanied by the Prince and Princess of Wales aboard the Royal Yacht *Osborne*, bound for Athens and the Royal wedding of the Prince of Wales' nephew to the sister of the German Emperor.

Just to make matters quite plain and to give them the Royal seal of approval, the Prince of Wales wrote to Lord Salisbury the Prime Minister expressing his great satisfaction with the way things had been handled. He had sent two Royal courtiers to visit Commissioner Monro to find out how things stood. He now hoped that if Lord Arthur ever visited England again, he might at least be quietly allowed to visit his parents without the threat of an abominable charge hanging over him.

As well timed as Ernest Parke's revelations were, they were not as diligently researched. Lord Euston had not fled to Peru. He hadn't been further in the last ten years than Biarritz and was still very much in London.

Lord Euston sued Ernest Parke and the *North London Press* for libel.

Jack was at home at 15 Old Compton Street when a young man called Ashley knocked at the door. Would Mr Saul see him? Mr Ashley was ushered in, sat down, and told Jack that he was from the office of Ernest Parke's solicitors. Though he had met all sorts in his line of work, Ashley was nervous at first. He was there to ask a particular favour. It was a difficult one to request of anybody, especially someone like Jack.

Eventually he broached the subject he had come about. The editor desperately needed someone to help him in his defence, which was to be one of justification. Parke was intending to say that essentially the libel was true and that Lord Euston had been a visitor to 19 Cleveland Street, as the newspaper had implied. Jack was someone who had actually taken his Lordship back to the brothel and had sex with him. Would Jack get up in court and say so?

Or put another way, would Jack stand up in court and admit to crimes that might end up in him going to prison himself?

Jack's first thought was how this solicitous young man had found him. He didn't look the sort who hung about Piccadilly chatting to rent boys until he found one who had been with Lord Euston.

There was only one way young Ashley could have tracked Jack down. Inspector Abberline.

Jack said he would have to think about it. Ashley told him that a subscription had been raised to help

Mr Parke and that expenses would be paid. This was a circumspect way of saying that it might be worth Jack's time, though no amount of money could obviously be worth the very real risk to his liberty.

It was the first time in Jack's life he had been asked to volunteer to go to court. This was no subpoena. Nobody was hauling him off and forcing him to make a statement. This was a plea for help, not from the police, but an individual. Ernest Parke, the man he was being asked to save, was a young man not very much older than himself, with a five-year-old son. Parke risked going to prison for simply naming those far more guilty than the poor clerk Newlove, now in Pentonville. Those who, by virtue of their position in society and inherent wealth, were almost untouchable.

Jack said he would think about it. Ashley came back the following day, and still Jack hadn't made a decision. The young man returned a second time the following Saturday morning. He was becoming more and more persuasive, and quite desperate. Had Jack made his mind up? Jack had. He said he would do it. They had something in common, Jack and Mr Parke. The unlucky young editor had been screwing the establishment for just a few months. Jack had been doing it for years.

Jack would try and do at least one good thing in his life. How and where he might be rewarded for his good deed remained to be seen.

* * * * * *

Chapter Notes

1. George Barber claimed to have been introduced to 19 Cleveland Street by someone called Ripley. The same man is

mentioned by Hammond in one of his letters home, written ungrammatically by Ames, dated 17 July 1889 while on the run. 'I have written to Mr Ripley and ask (sic) them to find everything out for me, as I do not think things are as bad as what people tell you.' The DPP's correspondence in the Cleveland Street files makes mention of an E.G. Ripley, but identifies him no further. Ripley was clearly someone, or so Hammond thought, in a position to find out what was going on in the early days of the police hunt. Montgomery Hyde in *The Cleveland Street Scandal* said that it was possible he was George Ripley, a younger son of the Yorkshire Baronet, Sir Henry Ripley. Being a lawyer, and also a gay historian, he must have had good reason for suspecting him. George Ripley was born in Halifax 1845 into a family that operated dyeing works in Bradford. His father was one of the Ripley Baronetcy of Rawdon in the county of York, and Bedstone, Shropshire. In October 1868 it was reported that a George Ripley, staying at the St George's Hotel in Albemarle Street, London, became involved in a fracas with sixty men at the notorious Alhambra, frequented by Jack Saul, Boulton and Park *et al*, most of whom were cadets belonging to the Royal Military Academy at Woolwich and the Royal Military College at Sandhurst, which sounds suspiciously like another case of someone with a passion for young men in uniform. Seven years later back in Bradford, he executed his will at the age of thirty, leaving the sum of five hundred pounds to Dr Harrington Tuke of 37 Albemarle Street, who ran the Manor Farm House asylum in Chiswick, a mental institution for gentlemen from the professional classes, and who was one of the most prominent physicians in the country dealing with psychiatric diseases. George Ripley died unmarried at 42 Paulton Square, Kings Road, Chelsea. The evidence strongly suggests that he was yet another homosexual man put away for a while in a madhouse for his sexual leanings.

2. The letter mentioning PAV resides in the files of the Director of Public Prosecutions kept at the National Archives in Kew. DPP 1/95/1-7

3. John Stricker. Hammond referred in a letter home to Adele Gayet's 'protector' as John Stoker. Records from Washington State Archives refer to him as John D Strachet or Stricker.

CHAPTER SIXTEEN

THE RESPECTABLE
MR VIOLET

There were forces operating, as they had in the Dublin scandals, of which Jack was unaware. Not all of them were benign.

It was no coincidence that the *North London Press* first mentioned the names of Lords Euston and Somerset. The same newspaper, over a number of issues, also published Hammond's letters from France, Belgium and ultimately from America. How did a radical newspaper with a circulation of about four thousand five hundred, which only a tiny percentage of Londoners read, get hold of Hammond's letters? After publication, Ernest Parke obligingly offered to pass them to the Attorney General should they be required in any future prosecution of Hammond and others. His offer was taken up, but not with urgency.

The letters can only have been given to him by the police, who had either obtained them from members of Hammond's family – Caroline and his brother Ted – or as seems much more likely, intercepted them. It is extremely unlikely that the family sold on the letters for much needed cash to help Hammond's flight.

Frustrated by inaction from those above, Abberline decided to leak to the press. Ernest Parke was only too pleased to be the first to mention Lords Somerset and Euston, but as a reward for the risk he took he was provided with the letters. No other newspaper was as privileged. When Lord Euston decided to sue for libel, the *Daily Star* newspaper started a subscription to help the beleaguered Parke as one newspaper helping another in times of trouble. By the end of the year the Fair Trial Fund had reached over three hundred pounds, with contributions from a wide variety of people, including fellow journalist and the founder of the *Star* newspaper himself, T.P. O'Connor, the Irish Nationalist MP.

It wasn't only the *Star* that came to Parke's defence. Realising that his actions had now got Parke into trouble, Abberline had offered him Jack. If Jack testified for the editor and Parke was acquitted, it would be a damning indictment against Lord Euston, and the Crown would be obliged to start proceedings against him, just as had happened when Gustavus Cornwall's libel action against *United Ireland* failed.

On the other hand, if Parke was found guilty of libel, then Jack's evidence would be in tatters and he himself might be tried for perjury and worse. It would also then allow Abberline to reveal Jack's statement which, at the moment, he was disinclined to do because of the reluctance of most of his superiors to embroil themselves in a witch-hunt among the aristocracy.

Either way, Abberline would win. Whichever way it went, Jack could only lose. In one of its December editions the *North London Press* published a short story called *Wild Jack – A Hero of the Streets*. The heading might have given Jack cause for excitement. But sadly it was not about him, though the timing was apposite. Rather, it was the story of the brave exploits of a tall, handsome and well-built Irish policeman.

It was that very different kind of hero of the streets who, the same Saturday afternoon of Ashley's third visit to him at Old Compton Street, walked down to the Westminster Detective Agency to make a statement. They were handling the inquiries and finding witnesses on behalf of Parke's solicitor. If he had known what kind of an operation he was walking into, Jack might have turned and fled.

Captain John G. Webb, seventy years old and a former sub-inspector with the Royal Irish Constabulary, now working as a private detective, was more than pleased to have Jack's services. He was having considerable trouble tracking down reliable witnesses to help Parke's case. Others were only identification witnesses who claimed to have seen Lord Euston entering 19 Cleveland Street, but they did not know him, except by sight. Jack was different.

An advertisement for the agency ran,

WESTMINSTER DETECTIVE AGENCY. Detective work undertaken. Agents everywhere. References, secrecy and despatch. 9 Carteret Street Westminster (opposite *Truth* office) London S.W. Telegraphic address, 'Touch, London'. Mr Henry Labouchere M.P. writes to the manager of the agency as follows. 'I can strongly recommend you, for I have found you – in a very difficult business – reliable, honest and intelligent.'

Ironically, this glowing reference was by the very MP responsible for the notorious clause in the Criminal Amendment Act, which had turned every homosexual man indulging in any act whatsoever, into a criminal overnight. He worked just across the road in the offices of *Truth*, a periodical in which he railed against vice and the sins of Babylon. Labouchere had employed Captain Webb who in turn had helped him out in some undisclosed sensitive matter.

A rather different reference would be provided by *The Hawk*, a fore-runner of today's *Private Eye*, whose editor Augustus Moore accused Captain Webb of being 'Labouchere's protege', and in calling himself a Captain was using an 'honourable title to which he has no right. He had or has a son who held a commission in a North of Ireland militia regiment, but I should hardly think this entitles his father to a military title.'

Webb wasn't running the Parke defence case on his own. He had help from a very tarnished quarter.

At the office, Jack was confronted by a thickset man with a handsome moustache and a refined English accent, leaning on a large stick. He was an ex-Scotland Yard man called Maurice Moser, whom Webb had sub-contracted. It was Moser's job to take witnesses with him and stand on street corners for hours waiting to catch sight of Lord Euston. The colourful Moser described himself as a master of disguise, and proudly advertised the fact that he employed lady detectives. One of them, Mrs Williamson, was also his mistress. Moser would later be cited as co-respondent in a divorce case by Mr Williamson.

Moser's professional reputation was already compromised. His own Anglo-Continental Inquiry Agency in Southampton Street off the Strand had recently been dissolved. He was notorious as the private detective who had been employed and paid a large sum of money by *The Times* newspaper to collect evidence against Charles Stewart Parnell, the Irish MP and nationalist, to implicate him in the Phoenix Park murders. The incriminating letters, which he obtained, supposedly written by Parnell, turned out to be forgeries. *The Times* printed one of the letters and was successfully sued by Parnell for libel. Richard Piggott, the journalist who forged them, blew his brains out in a Madrid hotel room.

It seemed that the cauldron of Irish politics was never far away from wherever Jack found himself.

Between them, Captain Webb and Maurice Moser would turn out to be more Inspector Clouseau than Sherlock Holmes.

Seated in the office, made to feel both comfortable and important, Jack was shown a photograph of Lord Euston, which he identified immediately. He was also shown a photograph of his friend Carrington, whom Webb and Moser were presumably anxious to trace as he had also taken Lord Euston back to the brothel. However, Carrington would not become one of their witnesses.

There was no need for Jack to spend even five minutes on a street corner with Moser, to identify a man with whom he had gone back to Cleveland Street in a cab and could describe intimately. From that moment on, Jack became Ernest Parke's star witness.

Captain Webb was duty bound to remind Jack that in giving evidence he would be incriminating himself. But Jack wasn't going to waver either. He sincerely believed that Parke was being unfairly treated. The establishment were out to get him. And were they not the same people who had been occupying his country ever since he was born and long before that?

Nevertheless, Captain Webb had no intentions of taking any risk with Jack and letting him slip through his fingers. Jack's habit of flitting from lodging to lodging could not continue for the duration of the run-up to the trial, which was due to take place just after the New Year. Neither could Jack's line of business, so to speak. It would look much better if Jack was to reside with respectable people, preferably a family.

Jack had no objection to being put up with a family, especially, as it turned out, his stay would stretch over the Christmas period. He could hardly go home to Dublin with this hanging over him, not after the last well-publicised scandal in which he had been involved, nor would Captain Webb have wanted him to. Webb could not take the risk of his chief witness vanishing into the mists of the Emerald Isle. Jack was promised free accommodation in London, as much food as he wanted to eat, and ten shillings a week.

He was grateful. At least he could send home something regularly to his mother.

A couple called Thomas and Eliza Violet of Akerman Road, Brixton, who took in boarders, were selected for the task. They were in their fifties with three grown-up children, a daughter who worked in a dress shop and two teenage sons who were clerks. Mr Violet was an agent for a fire and life insurance company and was probably someone whom Captain Webb had met through his dealings as an investigator. No doubt he was remunerated for his trouble.

What the Violets thought of this effeminate and somewhat theatrical young man in his early thirties, who arrived with his belongings to take up residence and spend Christmas with them, one can but guess at. They must have known he was to be a witness in a trial, though they may not have known the full circumstances. Still, he was a guest and had to be treated like a guest. Mr Violet clearly took a liking to Jack and felt sorry for him in his circumstances. Jack in turn took a fancy to a silver-headed cane that he spotted in Brixton market and Mr Violet gave him one and sixpence (15 pence) to buy it. He also lent Jack other small sums to send home to his mother.

For a few weeks he had his own comfortable room, his meals were cooked for him, and few of his needs were not met. Captain Webb kept in regular touch, informing him of the progress of the case and making sure he was happy.

Jack however still had plenty to worry about. Not only was he in the hands of two incompetent private detectives, he had been set up by the police and would have no opportunity to rehearse his evidence.

Not so with Lord Euston, who had already enjoyed a perfect opportunity to rehearse and test his entire 'story' in the full glare of publicity at Bow Street Police Court at the end of November during Parke's committal proceedings.

Euston had a surprise for his accusers.

* * * * * *

CHAPTER SEVENTEEN

JACK JUMPS OVER
THE CANDLESTICK

'One night in 1887 I was walking in Piccadilly. I cannot quite say the date. It was either the end of May or the beginning of June. A card was put into my hand which, on reading afterwards, I saw was headed *Poses Plastique*, Hammond, Cleveland Street. I do not remember whether Tottenham Court Road was on the card. About a week afterwards I went there. It was about half past ten or eleven o'clock at night. The door was opened to me by a man. He asked me to come in and then asked me for a sovereign. I gave it to him. I then asked him where these *poses plastique* were going to take place. He then said, "there's nothing of the sort".'

While Jack was treading the boards at Drury Lane as a Roundhead trooper fighting Royalist forces during the production of *The Royal Oak*, with the trial a full six weeks away, and before young Mr Ashley had come knocking on his door, the noble Lord was on his feet in Bow Street Police Court putting on a performance of his own. He intended pulling the rug out from under the feet of anyone who might accuse him of going to Hammond's brothel. Of course he had.

Poses Plastique meant striptease, and were often laid on in private houses. They were demonstrations of naked ladies in various poses, which a gentleman like Lord Euston, who had the reputation of being a ladies' man and had married an actress, might well be tempted to visit.

'Did you immediately leave the house?' Mr George Lewis, QC for the prosecution, led him.

'I did.'

'How long were you in the house?'

'Considerably under five minutes.'

'Have you ever been there since? Or previously?'

'No. I have no knowledge of anything in connection with that house.'

Such was Lord Euston's excuse for going to Hammond's brothel. He went on to say that he was shown into a sitting room on the right hand side of the ground floor, which was where his altercation with 'the man' took place.

No spending on the belly of male prostitutes picked up at Piccadilly Circus. Lord Euston was not of that ilk. It was purely by accident he had found himself in such a place.

Under cross-examination by Mr Frank Lockwood QC, for the defendant Parke, he admitted having made a statement about his visit to a friend in October. Why he had waited that length of time he didn't say. Neither did he give, and nor was he asked, the name of the friend except that it was someone he knew 'in society'. He had no idea where the friend was now.

He had told the friend because there were rumours about him.

Returning to the card, Lockwood asked him how long it was after being given the card that he read it.

'When I got home I think.' he said. 'I don't remember particularly. I think when I got home and took my coat off. I did not read it in the street. I just shoved it in my pocket and looked at it when I got home.'

'Was it a printed or lithographed card?'

'It was a lithographed card, but the words *poses plastique* at the top were in writing.'

'Was the gentleman giving out these cards promiscuously, or were you particularly favoured?'

Lord Euston laughed.

'I cannot tell you. He shoved one into my hand, and I put it in my pocket.'

'Was he giving them away to other people?'

'I really cannot tell you. I was walking along pretty smart home. I do not walk slowly as a rule.'

'Did you see him give a card to anyone else?'

'No. It was near 12 o'clock as I was walking home.'

'I suggest to you that you had not time to stop and read it?'

Lord Euston gave another chortle.

'Well, I did not stop to read it under a lamppost.

'I do not know what there is to laugh at.' Lockwood admonished him.

'Well it was a comical question.'

'How long between your reading it and your going to see whether the promises on the card would be carried out?'

'Oh, at least a week.'

'Then you kept the card the whole of that time?'

He had.

'Did you bring the card back with you? After your visit to the house?'

'I brought it home ... I destroyed it. I was disgusted at having been found in such a place, and I did not want to have anything more to do with it.'

'Did you burn it or tear it up?'

'Well I think I tore it up. I should not have a fire in my room at that time of year.'

'You tore it up in disgust?'

'Yes.

'In indignation?'

'Yes I was very angry with myself for having been brought there.'

'Lord Euston – from what passed in that house you had no doubt what the character of the house was?'

'Not the smallest.'

'It is a house, as I understand you to say, where crimes such as those alluded to in the libel were probably committed.'

'I should think they might be, and probably were, from what was said to me.'

What was said to him would have to wait until the trial. As he stepped down, Lord Euston felt satisfied. His explanation was perfectly coherent. The fact he had torn up the card, which Hammond had given him, absolved him from having to produce it with the *poses plastique* writing.

Lockwood hadn't been able to shake him even slightly. But then he was a member of the House of Lords. He had been in the Rifle Brigade. He was currently in the 1st Volunteer Battalion, Northamptonshire Regiment. He was an aristocrat and a soldier.

Six weeks later, on 15 January 1890, a young man in his best tight-fitting suit and starched collar and patent leather boots, grasping a silver-headed cane and with a sparkling ring on his finger, caught a cab from Brixton to the Old Bailey and prepared to do battle.

Parke was defended, as he had been at the committal proceedings, by Frank Lockwood who would later become Solicitor-General. He was an accomplished cartoonist who, during slack moments in court, liked to draw pictures of his contemporaries, many of which he later sold on to them. Leading the prosecution was Sir Charles Russell, QC, MP, led by William Matthews who would later become Director of Public Prosecutions. The judge was Mr Justice Hawkins, known as 'Hanging Hawkins'. Who exactly would be hung out to dry remained to be seen.

It was an array of formidable legal talent. Lord Euston was well aware of Gustavus Cornwall's failed libel case in Dublin and how it had led to his prosecution along with others. He could not afford to lose his case. Neither could a lot of other people, watching nervously from the sidelines, afford for him to lose.

In Cornwall's case, the Secretary to the Post Office had been put in the box first to give evidence of the libel, and then been subjected to a fierce cross-examination during which the names of witnesses with whom he had supposedly committed sodomy had been put to him, preparing the jury for the evidence in justification of the libel to follow.

Russell's tactic was very different. It was to put Lord Euston in the dock last. It was an unusual course, but Mr Justice Hawkins tacitly agreed to it. Russell would simply state the facts according to Lord Euston in an opening statement, describe the libel, call on the defence to justify it with their witnesses, then put the prosecutor in the dock at the end to give his evidence. It also meant that the prosecution would have the final word with the jury, provided that Lord Euston called no witnesses of his own, which was an important advantage.

Lord Euston hoped that would not be necessary.

The facts of the case, Russell began, were simple. The libel stated that Lord Euston had been one of the visitors to 19 Cleveland Street for nefarious purposes. Parke had made the dreadful blunder of stating in his newspaper that he had fled to Peru in the face of the investigation, a fact that was demonstrably untrue.

Almost immediately came the first shock to anyone who had not paid attention to the committal proceedings. Lord Euston may not have fled to Peru, but he *had* been to that house of ill fame, but in quite different circumstances than suggested by the *North London Press*. Russell now told a crowded Old Bailey courtroom how his Lordship had visited the premises under the mistaken assumption that he was going to see *poses plastique*, and that on discovering that young men were on offer and not young ladies, he had demanded to leave and threatened to knock down the owner, one Charles Hammond. Lord Euston had left and that, he said, was his sole connection with 19 Cleveland Street.

The case was handed to Mr Lockwood to do his best with the witnesses that Captain Webb and Maurice Moser had assembled, of which Jack was the only one of any real value. That was when it became abysmally clear that Parke's inquiry agent had done his client no great favours. For the others were a motley bunch, making up in entertainment value what they lacked in credibility. Laughter was not what Parke's defence team wanted, but laughter was what they got.

As in Dublin, Jack sat waiting his turn, now nervously playing with his cane, twisting the ring on his finger. This time he would be called. There was still time to back out. He could go into the box and say nothing. He chose to do neither. He would step into that courtroom with all the confidence and bravura he could muster and tell it as it was. He had been a Catholic all his life, and if there was a time to pray, it was now.

John O'Loughlin, a coal dealer and greengrocer, lived just round the corner in Savile Street but also had premises in Tottenham Street. He testified in an 'odd Irish manner' that he had seen a horse and carriage pull up and a gentleman get out and knock on the door of No 19 around the 20th of May the previous year.

'What happened then?'

'Nothing more, he went in.'

'Have you seen the gentleman since?'

'Yes.'

'Do you see him in court?'

O'Loughlin looked around and admitted that his sight was very queer. It was a brilliant start.

'No.' he said. 'But I saw him at Hyde Park Corner and I saw him outside this court.'

O'Loughlin had been taken to Hyde Park Corner by the private detective Maurice Moser, and there they had waited on a street corner near Grosvenor Square for nearly two hours waiting for Lord Euston to emerge from his home. Moser's sudden insertion into the evidence caused no end of nudges and winks as his reputation in the Parnell case was recent and well-known.

When asked if he had seen him today, O'Loughlin caused more laughter by replying,

'I have seen him today and he came for me tomorrow.'

O'Loughlin described Lord Euston as being about five feet eight ten inches in height. His sight was very queer indeed.

Lord Euston was asked to stand up, his true height becoming apparent to the court. O'Loughlin said he would like to see 'Mr Euston' walk. Euston took a few paces at which O'Loughlin remarked to much laughter,

'I should say that is Lord Euston.'

It transpired that O'Loughlin had most of his meetings with the elderly Captain Webb away from the inquiry agent's office in the relaxed and less intimidating surroundings of the nearby Westminster Aquarium, or to give it its full and proper name the Royal Aquarium and Summer and Winter Gardens, where Westminster Hall now stands, and where the coal dealer and the inquiry agent had met three times 'purely by chance'. If there was something fishy about this, the aquarium itself had very few fish. The management had become rather fed up with marine life and instead put lady swimmers in the main tank, which attracted a rather different kind of visitor.

Perhaps these aquatic distractions had interfered with Captain Webb's judgement in gathering witnesses.

Under cross-examination by Russell, O'Loughlin admitted that his eyesight had been deteriorating for ten years and was getting 'wusser', an exceedingly quaint Dickensian expression. When he confessed that he could not tell whether Lord Euston had come to Cleveland Street in a private carriage or a hansom, or how many horses pulled it because he knew more about coal barrows than carriages, O'Loughlin's evidence fell apart.

There was a further comic interlude when Russell asked him how much he had been paid. Less than ten shillings, he said. One inquiry agent had borrowed 'some baccy' from him and a shilling, and hadn't returned those either. But when O'Loughlin described Lord Euston's walk as 'like an old policeman who had done twenty years on the stones', his transformation from defence witness to comic turn was complete.

O'Loughlin's companion that day, John William Smith, a railway porter, did nothing to advance the defence. He said that the man he saw going into No 19 was five feet eight inches, whereas the court now knew that Lord Euston was very tall.

The third witness was O'Loughlin's son Michael, an unemployed barman who had the annoying habit of playing with his moustache and was told frequently to leave it alone. Michael O'Loughlin (not to be confused with Michael Loughlin, the rag merchant who owned 19 Cleveland Street) claimed to have seen Lord Euston at Royal Ascot two years previously, and since then he had seen him go in and out of 19 Cleveland Street three or four times, at the end of May and beginning of June. Asked if he had received or been promised any money from Captain Webb or anyone else in connection with his evidence, he said no.

'But I expect I shall get some,' he added cockily.

After lunch came Mrs Hannah Elizabeth Morgan who lived across the road at 22 Cleveland Street. By a stroke of irony, this was the house Charles Dickens had once lived in, when earlier in the century it was part of Norfolk Street. She was the first 'respectable' witness, being well dressed and middle-aged. Over the past year she had seen about fifty or sixty persons entering and leaving the house. She had identified one man as Lord Euston, after being driven down to Grosvenor Square by Maurice Moser, where they had waited to see him.

The fifth witness was another friend of the O'Loughlin clan, yet another barman called Frederick Grant. He had been going to a music hall with Michael O'Loughlin around the end of May and had noticed a gentleman coming out of number 19. O'Loughlin told him it was Lord Euston and informed him about the character of the place.

If that had been it, Ernest Parke's defence team might well have been advised to pack up and go home. Not one of the witnesses said they recognised Lord Euston because he was so tall. And there was too much dis-agreement about his clothes, including in one case the cut of his trousers. And as the court already knew, Lord Euston *had* been to 19 Cleveland Street. It would not have been surprising if he *had* been seen by *someone*.

Then Mr Lockwood produced the name of his next witness.

'Call John Saul.'

The charmed life of Mr Jack Saul, ready for a lark at any time, now hung in the balance. He strode into the court with the silver-headed cane he had bought in Brixton market and took up his position with all the confidence he could muster.

It was his moment. His day in court. Whether he regarded it as something to be proud of, or whether he was now regretting he had ever agreed to give evi-dence, it was now too late to back out. The last time he had been in a courtroom was eleven years earlier, accused of burglary. On that occasion, he had been lucky. During the Dublin trials, he had waited outside but not been called.

This time he had. He was not on trial, but he might well have been.

The *Star* newspaper described the atmosphere in the court, which had clearly anticipated Jack's arrival, as if the Royal carriage had just come into view.

> 'There was a buzz of excitement ... for he had something more to speak to than having seen Lord Euston go in and out of the house. Dramatic indeed was the situation when this young man, asked whether he recognised anyone in court having been to Hammond's house pointed to Lord Euston...'

Dramatic indeed. In reply to Mr Lockwood's question he pointed across the courtroom and, in an 'effeminate voice' according to the *Star*, and in a 'foreign accent' according to *Reynolds News*, said,

'Yes that one, I took him there myself.'

The *Star* reporter, who was clearly caught up in the moment, wrote that it seemed minutes before another question was asked, for 'so intense was the thrill which this declaration excited.'

'Which is he?'

'That gentleman there with the moustache.'

'Have you taken many men back with you?'

'Yes sir, I have taken quite a number of men.'

It was an admission that could earn him two years. For that reason, it created the next sensation. The expressions 'sensation, renewed sensation and great sensation' were often used by trial reporters in those days to describe the atmosphere in a courtroom. All three would be used in the first few minutes of Jack's examination.

Lord Euston stared across the court at the young man who clearly saw himself as the aristocrat's nemesis, who wasn't afraid to admit to being a criminal if it meant exposing the truly guilty.

'Was that the first time he had been there, this person you took there?'

'Yes, I believe so.' said Jack.

'When was that?'

'Some time in April or May, 1887.'

'Tell us where you met Lord Euston.'

'It was at Piccadilly, between Albany Courtyard and Sackville Street.' Jack was quite specific. 'He laughed at me and I winked at him. He turned sharp into Sackville Street and I followed him. He was known as the Duke. He spoke to me.'

This banal and slightly comical description of an encounter between a young male prostitute and a member of the House of Lords created the 'renewed sensation'. If Lord Arthur Somerset shaking hands with a private soldier outside the door of a brothel was something that offended the Victorian notion of class, a nobleman stopping to talk to a street youth who winked at him was quite beyond the pale.

'Tell me what happened.'

Lockwood guided him, aware that Jack's evidence was quite the most important in the case. He could not afford for the jury to go against Jack. Unfortunately, Jack's effeminate manner and the way he flourished his silver-headed cane had already caused Sir Henry Hawkins to bristle.

'He came after me and asked me where I was going. I said home. He asked me what sort of place it was, was it comfortable. I said yes. He asked me if it was quiet. I said yes.'

Jack then created the 'great sensation' by telling the court how they got into a hansom and went back to 19 Cleveland Street, where Jack let himself in with his own latchkey and took Lord Euston inside. This was a totally different story to the one the court already knew Lord Euston was going to tell. No mention of cards handed out in the street or *poses plastique*. Just a straightforward commercial sexual encounter.

When the mounting sensations had died down, Jack described how Hammond had come in with his tray of cards and a glass of champagne, at which there were sounds of laughter in court, as though such things were now completely beyond the comprehension of most spectators.

'There will be no more of that.' threatened Mr Justice Hawkins. 'It is brutal and disgusting.'

Not as brutal and disgusting as the sexual act which Jack then described, which no newspaper printed, though we know that it ended with his Lordship bent over Jack and climaxing onto Jack's stomach. Afterwards, Lord Euston had told Jack not to speak to him if he saw him again in the street. Jack had seen him back at Cleveland Street however. The second time, Hammond had excluded him from the room. The third time, Jack had observed him with Frank Hewitt, whom Jack informed the court had been 'sent abroad'.

It certainly seemed as though he had, for the young carpenter's son from the top of the Hampstead Road had disappeared. Jack was feeling he could do with some support. Henry Newlove, who had seen Lord Euston in the house, was in prison and hadn't been called. Parke's solicitor, Minton Slater of Ludgate Circus, had tried to get an interview with him in prison and to see the depositions produced at his trial, but the authorities had been obstructive. He was told he would have to subpoena the Crown to have them produced in court. And any communication between him and Newlove in prison would not be confidential. The nature of it, he was told, would be sent to the Secretary of State and the Attorney General for the 'due administration of public justice'. It would be hardly surprising if Newlove simply preferred to get on with his four-month sentence and say nothing more that might incriminate him.

Neither were Tom Wells, alias Clifton, or his friend Carrington there to help him.

Unlike the other witnesses, Jack was not asked by Russell to describe the height of Lord Euston. Had Jack been making up the whole thing, it would have been a simple matter to destroy his credibility in the same way by asking him how tall Lord Euston was. But Jack of course knew, and was not asked. At five feet five and a half inches, he was almost a foot shorter than Euston. Euston must have towered over him, especially in his top hat.

Jack explained how he had fallen out with Hammond and why he had left Cleveland Street. It had been over Hammond cheating him out of money and for bringing Post Office boys to work in the house, while he had to walk the streets.

'For what is in my face and that is my shame' he added.

The *Star* observed that he tossed back his head with a theatrical gesture at that point. It was the *London Daily News* which reported that, after admitting he had nothing in his face but shame, he brought out a handkerchief.

Jack was too controlled to cry in the dock. It might have done him some good if he had. Penitence about the life he had led would have gone some way to undoing the damage. Instead, it was Jack's assuredness and the way he relied on that cane to give him an air of authority that was burning into the judge's brain.

Sir Charles Russell then rose to cross-examine.

Instead of challenging the facts of the evidence, Russell concentrated on demolishing Jack's character, which hardly taxed his forensic skills. Jack was a lamb waiting to be slaughtered, and he had walked right into the abattoir.

'Have you any honest means of earning your bread?' Russell asked.

'No sir.' replied Jack.

Owing to his 'loss of character' in Dublin he had been unable to find gainful employment in London, other than washing and scrubbing the houses of gay ladies, and the occasion when he had been employed at Drury Lane Theatre.

He was taken through a litany of addresses at which he had stayed, one of them being the house where sodomy was carried on in Nassau Street, which in fact was only just round the corner from Cleveland Street.

Jack was pulled up short when asked if he had lived with a prostitute in a house near Leicester Square. Though the press did not report any more details, this was almost certainly a reference to Madame Clemence of 36 Lisle Street, the address Jack had been living at when he wrote *Sins*. Did someone in court have a copy of the book? Was it going to be produced at any moment and a particular page referred to where Mr Saul of Lisle Street admitted to being ready for a lark with free gentlemen?

Jack chose to give them no help, just in case. He denied ever knowing of that house. The subject passed. Jack was asked about his stay at Cleveland Street and about Hammond's 'very fine collection of telegraph boys', some of whom had given evidence at Veck and Newloves' trial. Jack felt very sorry for Newlove.

'I don't recognise some of the names but I might have met the boys themselves.' Jack answered noncommittally.

'Did you carry on these infamous practices in Dublin with a man called Kirwan?' Russell then put to him.

'Yes sir. As far back as 1875.'

Kirwan was out of danger now, so Jack had no compunction about admitting it. For a long time he had carried on these 'infamous practices' with the young Captain, then a Lieutenant, from County Galway. To talk about love, to tell a court of how, as a poor boy from the slums, he first became attracted to an older man from a far superior background who wore a handsome uniform – the Queen's uniform no less – was not an option to him. Had Jack been able to anticipate Oscar Wilde, he might have told the court of a love that did not speak its name and truly been the first 'gay activist'.

But Jack, while having Oscar's bravery and some of his vanity, did not have his wit and self-assurance. He felt morally obliged to talk of his life of shame, to agree with the makers of the law that their intimacy was criminal. As he truly knew and believed it was.

Russell dredged up the fact that Jack's evidence against Captain Kirwan had not been used at the Dublin Commission.

'Were you not told that your evidence could not be accepted because you were unworthy of credit on oath?'

'No, that is not so.' said Jack. 'My evidence was, I think, too old.'

It was the truth, but Russell created a very different impression.

'I see you have a ring on your finger?'

Jack glanced at it and brought the court to laughter.

'It's not my fault, or it would have been gone long ago. It's only paste.' he quipped'

'And a silver-headed cane.'

'Oh that is not much. Only about eighteen pence. A bargain buy.'

He explained how he had bought it in the Brixton Market while staying with respectable people, and how Mr Violet allowed him half a sovereign a week (actually the money came from Captain Webb's office, but it made him sound like a kept boy), which he sent to his mother. He told the court how he had also borrowed money for the same noble purpose. His present lodgings, he said, were free and very comfortable and he could have the best food to eat if he liked.

Mr Justice Hawkins' dislike of Jack reached a towering peak. He glowered at the witness from the bench. The comments he would make in summing up were already fermenting in his mind. In fact, they were boiling over.

'Since the second occasion, have you had any communication with Lord Euston?' asked Russell.

'No, sir. I have seen him in the street but we had the warning. If ever you see me in the street, don't talk to me.'

Jack explained how he hadn't known who Lord Euston was at first, until his friend Carrington pointed him out. He told the court how, at Captain Webb's office, he had been shown a photograph of Euston whom he recognised, 'by his face and by his big white teeth and moustache', and one of Carrington too.

Sir Charles immediately expressed his regret to the court that Jack had mentioned the name of Carrington, someone not before the court, and the judge agreed it had been unfortunate. Jack then stated he had last seen Lord Euston in the street the night before he gave his statement to Inspector Abberline in August.

The introduction of his statement to Abberline caused consternation. Abberline was in court and knew that it would, for he had been waiting for this moment. He had shown it to no one, except perhaps Commissioner Monro who was on his side.

Mr Justice Hawkins was outraged. If Inspector Abberline had possessed Jack's detailed statement of the comings and goings at Cleveland Street, why had nothing been done? Why had no arrests been made? This was January, a full five months on, and a lot of the people involved had been allowed to skip the country.

Russell put it to Jack that he had come forward with his story only because he had heard a considerable sum of money had been raised to help Parke. It was Jack's opportunity to say what many must have thought. Just how much money made it worth risking prosecution? Enough to buy a silver headed cane and a paste ring, and a few pounds to send back to his mother? But he said only that he thought the editor 'was acted very unfair with'.

'Your sense of justice prompted you to help him?'

'Yes.' said Jack.

Russell then asked him if he had ever lived in Church Street with a woman known as Queen Anne. It was a cheeky question, for Russell knew the sex of the person very well, and also because, like Carrington, Andrew Grant was not before the court either.

'No, he is a man.' said Jack. 'Perhaps you will see him later on.'

'Is he in attendance here?'

'Yes sir, he is a young fellow who knows a lot of the aristocracy.'

'Did you live with this man Grant, or Queen Anne, in Church Street, Soho?'

'No, he lived with me.' Jack replied.

Jack's assertion that the court might 'see him later on' suggests that he expected Grant to give evidence. Grant had neither been subpoenaed nor interviewed, but Jack didn't necessarily know that. As in Dublin, Jack had little idea about what was going on behind closed legal doors.

Jack's few minutes of fame were almost over. He concluded with the surprising information that the London police had been kind to him and let him go about his business unmolested, though they had advised him to give up his 'abominable life'.

'So I would' he said, 'as I am ashamed of it, but I cannot.'

'Do you mean they have deliberately shut their eyes to your infamous practices?' asked Sir Charles Russell in astonishment.

'They have had to shut their eyes to more than me.' Jack answered. 'I mean that they have let me go my beat. Sometimes they would tell me that I should do something better than that. But there are a great many young men at Piccadilly who carry on the same business as I do.'

Indeed there were. And not one of them came to help Jack out.

Lord Euston was the next to take the stand, the tall six-foot-four English aristocrat following the short fair-haired rent boy with the theatrical mannerisms and effeminate Irish accent. He created an equal stir. He had never seen Jack in his life before. He was not the young man who had handed him the card. He had never been out of the United Kingdom since 1882, when he had gone to Biarritz, and he was certainly not on the run in Peru. As all could see. His one and only visit to the house ended with him being tempted to punch the proprietor for being a blackguard and walking out.

Ernest Parke must have thought his case hopeless. There are moments in a trial when a conclusion seems inevitable. Lord Euston's tall and confident presence in the witness box was that moment. There had been, he said, no suggestion whatsoever that a warrant should be taken out against him for any offence.

Lockwood stood to cross-examine. It had the potential to be his finest moment. He lit the fuse-paper then produced a damp squib.

Who was the friend that Lord Euston had told about his visit in October, when rumours about him were circulating? It turned out now there were three.

'Lord Dorchester, Lord Dungarvan and Mr Bedford.' he said.

'Do you know Lord Arthur Somerset?'

'I know him, he belongs to some clubs to which I also belong.'

He said that he didn't tell anyone earlier because he was ashamed of having been trapped in such a position. Quite why he should start to tell his fellow noble Lords once rumours circulated wasn't gone into.

'You knew that *poses plastique* referred to a filthy exhibition?' Lockwood attacked his moral fibre.

'No, I understand it to refer to a nude exhibition.'

'Do you consider it a filthy exhibition?' Lockwood pressed him.

'I do not approve of it' Lord Euston admitted. 'But I have seen some *poses plastique* which are not filthy.'

And that was all. He was allowed to stand down.

Notwithstanding the unlikeliness of his story, Mr Justice Hawkins was in no doubt whose tale he believed. Perhaps members of the legal fraternity were not unacquainted with *poses plastique* in their leisure time.

In summing up, he asked the jury to consider – was Saul's evidence true?

'You can have only the oath of Lord Euston against the oath of *that man*. You will have to ask yourselves which oath you prefer. The oath of the man who according to his own account, if he spoke the truth, was liable to be prosecuted and sent into penal servitude, or the oath of the prosecutor (Lord Euston). So far I marvel that anybody could be found to take into his house a man professing to be the *revolting creature* that he is, and to treat him with all the luxuries that man could desire.'

Hawkins wasn't finished.

'Saul described that he was well housed and well fed and was given pocket money. When I think of *that creature* walking about the streets with his silver-headed cane and that ring on his finger, living off the fat of the land, pampered with luxury denied to a poor honest man, it makes my blood hot to think that such a condition of things can exist!'

Whether Mrs Violet's cooking could be reasonably called the fat of the land, it scarcely mattered. Like the ring, Jack had lost his sparkle.

The jury took the side of Lord Euston and found the libel proved. A horrified Ernest Parke was sentenced to twelve months imprisonment and Lord Euston despatched from the court without a moral stain on his character. Not so Jack.

Hanging Hawkins turned on him in front of the court, describing him as a melancholy spectacle, a foul creature and a loathsome object, and spoke the very words that Jack feared – that he ought to be prosecuted.

An editorial in the *Northampton Mercury* a few days later stated what a lot of people felt.

> 'Sir Henry Hawkins suggested that Saul ought to be prosecuted. A jury has arrived at the conclusion that he committed perjury. If this is correct, a more atrocious and wicked perjury cannot be imagined ... attention was recently called to the case of a poor woman who has passed twenty-two years in prison for having stolen provisions worth ten shillings. To say that a poor woman was justly punished in this fashion for the pettiest of larceny, and that a wretch like Saul is allowed to swear away the honourable good name of a person with impunity, without any action on the part of the public prosecutor, is an insult to law and justice.'

Melancholy spectacle and loathsome object as he might be, self-confessed rent boy as he most certainly was, occasional keeper of houses for gay ladies, a walking insult to law and justice, and a young man who had trodden a criminal path most of his life, Jack's story about Lord Euston not being an actual sodomite but a man who enjoyed foreplay before ejaculating on his partner's stomach had the ring of truth about it to anyone who knows about these matters.

Lord Euston's tale of going to 19 Cleveland Street believing he was going to see a female striptease and turning away in anger does not. Would Hammond really have had his cards printed and handed out to all and sundry with *poses plastique* written above, and would he, when a customer turned up looking for naked ladies, offer him a boy instead? Hammond was reckless and greedy but he was no fool. Conveniently Lord Euston lost the card. And no others were ever found.

There were aspects of the trial that were never discussed. Besides the obvious question as to why on earth Jack would put his freedom on the line just to come to court to tell a tissue of lies, if he *had* perjured himself a host of bizarre coincidences come into play.

How did he come to name the man he had taken back to No 19 in his statement to Abberline, the very man who later admitted he *had* actually been to the address though in such completely different circumstances?

Jack said it was in May 1887. Lord Euston said it was in May. The initial encounter in both stories had taken place in the West End. Jack said Lord Euston gave him a sovereign, which he put on a chest of drawers. Lord Euston said he gave a sovereign to Charles Hammond.

If Jack had been mistaken about the identity of his client, and it had been somebody else other than Lord Euston, it was an amazing twist of fate – and simply unbelievable – that the real Lord Euston had turned out to have met a young man in the West End, gone to 19 Cleveland Street, and parted with a sovereign.

Jack came very close to prosecution. Closer than he knew.

Later that month, the statement he gave to Abberline was passed to the Secretary of State. Sir Augustus Stephenson, the Treasury Solicitor and also the Director of Public Prosecutions, wrote to Sir Richard Webster, the Attorney General, asking for his direction as to whether any proceedings should 'be taken against Saul for perjury or sodomy'. He also asked that with regard to the numerous names given by Saul in the statement, whether 'any profitable enquiries should be made" into the people mentioned.

Sir Richard Webster considered it carefully then concluded,

'No proceedings should at present be commenced against Saul. As regards perjury, I see no means by which sufficient evidence can be produced to prove the offence of perjury. As regards sodomy, it would be both unprofitable and in my opinion improper to try Saul for the offence, the only evidence against him being his own confession contained in his statement.'

Unprofitable. Indeed it was. Improper. Of course it would be. Nobody wanted to sully their hands any further with this dreadful business. No one knew what else he might say in court in his defence.

An editorial in Labouchere's *Truth* demonstrated just how lucky Jack had been. It was taken up verbatim by a number of provincial papers and was unflatteringly headed,

THE "CREATURE" SAUL

'Why was he not brought to justice? The Public Prosecutor has made up his mind not to prosecute the "creature" Saul for perjury. If this be so, a more scandalous decision never was taken. A jury has declared that the "creature" committed one of the most horrible perjuries on record – a perjury for which the longest sentence permitted by the law would not be sufficient.'

Whatever it was about Jack that merited the description 'creature' three times, it had certainly got up Labouchere's nose. Perhaps it was the unashamed way he laid his intimate life bare, something rarely seen in any court let alone the Old Bailey. Perhaps it was his all too grand and confident air. Late Victorian society was simply not ready for him, in the same way that it would not be ready for Oscar Wilde.

Jack be nimble. Jack be quick. Jack jump over the candlestick.

And so Jack walked away from it, singed but not burnt, as he had done many times before, avoiding prosecution, presumably for the police to continue to turn a blind eye to his activities. He carried on with his lifestyle, unabated. But it would become another watershed moment in his life and it did make him think about the future. He wasn't going through this again. He would take the advice of the bobbies on the beat and try to find something else to do. It was time.

The English press never heard of him again. But Jack was there. He just lay low, and got on with his life. He was never very far away from his old stamping grounds of Dublin and London's West End.

Charles Hammond might be making a new life for himself in the States, but Jack knew nowhere else.

CHAPTER EIGHTEEN

WHATEVER HAPPENED TO JACK SAUL?

Villiers Street, which runs down from Charing Cross to the Thames Embankment, was not a million miles from Jack's old cruising ground of Piccadilly Circus, Leicester Square and the Haymarket. In fact it was right on the edge of it, and only a short step from the Strand. It has had mixed reputations. Rudyard Kipling lodged there, and many members of the legal fraternity from nearby chambers had rooms, alongside pubs and hotels and prostitutes and the occasional brothel. Now, it is home to the most famous gay nightclub in London, Heaven.

Under the famous arches, formed during the building of Charing Cross Station and now also the home of shops and a London theatre, but then rather disreputable, *poses plastique* were known to take place. Lord Euston please take note.

Almost where the historic and well-known Gordon's Wine Bar is now, the Marlborough Hotel then at No 23 was run by Arthur Dalton and his wife Alice. It was here soon after the trial that Jack got a job in service again. Dalton was a young man, about the same age as Jack, and may not have needed references. Jack still had the old Irish gift, a touch of the blarney, and was capable of talking his way into a situation – as he had talked himself many times in the past, though not always into situations of employment. Dalton may not have known about Jack's past, though he was a Londoner from the Hackney area, which was served by Ernest Parke's *North London Press*.

It was a small family run hotel. The Dalton's two young children, Charles and Alice, lived on the premises. Being the only male servant other than the porter, and the eldest, Jack was put in charge of four female servants. To be trusted again was important to Jack after what he had been through. No one ever officially informed him that he was not to be prosecuted after giving his evidence in the Parke trial. As far as he knew, it was still hanging over him.

The Attorney General had written that *at present* no proceedings should be commenced. Had Jack known, it would have concerned him even more. The police had been severely criticised for letting him carry on unmolested picking up men around the West End. Inspector Abberline had been mauled for not acting on his statement. At any moment, now that the dust had settled, the police could come for him. There were scores of people who would not bat an eyelid at giving evidence against Jack if it meant saving their own skins.

Jack worked, and waited. Perhaps if they came now they would find him in a respectable place with respectable people, just like Mr Violet had been. Jack always wanted to be among respectable people. When the census enumerator came round at the end of March 1891, having failed to find him ten years previously, under employment, as well as servant, Jack put down the occupation 'chemist'.

A servant who is a chemist is a decidedly odd combination – probably unique – but enumerators only put down what the occupants of premises told them. It was no more peculiar than Charles Hammond calling himself a Professor of Languages on his marriage certificate, or George Veck called himself Reverend. Years later when Veck was charged again, this time for theft, he would be an 'inventor'. Jack was an inventor too, of himself. Perhaps he was mindful of what he had learned about making up drugs as a servant at Dr Cranny's, and the homespun medicines all slum dwellers learned at their mothers' knees in Dublin.

Jack Saul, resident chemist at the Marlborough Hotel. It sounded good. Mr Saul will see you now. A tonic for that dreadful hangover you got last night at the Alhambra sir? Something to soothe the dreadful pains in your stomach from that meal last night – not at our establishment of course. Something to help you sleep? Doctors were expensive, and the kind of people who stayed at the Marlborough were not wealthy. What better service could a small hotel supply. In Dublin, sir, we had a cure for everything. We had to, to be sure.

If they came now for him they would find him an indispensable member of the staff. He had done what the police advised. Given up his way of life. He was thirty-three (though he vainly said he was twenty-nine).

Once again it would please his family and give him a regular income to send home. If there was something Jack never failed to do, it was look after Eliza with whatever money he could spare. He wasn't maybe the best Irish son, but he was the best one he was capable of being.

While Jack was picking up the threads of his life, Charles Hammond in America was rapidly losing the threads of his.

The press pursued him relentlessly on his arrival in New York, and after his arrival in Seattle where Caroline and his young son Charlie soon joined him. Seattle was very much a frontier town, one that had just recovered from a devastating fire which destroyed twenty-five blocks of the city. Hammond's arrival on the west coast coincided with its rapid rebuilding.

The West certainly turned out to be wild. Adele Gayet, said to have been a niece of Caroline's, was a prostitute whose protector, John Stricker, Hammond had known in London. Stricker got arrested for shooting at the police when they raided a brothel he ran, probably the same place in which Adele worked. The American newspaper fraternity were soon on to Hammond, who was still calling himself Boulton and who professed total surprise at being discovered.

Perhaps to throw them off the scent, and to demonstrate that nothing he said should be believed, he concocted fantastic stories about how his wife had owned a chateau near Paris and how he was a descendant of French Royalty, was related to the late Emperor of France and to Israeli financiers in the same country, as well as rich mine owners in the north of England. This highly unlikely family tree, typical of Hammond's bluster, didn't lessen their interest.

Herbert Ames, whom Hammond said had accompanied to America with the full consent of his parents, was spotted handling what a reporter thought looked like diamonds. He and Hammond's young son promptly became connected with 'nobility and the Royal Family in England.' The Princes in the Tower perhaps.

The American press dared to go where the British newspapers feared to tread, and on the way they fell over themselves. Hammond, they said, was the chief witness against the heir to England's throne. Another article even described him in its bold heading as 'the friend of the Duke of Clarence'.

Newton's lowly clerk Fred Taylorson, who had accompanied Hammond on his escape to America, was elevated to the status of an 'English Lord' in the American newspapers when he returned across the sea to England.

It probably amused Hammond as much as did their description of him as a man who had the bearing of a highly educated gentleman whose family in London were much respected. He spoke French to the boys, and was fluent in Spanish.

This new Hammond, the brushed-up, multi-lingual respectable gentleman of Seattle, friend of Royalty, continued to deny any involvement with the Cleveland Street brothel. It had not been his house. It had been another house. He had been paralysed at the time and could not have operated such a place. Then he had been blind. His house had been confused with another one in the Euston Road run by a C.J. Hammond. London was full of brothels, which catered for the English disease, didn't you know? A doctor could testify that he was not responsible for what went on. Just leave me alone.

There was no chance. He then started claiming he had $250,000 dollars of hush money at his disposal in the Bank of California, placed there by wealthy Englishmen. Hammond had become by reputation an international blackmailer who possessed incriminating letters (and presumably still the Cleveland Street appointments book) and certain members of the aristocracy would stop at nothing to get them back.

In yet another interview, he said he would never betray the men who used his house in London. Nothing he ever said made much sense.

The story of Hammond in America then begins to take on the aura of an Sherlock Holmes mystery.

He bought a bar in Seattle called The Haymarket – or more likely he named it that himself as a reminder of home – and set himself up as a saloon bar keeper. One of his customers was Micajah Fible, a young journalist graduate from the Harvard Law School who worked for the *Chicago Tribune*. According to Hammond, he had plenty of money and spent it lavishly. Champagne was his favourite drink, and Hammond, being a keen dispenser of champagne, spent many hours drinking and making friends with Fible. But it turned out Fible was more interested in the 'London affair'. He offered Hammond $4,000 for the story, and for any letters or documents he possessed, and wanted Hammond to go with him to Chicago. A twenty-column story was being prepared in the *Chicago Tribune* and Fible was reputed to have obtained from Hammond a number of letters.

Then Fible disappeared. Questioned about it by a reporter from the *Seattle Daily Times*, Hammond said they had last been together in Tacoma, a city about thirty miles away, and that Fible had returned from there to Chicago on his own. The story circulated that Hammond had got rid of Fible. Fible family records state simply that he died in 1890 while on assignment for the *Tribune* in Seattle. His disappearance and death supposedly by drowning have never been adequately explained, though it became generally accepted that he had lost money through gambling and had become depressed.

Then a so-called 'English detective' calling himself Alexander Todhunter, 'formerly of the Metropolitan Police' arrived in Seattle, it was said, to retrieve Hammond's incriminating documents at the request of a number of well-placed persons in England. He took an undercover job as a barman in Hammond's saloon but it was also rumoured that he was there to get Hammond back onto British soil, though why the same well-placed persons, who were presumably being black-mailed by Hammond from across the pond, should have wanted Hammond back, except to murder him, remains a mystery.

Todhunter had previously tried to get Hammond to go with him to the Queen's jubilee celebrations in Victoria, Australia, but Hammond refused to set foot again on English territory.

The mysterious detective Todhunter however was said to have achieved at least one thing. Hammond was accused by Mrs Augusta Simmons, the wife of a bar keeper, of stealing her sealskin jacket and a gold watch after a night in which they caroused at the bar of his tavern and got drunk together. Hammond was arrested and charged with grand larceny.

Despite his protests that the case had been got up against him by Todhunter, he was sentenced at the Superior Court of Seattle to two years imprisonment in the State Penitentiary at Walla Walla.

It transpired at the trial that Todhunter was not a detective after all, but a hotel keeper from England who had lived in Seattle for some years. He had a brother in Los Angeles who was a clergyman. His grandfather was a Russian count. Nevertheless, the feeling persisted and grew that he had set Hammond up, for reasons better known to himself.

Young Charlie Hammond, who was clearly more literate than his father, penned a sad letter to the Governor of the State.

> '...I beg of you to pardon him as he has been a good and kind father and if he went to prison I know it would kill him, and his health is very bad having been told us by one of the most prominent physicians of Seattle Dr (unreadable). I trust you will do us this favor as he is entirely innocent of the crime of which he is accused. I am, Yours etc, Charlie Hammond.' (1)

Herbert Ames, his employer now safely behind bars, made a sworn statement saying that he had been scared to talk before because of Hammond's threats of personal violence and that he had indeed written many letters for Hammond to English noblemen asking for hush money. He spilled the names of people who had visited 19 Cleveland Street, some of them not yet in any domain, including a Dr Maitland, Percy Stafford a capitalist, and the stockbroker Hugh Weguelin, whom the American press called Hugh Waglin.

Young Ames went further. He said that Hammond had offered him a glass of whisky but that he had declined it, as there was something suspicious in the bottom, leaving the impression that Hammond had tried to poison him.

Ames may have been covering his own back. There is no other evidence Hammond was ever violent, or a potential murderer. If he did possess a quarter of a million dollars of money from English aristocrats, it is strange that his family fell into destitution while he was inside and became county paupers. An official visited them and had to give them eight dollars for groceries. Caroline Hammond was infirm and suffering from heart disease, but despite her poor health continued to visit him whenever she could in prison.

Hammond refuted everything Ames said. The boy had stolen some money from his wife and she had refused to let him back into the house. That was the reason for him telling stories about hush money and English aristocrats, much the same stories that Hammond himself had foisted on a gullible press.

There was a petition for Hammond, organised by those who believed he had been set up, from a number of the 'residents' of Seattle – mainly Hammond's friends – on the grounds that he was innocent and had a family dependent on his support. He fell ill with pneumonia. Even the warden of the penitentiary became his ally, and two ex-convicts offered to give evidence on his behalf that the whole thing had been a conspiracy. It worked. In February 1892, he was reprieved by Governor Perry. He walked out of Walla Walla penitentiary to resume his career as a saloon bar and lodging house keeper, and to achieve the obscurity he no doubt desired.

Jack left his employment with the Marlborough Hotel, possibly after a change of management the following year, and returned to Dublin. He had supported his mother as best he could while he was in London, even if it meant she subsisted part of the time on immoral earnings. He returned to a family who now knew all about his life and background. Not only had he been involved in a scandal in Dublin, but he had been in the box at the Old Bailey, branded a liar and a lot more besides by an English judge.

Both his brothers Edward and James were fully-fledged jarveys, and cab drivers were a notoriously hard breed, often hard drinkers too. Edward had been fined for driving his carriage while under the influence of alcohol. Being out in all weathers and catering to a public who frequently complained about them, they had developed a blunt way of dealing with people. They were not 'musical' in the way that the witnesses in the Dublin scandals were, and Jack was quite definitely not of their world. He was still a criminal in their eyes, even though he had only once been charged with something and had never been found guilty of anything.

His rather snobbish airs and graces and effeminate theatrical manner alienated a lot of people. Dublin was just as much a deeply conservative place as it had been when he left. Still, he was family, and if Edward had good reason to resent Jack, his younger brother James still supported him and indeed would step up to the plate when it was called for. James was, after all, Jack's blood brother.

Eliza Saul died on 17 April 1897 of Bright's Disease, an obsolete name for nephritis, a kidney condition. It can be caused by infectious diseases like pneumonia, measles or hepatitis, or by having too little potassium or too much calcium in the blood. The unhealthy living conditions in which the Sauls lived for many years, combined with poor diet, likely contributed.

Eliza's death changed everything, as mothers' deaths always do when there is conflict within a family. They hold things together and patch up relationships. When they go, the fractures widen. She passed away while staying with Edward, who had moved round the corner to 6 Frederick Lane. The funeral procession carried her on her last journey to Glasnevin Cemetery where she was interred in the Saul family plot, alongside her husband, mother and two children.

Edward had given their mother much reason to be proud in the last years of her life. Having supported the family almost single-handed since he was a teenager, Edward had now built up his own successful business as a cab proprietor. She lived to see him win a prize at the Dublin Horse Show in Ballsbridge with his seven-year-old bay mare Rosey. The show was a Dublin institution. Edward would go on to win prizes in subsequent years with his horses and fine carriages. He was well-known for what the press called his 'fine trotting horses' and a sale of them at the stables at the back of his house in Frederick Lane was well attended.

James was in the same business and like his brother would go on to win prizes at the show. Both brothers were unmarried yet they did not live together, Edward residing in Frederick Lane and James in South Frederick Street just round the corner, with their sister Annie staying with him as housekeeper. It was not unusual for a spinster sister to step in as housekeeper for an unmarried brother. But for two unmarried brothers with no families of their own, and in the same business, to live apart yet so close to each other is highly unusual, though they stabled their horses together next to the Kildare Street Club (of which Captain Kirwan had been a member). Jack may well have been the reason for them living separately, not welcome at one but at the other just so long as he didn't frighten the horses, until he too found a job and a place of his own.

Just as leopards do not change their spots, Jack did not completely give up his way of life. A few months after their mother died, he found himself on the right side of the law for a change. He was walking along by the south side of Trinity College, a few yards from where his brothers lived, between eleven o'clock and midnight, when he was accosted by a thirty-three-year-old man called John McCormack who snatched his brass watch chain and ran away, in hot pursuit by a policeman.

There was very likely a less innocent side to the encounter, though to give him the benefit of the doubt he may just have been walking home after visiting his brother. The newspaper made a point of reporting that a standholder's ticket for the Dublin Horse Show was found in the prisoner's possession, with the implication that he had stolen it from Jack too. McCormack was sentenced to a month's imprisonment with hard labour.

During the interim years, Jack kept his eye on what was happening back in London. He had got out in time.

The police and courts finally caught up with the fact that the notorious Labouchere addition to the Criminal Law Amendment Act had become a blackmailer's free-for-all, thirteen years after the event. In 1898, there was a series of blackmail trials at the Old Bailey. Right at the centre of them was Jack's old friend Andrew Grant, alias Queen Anne, 'who knew a lot of the aristocracy'. Grant was now running a lodging house off Regent Street.

He and his two accomplices, Henry Coulton, who had already served time for the same kind of offence, and a youth called Albert Edward Thorpe, inveigled one Joseph Stanley Matheson from Braintree in Essex to go to a house near St James Park with them, after which he parted with £1,500 to stop them accusing him of an 'infamous crime'. It was stated in court that Grant had been engaged in the business of extortion and blackmail for twelve years; from the time he had known Jack.

Grant came up before Mr Justice Hawkins, the very same judge who had branded Jack loathsome. No such word was applied to Grant, though he was given life imprisonment and sent to Parkhurst Prison on the Isle of Wight. He would serve almost twenty years before being released. Coulton and Thorpe received twenty years and fifteen years respectively.

Grant, Coulton and Thorpe were only part of a much larger gang. William Allen, the former valet, and Robert Cliburn, one time telegraph messenger and butcher's boy, were given seven years each for a similar crime committed against a different victim. It was only two years after their names had been dredged up in Oscar Wilde's disastrous prosecution of Lord Queensberry for libel, as having attempted to blackmail the playwright with a passionate letter he had written to Lord Alfred Douglas. Both had gone on the run at the time of the trial but had been tracked down. There was no escape for them now. It is reputed that Cliburn told Oscar Wilde that Lord Euston had been one of his blackmail victims. That is quite likely. Cliburn had received through a solicitor an annuity of one hundred pounds from a gentleman he had been blackmailing for several years.

All in all, eleven young men were tried, including two German waiters who dressed in female attire to ensnare their victims. It was said in court that there were 'a number of persons of this class who infested the West End to carry on their business.'

Jack recognised some of the names. Others were new. So too in Dublin there was another generation of renters, just as hard-edged, while those Jack had known in Dublin were, like him, drifting towards middle age. Bill Clarke was still living with his family and working as a cooper, forty years old and long past the age when he could make extra money in a male brothel. Others had simply vanished, emigrated perhaps. Like old soldiers, rent boys never died. They just went to prison or faded away.

The next few years of Jack's life are sketchy but he had presumably found a job back in service, for by 1901 he had elevated his status from servant to butler though he was living on his own in a single room of a three-storey tenement at 23 Luke Street, near to the Liffey and George's Quay. The fact that the rest of the house was occupied by general labourers and cab drivers and their families, where two families of seven and one of six lived in a single room each, suggests that by that time he was once again out of a situation. He was also claiming to be thirty-two whereas he was actually forty-three. While vanity obviously once again played a part, the Irish traditionally used the Government census as a way of getting one over on their English rulers by lying through their teeth at every opportunity.

Ironically, 23 Luke Street was next door to the notorious Lock Hospital, which treated prostitutes suffering from incurable venereal diseases. It is interesting to speculate what diseases Jack might have brought home with him. A young man of his occupation would have to have been very lucky, or blessed by the saints, to have avoided catching the dreaded syphilis.

Jack be nimble, Jack be quick. Jack jump over the candlestick.

But the flame on the candlestick was beginning to burn ever higher.

He moved again, just round the corner into Poolbeg Street, home of Mulligan's, that most well-known of all Dublin pubs through the door of which has passed almost anyone famous who ever drank a pint in the city. It was in his lodgings in Poolbeg Street that the cough would have started. It always started with a cough, a racking, rasping cough that wouldn't go away. He developed a fever and began to have night sweats, and it wasn't long before he was losing weight. Then blood came up with the sputum.

Dublin had the highest rate of tuberculosis in Europe. Jack may not even have caught it in Dublin. Many people can carry the infection and show no symptoms until it progresses from a latent phase into consumption, so named as the body seems to consume itself. TB was not always fatal, but there was no cure other than rest in a sanatorium, which was beyond the means of most.

When Jack became unable to look after himself, his younger brother James took him into his home. Whatever family differences there had been, James could not see his eldest brother die alone in a damp room near the Liffey. It was summer and the stink from the river was just as bad as when a juror had once complained of having to spend the night there.

James had only just got married to a stevedore's daughter, Annie Donohue, so it was a terrible risk to himself and his young wife. Their sister of the same name had married a cousin who was a plumber and moved out to the healthier suburbs. Jack was beyond family help however. He knew he was going to die. And so did they.

Jack was taken to spend his last days at Our Lady's Hospice in the south of the city, on raised ground near the Grand Canal in the small community of Harold's Cross. It was a handsome late eighteenth-century mansion that had previously been owned by the Society of Friends (Quakers). The name was originally Greenmount, which was a fitting one for the location as the air was cleaner there. It had operated as a charity since the year of the smallpox epidemic, the same year that Jack had left Dublin. There was no hospital in the city which would take in fever patients who were infectious. Such admission policies were common to most hospitals, where only those who could be treated and helped were given beds. People were expected to die at home.

The hospice had been founded by the Religious Sisters of Charity, who still ran it. The order was the brainchild of a Cork lady, Mary Aikenhead, who converted to Roman Catholicism. The Sisters eventually realised the dire need for a place where the destitute and the dying could come and be treated, not with medicine, but with dignity in the final weeks of their lives. In the beginning, the hospice had just nine beds. By the time Jack arrived in the summer of 1904 there were forty.

The Mother Superior was also the matron. She was Agnes Gertrude Chamberlain, who 'ruled with firm and gentle sway'. She had taken over from the first Superior of the hospice, Anna Gaynor, who had been in the job seventeen years.

An impression of the quality of the food there and general atmosphere of care was summed up by Sara Atkinson, the biographer of Aikenhead, who said 'one thing at any rate is certain, the Irish as a rule know how to die.'

The Sisters knew how the dying wanted to die. They could not be treated as ordinary patients but had to have a better diet than would be offered in any hospital. Tubercular patients tended to have increased appetites so the food bill was high. Charitable bequests made up a substantial portion of their funds.

Jack was well fed for the remaining weeks of his life. (Which would probably have annoyed hanging Judge Hawkins if he had known). The ward into which Jack was placed was kept as cheery as possible by the Sisters. The four poster beds were covered by pink and white dimity curtains, and there was an open fire with a singing kettle for constant hot water and soothing drinks at any time of the day. One nun with one maid ran each ward.

When not in bed, Jack had the use of a large sitting room, and for fresh air – regarded as essential for tubercular patients – there was a balcony at the back of the hospice. In the grounds was a smoking pavilion. If one did not wish to smoke, one could walk in the rose garden.

Not all of the patients with whom Jack shared Our Lady's Hospice were poor. Nor were they all Catholics, for the Sisters did not make any division between religions. Protestants, doctors, solicitors, soldiers, sailors and members of every class came under the mantle. Jack must have felt quite at home.

Treatment was palliative. A doctor made his daily rounds – during Jack's stay the resident physician was Michael Francis Cox, who remained for a quarter of a century in the post – but his resources were few. He had morphine and aspirin for pain, purgatives for constipation and tonics for exhaustion, strychnine and spirits for sedation. There was little more that one could do for the dying, except wait with them.

Jack Saul, registered under his given name of John Saul – died on 28 August, 1904. He was forty-six years old, though his death certificate stated his age as forty-two. It recorded the fact that he had died of TB, was single, and indeed a butler.

Like he cheated most things in life, Jack deprived posterity of any official mention that he might have died of, or also suffered from, something more shameful.

Although there was a cemetery at the rear of the house, Mount Jerome, most funeral processions, which included Jack's, headed north across the Liffey to Glasnevin where – Jack would have appreciated it – almost everyone who was anyone in Dublin was buried. Besides, the family plot was there.

Jack may not have got on with everybody in his family in life, but in death he was one of them, in spite of his sins. There, only a couple of minutes walk from the tomb of Daniel O'Connell, and where so many Irish nationalist heroes including Michael Collins would be buried, he was laid to rest in the same grave as his mother Eliza, his father William, his grandmother Eliza Revington, and his two siblings Susan and William who had died in childhood. Though his grave can be identified, there is no stone marking the family plot. Stones and monuments were for those who could afford them. The majority of graves at Glasnevin were, and are, unmarked.

Edward Saul continued in business as a cab proprietor and died in 1932. He also lies at Glasnevin, in the section known as St Patrick's, and is the only one of the family to have a headstone. James died in 1944, aged sixty-nine, a motor driver, his widow Annie surviving him by eleven years. Four of their children never married, just like their famous uncle Jack. Gerald, a clerk, died single aged seventy-seven in 1987. Arthur, who became an accountant, died a bachelor aged forty-one in 1950. Two sisters died in middle age, both spinsters. One wonders.

Martin Oranmore Kirwan of Bawnmore and Cregg died three months before Jack in his native Galway at the age of fifty-seven. He was little heard of outside of the county in the two decades between his trial and 17 May 1904 when after two years of illness he succumbed to a cerebral haemmorhage at the family seat in Bawnmore. He never married. In the intervening years he was a Justice of the Peace for Galway, one of the governing body of the County Galway Hospital, a member of the Galway Board of Guardians, and was regarded according to his obituary in the *Tuam Herald* as a considerate, amiable and intelligent landlord, held in high esteem by his tenantry, much like his father. His remains were sent to Galway City, en route for Dublin. He was interred next to his parents in Mount Jerome Cemetery at Harold's Cross, only a few hundred yards from the hospice at which Jack would lay dying. Any stigma that had become attached to him after the sodomy trials seems, on the surface, to have been wiped away.

When the author sought out Bawnmore House, quite a modest property compared to Cregg Castle, he spoke to a middle-aged lady in her car who had been born and brought up there. On being asked if she wouldn't mind helping with some information, she drove away at speed. Which, given what has happened in Ireland since, regarding changes in the law, seems a shame. Perhaps there are still those who do not want to remember the past.

Martin Oranmore Kirwan was succeeded in line by his nephew, Dennis Agar Richard of Cregg. It was said of him that as one of the 'old stock' he 'resumed the tradition of hospitality at Bawnmore, the same spirit of hospitality and friendship that his uncle had fostered within the stone walls.

Of the visitors to 19 Cleveland Street, Lord Arthur 'Podge' Somerset spent the rest of his life in exile on the French Riviera, perhaps not a bad place to live in the shadow of disgrace. For many years he enjoyed the companionship of a male friend and fellow Englishman, James Andrew Neale. Somerset died at the Villa Sophie in the resort of Hyeres in 1926, and was buried in the English section of the town cemetery. Three years earlier, another visitor to Hyeres died in the town, Roland Yorke Bevan the banker, at the age of seventy-four. Hyeres was a popular resort with British tourists. It would be interesting to know if the two men met and reminisced about their mutual experiences at Hammond's brothel.

In spite of being nicknamed the Duke by the boys at Piccadilly Circus, Lord Euston never became a real one as he died before his father, and did not inherit the Dukedom. He did however become Grand Master of the Mark Master Masons, and was appointed an ADC by King Edward VII in the year of the coronation. His admission at the Parke trial to enjoying *poses plastique* had no effect whatsoever on his later career.

Hugh Weguelin continued to prosper financially. When he died aged sixty-four in 1923 he left an estate valued at £38,948. A thousand pounds was left to his valet. He had been a member of the Stock Exchange for forty-three years.

None of those mentioned in Jack's statement or by Hammond's boys were ever prosecuted.

Of the occupants of the house, the self-styled Reverend George Daniel Veck was perhaps proof of the adage that God pays his debts without money. Although he lived to the ripest old age, it was certainly not the happiest. He became a doctor's assistant but, by his late sixties, he was destitute, an inmate of St Marylebone Workhouse. Veck lingered on for another three decades until 1937 when he died 'of no fixed abode' and in extremely bad health at the age of ninety-eight.

The boys who worked at the house enjoyed mixed fortunes. Algernon Allies, in the aftermath of the scandal, took a ship to America where he married a girl from Kansas and settled in Chicago, Cook County, working as a waiter and barman. Whether he ever got his under linen, two suits, boots and a hat is not recorded. Charles Ernest Thickbroom, after being dismissed from the Post Office, became a draper's porter in Shoreditch. He too married, and went to work as a cowman on a farm in Southampton. They appear to have had no children. By the eve of the Second World War, he was as an old-age pensioner, living with his wife in Winchester. He died, aged eighty-one, in 1953.

Henry Newlove, after his release from Pentonville, returned home to live with his mother. He worked as a shop assistant and as a railway clerk, then on the death of his mother, he moved in with his brother William, who was a bookbinder in Holloway. He too lived to be an old-age pensioner, a retired clerk living in a lodging house in Tottenham. He died in Ealing, aged eighty-four, unmarried, in 1961. The only telegraph boy to have the good fortune to be allowed back into the Post Office service was William Meech Perkins. He became what most telegraph boys aimed to become – a fully-fledged postman. Possibly his part in the Cleveland Street scandal was seen as slighter than that of the others.

Charles Thomas Swinscow, the boy whose misfortune it was to be found with fourteen shillings in his pocket, the event that led to the unfolding of the scandal and the police investigation, married a Kentish girl Mabel Eveline Cecilia Joy in 1900, raised children, and continued to live in Islington. Ten years later he joined the Gloucestershire Regiment as a reserve, and during the war was posted to Malta as a Company Quartermaster Sergeant. He had a flair for mathematics. When his service came to an end in 1921, the army offered him a position in accounts but he turned it down, taking instead a job with the Department of Works at Kew. Mabel Swinscow was a midwife, and when their two daughters' marriages broke up Charles and Mabel took in a pair of grandsons and brought them up. One of their adopted children remembered Charles as being kind but aloof, walking to work wearing a monocle, plus fours and always smartly dressed. During the Second World War, he became an ARP Warden, left Mabel and took up with another woman, though he remained in Islington. He died in 1945, and is buried in Finchley Cemetery.

After Charles Hammond walked out of Walla Walla Penitentiary, cleared of robbing Mrs Augusta Simmons, the press appeared to lose interest in him. He returned to manage the saloon at the corner of Front and West Streets, which Caroline had run in his absence, serving the good people of Seattle who had taken him so warmly to their bosoms.

But his apparent nemesis, the 'ex-Metropolitan police officer' Mr Todhunter, surfaced yet again a few months later. He was given the job of escorting a prisoner, Robert Dann, who had stabbed a ship's captain on board a vessel on which he was the first mate, back to England on an extradition order. This time the Todhunter concerned turned out to be exactly what they said he was – ex-Metropolitan Police, even though he had been dismissed from the force after only eleven months.

He was not the barman and amateur detective *Alexander* Todhunter however, whom Hammond had accused of fitting him up, but Alexander's brother, Frank Cecil Todhunter, who really had been a London police officer.

Perhaps after all there was much more to his brother Alexander's undercover work than met Hammond's, or anyone else's, eye. (2)

Charles Richard Hammond is still on the run today, which befits a man as wily and slippery as he proved to be. One might catch him in the 1930 US census for the city of San Jose in Santa Clara County, California, working as a presser in a laundry where he had been engaged for twenty years. One might think it something of a comedown for a man who entertained the landed gentry and possibly Royalty in a house with yellow silk pillows and velvet curtains, to end up taking in other peoples' washing. Born in England, this Charles R. Hammond, widowed, aged seventy-five, unnaturalised and still an alien, who emigrated to the USA according to the information he gave, in 1890 (a year later than he actually did) fits the bill almost perfectly. One might pronounce the same Charles R. Hammond dead on 11 September 1933 at the age of seventy-nine.

Or one might not. In previous censuses, Mr Charles R. Hammond, laundry presser, apparently came to the country in both 1880 and 1883. It would be typical of the notorious male madame of Cleveland Street and fugitive from justice to cover his tracks, wherever they might be and wherever they might lead.

Of his wife and son, I have not found a trace.

Ernest Parke came out of prison, broken but not bowed, and resumed his journalistic career, though the *North London Press* was no more. He became editor of the *Star* newspaper, which had risen so gallantly to his defence, and five years after his trial a reporter from the *Sketch* visited him in his office to write a profile of 'Mr Star' and described him as priestly and intellectual. Parke was in a bad temper during the visit, complaining of being pestered by lawyers, whom he termed the mosquitoes of the Press world, wanting damages for an 'alleged libel'. He did not state if his adversary was

THE SINS OF JACK SAUL

still Lord Euston, desiring his pound of flesh. It may well have been a fresh libel. In later years, despite his sentence, he became a Justice of the Peace in his native Warwickshire, and a member of the National Liberal Club. His career was marked by the radical causes that remained so dear to his heart.

Inspector Abberline was promoted to Chief Inspector, but became known – somewhat unfairly – as the man who failed to catch Jack the Ripper, who did not act on Jack Saul's statement in the Cleveland Street case, and let important people flee the country. They were his last 'big cases'. After retiring from the force, he joined the Pinkerton Detective Agency for a while and operated as a private detective. He retired to Bournemouth where he died in 1929. His wife died three months after him, and as there were no children, his grave, like Jack's, was unmarked by any stone. In 2001, by which time the Ripper industry was in full flow, the Cloak and Dagger Club, (now known as The Whitechapel Society), erected a headstone on his grave.

There is no Jack Saul industry to erect a stone in Glasnevin Cemetery. The plot of neat, green grass across the Irish sea will likely remain such for a very long time, unvisited and largely unknown.

I try to think of an epitaph for Jack Saul. Possessed of a time machine and given three separate days to go back and observe him, I would choose the day he got arrested as a teenager with Bill Clarke for 'stealing' that overcoat, the day he took Lord Euston back to Cleveland Street, and the day on which he stood up in court and defended Ernest Parke against his libel charge.

GLENN CHANDLER

But one can only follow his footsteps as best as one can. The streets of Soho that he knew are still there and if he came back today he would know his way around. 19 Cleveland Street has gone, swept away for redevelopment.

At the corner of Old Compton Street and Dean Street, the house in which Jack lived when the young solicitor's clerk Ashley came knocking on his door is still there. The ground floor is now a legitimate gay business.

In Dublin the slums have virtually all gone. Where Jack was born, at the junction between Upper and Lower Kevin Streets, there is now a large empty space, a busy traffic intersection. Ferns Court is no more. The old police barracks, which were once the training depot of the Dublin Metropolitan Police, later taken over by the Gardai, are still there. Up the road in Golden Lane, modern flats are little prettier than the slum tenements they replaced. It is hard to imagine brothels now in Golden Lane.

The house at 5 Duke Lane has disappeared. In its place is a high-class gentleman's boutique with flats above. Next door, Kehoe's pub on the corner of South Anne Street has stood the test of time. I sank a pint of the black stuff in its almost unchanged interior and wondered how many times the Sauls passed through its doors. Jack drank here. The family dramas that were enacted within these walls and in the condemned house that once stood next door must have been legion.

Finally, the trail takes one to Glasnevin. For lovers of cemeteries, there are few its equal. Quite apart from its famous residents, Michael Collins, Eamonn de Valera, Daniel O'Connell and so many others, the vast

Angels Plot pulls one up short. Many, though not all of the children buried here, were never born. Glasnevin was one of the few cemeteries which allowed the burial of stillborn and unbaptised babies. About their myriad plots are strewn the toys with which they never played. It is testament to the abiding faith in an afterlife, the belief that their unpolluted souls may be sitting with the angels.

Whether Jack is sitting with the angels is another matter. He lies only a few feet from the high wall separating the cemetery from the Botanic Gardens. On the other side are the neat paths and hothouses which Lieutenant, later Captain Martin Kirwan, so enjoyed with Jack and his other young men. It was the most pleasant place to go courting in Dublin in the rare old days.

I sat for a while by the unmarked grave then returned to the city.

That night I went to the George Pub in South Great King Street, a short walk from Jack's old home. It is the biggest, brashest gay pub in Dublin and the referendum on gay marriage had concluded only a few days before. The result was an overwhelming vote by the people of Ireland themselves to legalise same sex marriages. The atmosphere was electric. Rainbow flags and hats abounded. An outrageously blue drag act was taking place and the bar was packed with revellers. I couldn't help thinking of Jack and what he would think if he came back and saw this. What they would *all* think.

We lose touch with our past at our peril. Pendulums swing, and swing back again. What was a dreadful unmentionable sin then is no more, at least in the eyes of the law. Others see it differently. There will always be others.

In the course of his sins, Jack Saul undoubtedly gave a lot of pleasure to a lot of people. I only hope he got some in return.

Let that be his epitaph.

THE END

Chapter Notes

1. Charlie Hammond's letter is from a scan of the original in Washington State Archives. JTR Forums.

2. One of the many coincidences that besets the Cleveland Street case is that Roland Yorke Bevan was closely connected with a Joseph Todhunter of Walthamstow, a fellow member of the Essex Hunt, a Justice of the Peace, and a wealthy farmer. While I have been unable to make any connection between the Todhunters of Walthamstow and the Todhunters involved in the pursuit of Hammond, the possibility of there being a family link is an intriguing one to say the very least.

ACKNOWLEDGEMENTS

Uncovering the life of Jack Saul, and treading the murky byways of the Cleveland Street scandal, would not have been possible without the help of numerous bodies, The National Archives, Dublin; the National Library of Ireland; The Glasnevin Cemetery Trust; Mount Jerome Cemetery, Dublin; the National Archives, Kew; the British Library; the British Newspaper Archive; the Irish Newspaper Archive; Chronicling America; Gravesend Library; Westminster Archives; the Post Office Archives; The Victoria and Albert Museum Theatre Collection; Camden Library; Our Lady's Hospice, Harold's Cross, Dublin. The expanding plethora of Irish genealogy web-sites has been invaluable, particularly Roots Ireland and Irish Genealogy ie. The JTR (Jack the Ripper) forums have also provided helpful information.

The following books were immensely useful in my research.

The Cleveland Street Scandal, H. Montgomery Hyde, 1976

The Cleveland Street Affair, Colin Simpson, Lewis Chester, David Leitch 1976

Terrible Queer Creatures, Homosexuality in Irish History, Brian Lacey, 2008

A Secret History of Piccadilly Rent Boys, Jeremy Reed, 2014

Ripper Hunter, Abberline and the Whitechapel Murders, M.J. Trow, 2012

125 Years of Caring, Our Lady's Hospice, Harold's Cross, T.M. Healy 2008

To Hell or Monto, Maurice Curtis, 2015

Dublin Slums, Jacinta Prunty, 1998

Dublin Tenement Life, an Oral History, Kevin C. Kearns, 1994

Who was that Man? Neil Bartlett, 1988

The Sins of the Cities of the Plain, privately printed 1881, 1st Valancourt Books edition 2012

Letters from Laura and Eveline, privately printed 1883, 1st Valancourt Books edition 2012

Finally I would like to thank Maura Harvey for her photographs and much useful information; Stuart Swinscow and Debbie Jarvis; Valancourt Books for permission to quote from *The Sins of the Cities of the Plain*; Jon Bradfield for his cover design; my agent Diana Tyler for all she has done over the years; Peter Bull at Above The Stag Theatre who gave me the opportunity to produce *Cleveland Street The Musical*, which ignited my interest in Jack Saul, and who at the time of writing is soon to produce a musical based on this book; Piers Dudgeon for his help with the manuscript and enthusiasm for the subject; Christopher Delaney who read numerous drafts and whose help has been invaluable; and Justin O'Hearn of the University of British Columbia whose shared intrigue in the true identity of Jack Saul has long been an inspiration.

INDEX

Lightning Source UK Ltd.
Milton Keynes UK
UKOW04f2056190717
305647UK00001B/1/P